Shakespeare and Feminist Theory

ARDEN SHAKESPEARE AND THEORY

Series Editor: Evelyn Gajowski

AVAILABLE TITLES

Shakespeare and Cultural Materialist Theory
Christopher Marlow
Shakespeare and Economic Theory David Hawkes
Shakespeare and Ecocritical Theory Gabriel Egan
Shakespeare and Ecofeminist Theory Rebecca Laroche and
Jennifer Munroe
Shakespeare and New Historicist Theory Neema Parvini
Shakespeare and Psychoanalytic Theory Carolyn Brown
Shakespeare and Postcolonial Theory Jyotsna G. Singh
Shakespeare and Posthumanist Theory Karen Raber
Shakespeare and Queer Theory Melissa E. Sanchez

FORTHCOMING TITLES

Shakespeare and Adaptation Theory Sujata Iyengar
Shakespeare and Presentist Theory Evelyn Gajowski
Shakespeare and Race Theory Arthur L. Little, Jr.

Shakespeare and Feminist Theory

Marianne Novy

THE ARDEN SHAKESPEARE
LONDON • NEW YORK • OXFORD • NEW DELHI • SYDNEY

THE ARDEN SHAKESPEARE
Bloomsbury Publishing Plc
50 Bedford Square, London, WC1B 3DP, UK
1385 Broadway, New York, NY 10018, USA

BLOOMSBURY, THE ARDEN SHAKESPEARE and the Arden Shakespeare logo are trademarks of Bloomsbury Publishing Plc

First published in Great Britain 2017
This paperback edition published 2019

Copyright © Marianne Novy, 2017, 2019

Marianne Novy has asserted her right under the Copyright, Designs and Patents Act, 1988, to be identified as the author of this work.

For legal purposes the Acknowledgements on p. xi constitute an extension of this copyright page.

Cover design: Sutchinda Thompson
Cover image: X-Ray of a Jack in the Pulpit flower (© Ted Kinsman / Alamy)

All rights reserved. No part of this publication may be reproduced or transmitted in any form or by any means, electronic or mechanical, including photocopying, recording, or any information storage or retrieval system, without prior permission in writing from the publishers.

Bloomsbury Publishing Plc does not have any control over, or responsibility for, any third-party websites referred to or in this book. All internet addresses given in this book were correct at the time of going to press. The author and publisher regret any inconvenience caused if addresses have changed or sites have ceased to exist, but can accept no responsibility for any such changes.

A catalogue record for this book is available from the British Library.

Library of Congress Cataloging-in-Publication Data
Names: Novy, Marianne, 1945- author.
Title: Shakespeare and feminist theory / Marianne Novy. Description: London; New York: Bloomsbury Arden Shakespeare, 2017. | Includes bibliographical references and index.
Identifiers: LCCN 2017012855| ISBN 9781472567079 (hardback) | ISBN 9781472567093 (epdf)
Subjects: LCSH: Shakespeare, William, 1564-1616–Characters–Women. | Feminism and literature–England–History–16th century.
Classification: LCC PR2991 .N68 2017 | DDC 822.3/3–dc23 LC record available at https://lccn.loc.gov/2017012855

ISBN: HB: 978-1-472-56707-9
PB: 978-1-472-56706-2
ePDF: 978-1-472-56709-3
eBook: 978-1-472-56708-6

Series: Shakespeare and Theory

Typeset by Fakenham Prepress Solutions, Fakenham, Norfolk NR21 8NN
Printed and bound in Great Britain

To find out more about our authors and books visit www.bloomsbury.com and sign up for our newsletters.

For my daughter, Liz Carrier, and her generation

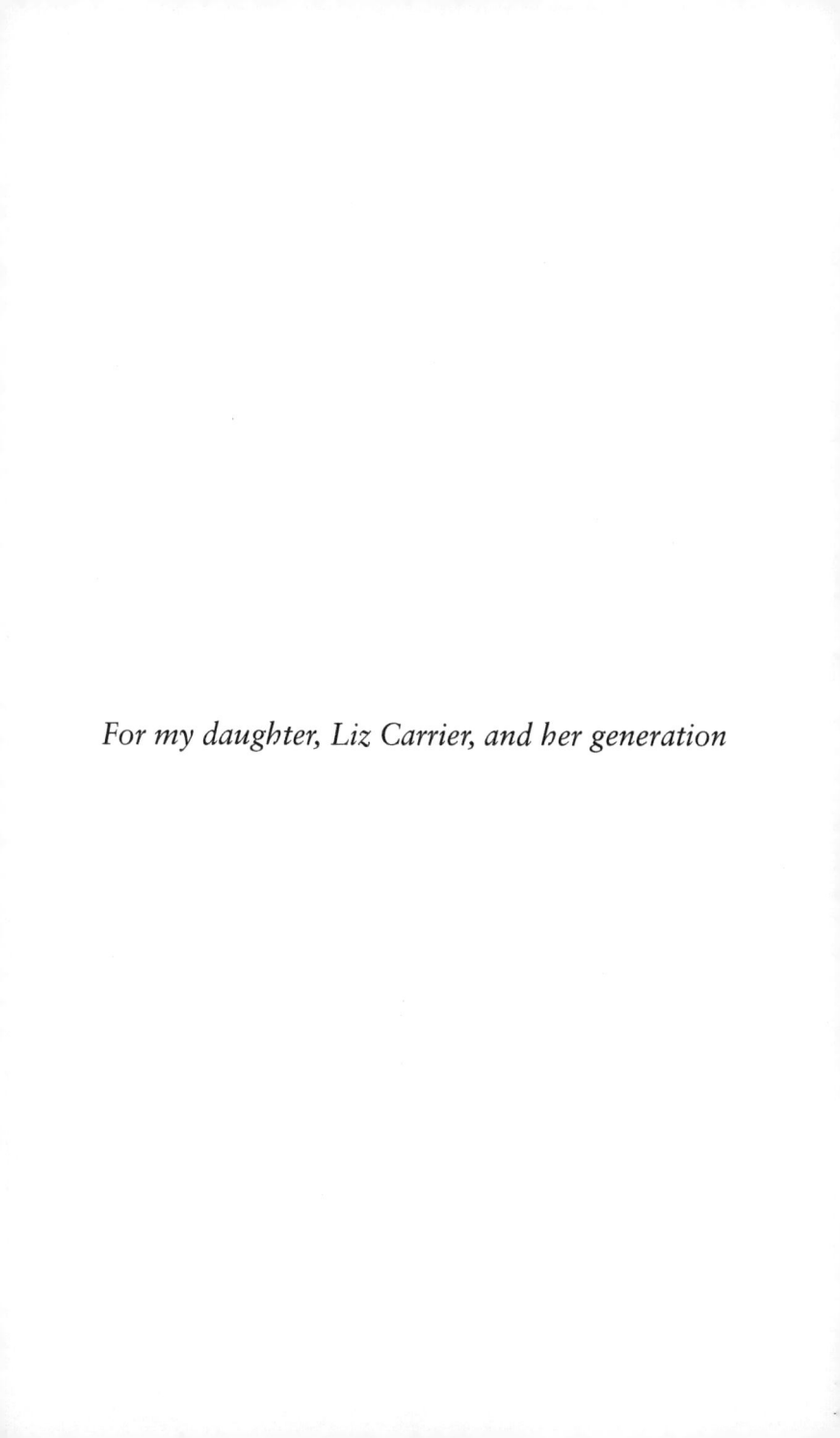

CONTENTS

Series Editor's Preface viii
Acknowledgements xi

    Introduction 1

1 Likeness and difference 13

2 Desire 31

3 Marriage 51

4 Motherhood 75

5 Language 103

6 Between women 121

7 Work 145

Appendix 160
Notes 162
References 176
Index 195

SERIES EDITOR'S PREFACE

'Asking questions about literary texts – that's literary criticism. Asking "Which questions shall we ask about literary texts?" – that's literary theory.' So goes my explanation of the current state of English studies, and Shakespeare studies, in my never-ending attempt to demystify, and simplify, theory for students in my classrooms. Another way to put it is that theory is a systematic account of the nature of literature, the act of writing, and the act of reading.

One of the primary responsibilities of any academic discipline – whether in the natural sciences, the social sciences, or the humanities – is to examine its methodologies and tools of analysis. Particularly at a time of great theoretical ferment, such as that which has characterized English studies, and Shakespeare studies, in recent years, it is incumbent upon scholars in a given discipline to provide such reflection and analysis. We all construct meanings in Shakespeare's texts and culture. Shouldering responsibility for our active role in constructing meanings in literary texts, moreover, constitutes a theoretical stance. To the extent that we examine our own critical premises and operations, that theoretical stance requires reflection on our part. It requires honesty, as well. It is thereby a fundamentally radical act. All critical analysis puts into practice a particular set of theoretical premises. Theory occurs from a particular standpoint. There is no critical practice that is somehow devoid of theory. There is no critical practice that is not implicated in theory. A common-sense, transparent encounter with any text is thereby impossible. Indeed, to the extent that theory requires us to question anew that with which we thought we were familiar, that which we thought we understood, theory constitutes a critique of common sense.

Since the advent of postmodernism, the discipline of English studies has undergone a seismic shift. And the discipline of Shakespeare studies has been at the epicentre of this shift. Indeed, it has been Shakespeare scholars who have played a major role in several of the theoretical and critical developments (e.g. new historicism, cultural materialism, presentism) that have shaped the discipline of English studies in recent years. Yet a comprehensive scholarly analysis of these crucial developments has yet to be done, and is long overdue. As the first series to foreground analysis of contemporary theoretical developments in the discipline of Shakespeare studies, *Arden Shakespeare and Theory* aims to fill a yawning gap.

To the delight of some and the chagrin of others, since 1980 or so, theory has dominated Shakespeare studies. *Arden Shakespeare and Theory* focuses on the state of the art at the outset of the twenty-first century. For the first time, it provides a comprehensive analysis of the theoretical developments that are emerging at the present moment, as well as those that are dominant or residual in Shakespeare studies.

Each volume in the series aims to offer the reader the following components: to provide a clear definition of a particular theory; to explain its key concepts; to trace its major developments, theorists, and critics; to perform a reading of a Shakespeare text; to elucidate a specific theory's intersection with or relationship to other theories; to situate it in the context of contemporary political, social, and economic developments; to analyse its significance in Shakespeare studies; and to suggest resources for further investigation. Authors of individual volumes thereby attempt to strike a balance, bringing their unique expertise, experience, and perspectives to bear upon particular theories while simultaneously fulfilling the common purpose of the series. Individual volumes in the series are devoted to elucidating particular theoretical perspectives, such as adaptation, cultural materialism, ecocriticism, ecofeminism, economic theory, feminism, film theory, new historicism, postcoloniality, posthumanism, presentism, psychoanalysis, queer theory, and race theory.

Arden Shakespeare and Theory aims to enable scholars, teachers, and students alike to define their own theoretical strategies and refine their own critical practices. And students have as much at stake in these theoretical and critical enterprises – in the reading and the writing practices that characterize our discipline – as do scholars and teachers. Janus-like, the series looks forward as well as backward, serving as an inspiration and a guide for new work in Shakespeare studies at the outset of the twenty-first century, on the one hand, and providing a retrospective analysis of the intellectual labour that has been accomplished in recent years, on the other.

To return to the beginning: what is at stake in our reading of literary texts? Once we come to understand the various ways in which theory resonates with not only Shakespeare's texts, and literary texts, but the so-called 'real' world – the world outside the world of the mind, the world outside the world of academia – then we come to understand that theory is capable of powerfully enriching not only our reading of Shakespeare's texts, and literary texts, but our lives.

***

I am indebted to David Avital, publisher at Bloomsbury Academic, who was instrumental in developing the idea of the *Arden Shakespeare and Theory* series. I am also grateful to Margaret Bartley and Mark Dudgeon, publishers for the Arden Shakespeare, for their guidance and support throughout the development of this series.

Evelyn Gajowski
Series Editor
University of Nevada, Las Vegas

ACKNOWLEDGEMENTS

Thanks to Evelyn Gajowski for the invitation to write this book. She, Jennifer Waldron and Carol Thomas Neely provided helpful feedback on chapter drafts; Carol gave an especially detailed commentary and sent me a prepublication copy of her entry on feminism and feminist criticism of Shakespeare for Patricia Parker's *Shakespeare Encyclopedia*, online from Stanford University Press in 2018. Phyllis Rackin and an anonymous reader gave support and good suggestions when it counted most.

University of Pittsburgh undergraduates Stephanie Dofitas and Sarah Kuethe searched bibliographies as part of the First Experiences in Research Program. Evelyn, Jennifer, and Nancy Glazener provided reading lists from their relevant courses. Good contexts for this work came from the students in my two most recent Shakespeare classes, my colleagues Carol Mastrangelo Bové and Bill Scott in a feminist theory discussion group and Susan Andrade in less formal feminist conversations. The Shakespeare Association of America and its conferences have been crucial to my scholarship. My chair, Don Bialostosky, and Senior Associate Dean James Knapp approved an indispensable sabbatical year.

I also want to thank my dear husband, David Carrier, for, among other things, the many books he has given me on both feminist theory and Shakespeare since 1979.

All quotations from Shakespeare are taken from the Arden Shakespeare, *Complete Works*, Revised Edition, ed. Richard Proudfoot, Ann Thompson and David Scott Kastan (London: Bloomsbury, 2011).

Marianne Novy

Introduction

The word 'feminism' first appeared in English in 1895, according to *The Oxford English Dictionary* (*OED*), which includes theory in its definition: 'Advocacy of the rights of women (based on the theory of equality of the sexes)' (1987: 263). But how can feminist theory be relevant to plays written about three hundred years earlier? Unlikely as it may seem, Aemilia Lanyer, as early as 1611, included a call for women's equality in her poem *Salve Deus Rex Judaeorum* (1993 [1611]). The historian Joan Kelly identifies as feminist theory a perspective in other early modern women writers in England, France and Italy: they see women as a social group, discuss the influence of culture, education and custom on women and point out examples of bias against women in other writing (1982).[1]

Are Shakespeare's plays feminist by this definition or, indeed, that in the *OED*? A few of his characters, such as Emilia in *Othello*, view women as a social group; Emilia, among others, implicitly criticizes the influence of custom. Many plays, *Othello* most pre-eminently, disprove misjudgements caused by bias against women. But feminist theory is relevant to his plays whether the plays themselves are feminist or not. Some feminist critics believe the plays show women as equal to men. Others argue that they promote the subordination of women. Others still take different viewpoints, which emphasize variations among plays or even within plays. Part of the reason for these disagreements is that critics rely on different traditions within feminist and literary theory.[2] But Shakespeare's plays treat topics and exemplify dynamics that feminist theorists discuss, and gender is relevant to how plays are edited and taught and how productions are staged and filmed.

Feminist movements and feminist theories

The best-known feminist theorist before the twentieth century is probably Mary Wollstonecraft, whose 1792 tract, *Vindication of the Rights of Woman* (1975 [1792]), influenced by the Enlightenment, emphasized women's natural equality to men based on their possession of reason, and criticized the influence of their customary education. While movements for women's rights were active in the US and UK in the nineteenth century, after suffrage was won in the early twentieth century the movements split and became less visible. Feminist analysis did develop further, most importantly in Virginia Woolf's *A Room of One's Own* (1989 [1929]), but there was no large audience for feminist theory at the time. In 1949, Simone de Beauvoir published *La Deuxieme Sexe*, translated into English as *The Second Sex* in 1952. Insisting that 'one is not born, but rather becomes, a woman', de Beauvoir emphasized the difference between biological necessity and social construction, and called for women to lead lives of transcendence, like (privileged) men (1974 [1952]: 249). For these books, and feminism, in general, to become influential, however, more activism was required.

Especially important in the US was *The Feminine Mystique* (1963), in which Betty Friedan argued that exclusion from meaningful work outside the home was women's main problem. At a 1966 meeting of the National Commission on the Status of Women, Friedan and others began the network that became the National Organization of Women, with Friedan as its first president. As the civil rights and peace movements developed, women began to see that even within them they were not treated as equals; they thus began to organize separately. In 1968, a month after a strike by workers and students shut down Paris, women workers in an auto plant in Dagenham, East London, went on strike against their low pay; there were similar strikes by women across the country, protests that eventually led to the UK's Equal Pay Act of 1975. Such events in the 1960s began what is often called the 'second wave' of feminism, recognizing earlier activism for suffrage and other women's rights issues in the nineteenth and early twentieth century as the first.

As women graduate students, faculty, freelance writers and others joined or identified with a feminist activist group, a large community with interest in feminist theory and feminist criticism developed. They suddenly had a lot to read, including early books that analysed literature as part of broader cultural, historical and theoretical analysis. Germaine Greer attacked women's socialization in *The Female Eunuch* (1971 [1970]). Kate Millett's *Sexual Politics* (1970) critiqued writers and thinkers – most importantly Marx and Freud – who provided rationales for male domination. Soon after, Sheila Rowbotham showed that feminists could use a revised version of Marxist theory emphasizing economics, later often called materialist, in *Women's Consciousness, Man's World* (1973), and Juliet Mitchell did the same for psychoanalytic theory in *Psychoanalysis and Feminism* (1974).

The currently most salient contrast in feminist theory is between two positions sometimes referred to as equality feminism and difference feminism. Equality feminism, as in the Oxford definition, believes in women's inherent equal rights, emphasizes what men and women do or might have in common and explains many of their differences as due to upbringing, education, law or customs – in general terms, social construction or in the more political terms of some, male domination – and this is the emphasis of all the writers just mentioned. Difference feminism emphasizes differences between men and women and the value of qualities and experiences traditionally associated with women. Because it celebrates women's differences and women's culture, it is also called cultural feminism or 'gynocentric' feminism. One early and influential feminist of this kind, Susan Griffin, celebrates the connection between women and nature (1978).³ However, some aspects of equality feminism and difference/gynocentric feminism can be combined – arguing, for example, that more nontraditional careers should be open to women because of the special skills that women would bring or emphasizing how deeply rooted in prevailing family structure is women's socialization.[4] Today, in fact, many feminists hold a combination of these positions. Even Katha Pollitt, who in 1992 critiqued difference feminism in an article titled 'Are Women Morally Superior to Men?' has modified her position and writes:

> Denying essentialism [the view that the sexes are essentially different] can slip over into valuing women most when they are most 'like men'. But don't we deserve a little credit for the fact that in no society on earth do women commit more than a small fraction of murders? (Reed and Pollitt 2015: 56)

Western culture has constructed a set of polarities in which one side is usually thought of as feminine and the other as masculine – for example, body, changeability, night and mercy are feminine and mind, stability, day and justice are masculine, although the allegorical figure for justice is female (Stimpson and Herdt 2014: 5). Cultural feminists often argue that women should affirm such associations and try to raise their cultural value, while other feminists favour instead deconstructing cultural ideas of masculine and feminine.[5] Which is worse for women – lack of equal pay for equal work, the assumption that they are less competent in their careers or the fact that nurturing qualities women may have are not valued highly in our culture? Liberal equality feminism emphasizes the first and second (while arguing for improved negotiating skills and greater individual effort, 'leaning in'), materialist equality feminism the first, with unionization and other collective efforts if possible, and cultural feminism the third. Still others, including some psychoanalytic feminists, would add that the lesser valuation of nurturing qualities also harms the nurturing potential in men, and society as a whole.[6]

INTRODUCTION

> *Guilt, insecurities of men led to their behaviour/treatment to women etc...*

Is it good to welcome both 'masculine' and 'feminine' characteristics in both women and men or should the terms themselves be abandoned because they maintain divisions and associations that should be broken up? <u>Shakespeare's plays often suggest that the men who call women changeable, deceptive and emotional may well have as many of these qualities themselves.</u> Will this be more obvious if we stop associating changeability with femininity? Or should we value changeability positively, using words like 'flexibility' and 'versatility' instead, and be glad that they are associated with women?

[Othello]

[King Lear?]

Equality feminists emphasize the importance of women's choice and women's access to the same rights as men. From this standpoint, <u>women's ability to choose a husband and not just accede to a marriage arranged by their families is an important feature of many of Shakespeare's plays.</u> But equality feminists might also bring into consideration the sexual double standard in marriage, and materialist feminists among them adduce as well the material conditions of marriage in Shakespeare's time, and might critique as fantasies textual suggestions of female power continuing after marriage. The actual practice of feminist Shakespeare critics often combines many different theoretical approaches.

[Romeo + Juliet]

Feminist Shakespeare criticism

While most influential works of feminist theory analyse women's subordination, the first book of feminist Shakespeare criticism, <u>Juliet Dusinberre's *Shakespeare and the Nature of Women*,</u> celebrates the characterization of women in his plays. Dusinberre argues that the power of Shakespeare's female characters resulted, in part, from the influence of religious reformers of the time, who criticized enforced marriage, the ideal of virginity and the double standard. Dusinberre follows the equality tradition in looking for women's agency and avoidance of stereotypes, concluding: 'Shakespeare saw men and women as equal in a world which declared them unequal' (2003 [1975]: 308).

Coppélia Kahn, another early feminist Shakespeare critic who praises Shakespeare's vision, focuses instead on his portrayal of men and their fantasies and fears in *Man's Estate* (1981). She finds his male characters have fantasies similar to those Freud identified in men and argues that Shakespeare questions and critiques those fantasies. By contrast, other early feminist critics maintain that the plays promote the subordination and exclusion of women. Clara Claiborne Park argues that there is subordination even in the romantic comedies in 'As We Like It: How a Girl Can be Smart and Still Popular' (1980).[7] Lisa Jardine's *Still Harping on Daughters* faults previous feminist criticism for treating the characters too much as real women and thus forgetting the impact of the boy actors who played them, and argues that reformers' ideas about marriage did not actually improve the position of women, and that in some respects the position of women worsened (1989 [1983]). This contrast between emphasizing women's agency and emphasizing women's containment – a contrast that does not consistently map onto other theoretical differences – has been central in the development of feminist Shakespeare criticism, though a critic might acknowledge both and analyse their interaction. Madelon Gohlke [Sprengnether] argues that the heroes of Shakespeare's tragedies are violent against women because those men feel weak in relation to them; the strength of women in these plays gives 'a rationale for the manifest text of male dominance' (1980).[8] Kathleen McLuskie's materialist feminist contribution to *Political Shakespeare* maintains, discussing *Measure for Measure*, that 'Feminist criticism … is restricted to exposing its own exclusion from the text', though she also imagines that it might make 'a text reveal the conditions in which a particular ideology of femininity functions' (1985: 97, 106).

Other early works of feminist criticism argue for variation in gender representations among Shakespeare's plays. Linda

Bamber emphasizes generic contrast in *Comic Women, Tragic Men* (1983). While Peter Erickson underlines the male-centricity of Shakespeare's plays in *Patriarchal Structures in Shakespeare's Drama*, stressing the importance of patriarchy even in *As You Like It* and *The Winter's Tale*, he distinguishes harsh from gentle patriarchy and sees more flexibility of gender roles in *Antony and Cleopatra* (1985). The British materialist feminist Catherine Belsey analyses both the loss of a speaking position for women in Shakespeare's and other tragedies (1985a: 183) and the free play of plural identifications in the comedies (1985b). In *Broken Nuptials in Shakespeare's Plays*, Carol Thomas Neely considers innovation in traditions of genre along with feminist psychoanalytic insights and close textual awareness as she shows how disruptions of the movement towards marriage reveals gender conflicts (1985).

Feminist Shakespeare criticism and other approaches

The field of literary study was changing in a number of ways in the 1980s and all affected feminist criticism. By this point, recent French feminist criticism had been translated into English, some of it responding to the French-originating deconstruction and Lacanian structuralism that were also influencing the field. Deconstruction is a mode of literary analysis associated particularly with Jacques Derrida. It involves breaking down binary oppositions, showing how the apparently more favoured pole actually depends on and involves its opposite: the 'self', for example, needs an 'other' to define itself against and projects aspects of itself into the other. The feminist implications of this approach include the idea that patriarchal societies overvalue what is considered masculine (e.g. rationality, public life) and deny its dependence on (and inclusion of) on what is considered feminine (e.g. emotions, private life). Jacques Lacan argues that a sense of identity develops from mirroring others, and that the child enters the world of public discourse only by identifying with the father. Like Freud, he defines all sexual desire as masculine, and thus he argues that 'woman' can enter into language only by imagining herself as men imagine her.[9]

Deconstruction is more congenial to feminist analysis than is Lacanian structuralism. Hélène Cixous, like Derrida, is interested in breaking down binary oppositions, and argues that woman's body and what she calls '*écriture féminine*', women's or feminine writing, do this also: 'women have a pre-conceptual, non-appropriative openness to people and to objects' (Jones 1985: 89). She believes that some male writers – especially Shakespeare – also break down oppositions, and writes at some length about *Antony and Cleopatra*, in which she emphasizes the gender fluidity of both title characters (1986). Luce Irigaray writes against the exclusion of women from the symbolic, trying to develop a language for women's desire (Jones 1985: 83–5). Julia Kristeva focuses on the importance of a pre-linguistic state associated with the infant's relationship with the mother, which she thinks experimental writers both male and female can evoke in their writing (Jones 1985: 85–6): she has analysed how the complicated feelings of this state appear in *Romeo and Juliet* (Kristeva 1987: 211). By contrast, Monique Wittig argues against the whole psychoanalytic framework and glorification of metaphorical '*fémininité*' of the other three. Instead she writes against the myth of 'woman', tries to destroy 'the material and conceptual stranglehold of heterosexuality' and writes fictions imagining a group of women in traditionally male positions, e.g. *Les Guerillères* (the warriors, gendered feminine) (Jones 1985: 91). This could be considered a precedent for recent all-female productions of some of Shakespeare's most male-dominated plays, such as *Henry IV*.[10]

Some feminist Shakespeare critics have used French psycho-analytic theory, feminist and not, to analyse Shakespeare's characters – for example, Carol Cook questions whether Beatrice offers an alternative to the militaristic value system of

Much Ado about Nothing (1995 [1986]), and Catherine Belsey uses Kristeva's advocacy of disrupting sexual identity to show that cross-dressed figures in *As You Like It* and *Twelfth Night* have not a unified subjectivity but a multiplicity of possible identifications (1985b). The strategies developed by Cixous, Irigaray and Kristeva, of looking for gaps and, in particular, gaps that suggest the absences of a mother have been used by many Shakespeare critics – notably Coppélia Kahn, showing that although there are no actual mothers in *King Lear*, a fantasy mother terrifies Lear's disturbed mind (1986).

Two other approaches that have influenced feminist Shakespeare criticism are new historicism, mostly American, pioneered in Stephen Greenblatt's *Renaissance Self-Fashioning* (1980), and cultural materialism, mostly coming from British sources, appearing in the collections *Alternative Shakespeares* (1985) and *Political Shakespeare: New Essays in Cultural Materialism* (1985), which also included new historicists. Both of these movements deny the view that the plays should be interpreted with reference to an eternal human nature or to a single dominant ideology of their time. In this respect, they can be allied with feminists who point out historical changes in the conditions of women. Cultural materialists frequently look for places in Shakespeare's texts suggestive of transgressive moments or revolutionary movements in early modern culture or analyse how his plays have been politically appropriated in performance, by critics or in the educational system. New historicists often juxtapose well-known literary texts, such as Shakespeare's, with more obscure and/or non-'literary' historical texts or anecdotes. As Jean Howard writes, they emphasize gaps and discontinuities between past and present, and contradictions within texts and cultures (1986). All of these approaches are also useful for feminist critics. Initially feminist emphasis on gender was in tension with cultural materialists' focus on class and new historicists' focus on state power and how subversion is contained and recuperated. However, many feminists eventually found that they could deploy strategies and ideas of both movements

(Catherine Belsey and Kathleen McLuskie were part of cultural materialism from the beginning), and more of their colleagues brought gender into their analyses and also moved beyond the arguments in which new historicists argued that in Shakespeare's plays state power always contained challenges while cultural materialists argued for the continued possibility of subversion.[11]

More recent feminist Shakespeare criticism

Fewer contemporary critics would now claim to interpret the plays in terms of a consistent ideology held by Shakespeare, whether feminism, patriarchy or something else; they are more likely to look for tensions and omissions. Today the dominant practice in feminist Shakespeare criticism involves invoking history in some way, whether it is from archives of Shakespeare's time, of later performances or films or the editing or criticism or creative revision of his texts. However, this use of history is by no means a retreat to the past; many find that the most interesting criticism is driven by a concern also relevant to its own time of writing.[12]

The range of issues considered has changed greatly since the early days of feminist Shakespeare criticism, most of it correlating with the expansions of concern in other forms of feminist criticism. Feminist Shakespeareans can now discuss the intersection of gender and race, in analyses pioneered by Karen Newman (1987), Ania Loomba (1989, 2002), Margo Hendricks and Patricia Parker (1993) and Kim Hall (1995). Such analyses are not limited to discussing the representation of black characters but also discuss the construction of 'whiteness' as part of the conventional idea of beauty, and particularly the use of the term 'fair', and also, like Ayanna Thompson, performance issues such as colour-blind and colour-conscious casting (2006). Loomba, who brings appropriations of Shakespeare in India into the picture, is a leader in combining feminist and postcolonial analysis, a move that becomes especially important today as Shakespeare performance and study is clearly a global phenomenon.

Feminist criticism has further benefited from and contributed to analyses considering the history of sexuality. Like race-conscious analysis, this goes further than studying certain marked characters – identified, in this case, as gay or lesbian. As Valerie Traub most influentially has shown, critics can study how desire circulates, considering the plays' text and performance and other evidence from social history. She shows how desire can be ambiguously both same-sex and opposite-sex because of the use of boy actors as female characters and female characters' male disguises (1992, 2002). Feminist criticism of Shakespeare now also considers such varied topics as the relation of women to the environment and to animals, to categories such as religion, nation and class, and to work within both the household and the theatre (Laroche and Munroe 2017; Wall 2002, 2016; Korda 2011). Women with feminist viewpoints are editing Shakespeare and analysing how bias has influenced preceding editions (Maguire 2000) and writing feminist criticism of performances and adaptations (Hodgdon 1998).

In the following chapters, this book discusses Shakespeare's plays with regard to key issues in feminist theory. Basic questions about gender are discussed in Chapter 1, 'Likeness and Difference'. Feminist psychoanalytic theory is especially important in Chapters 2 and 4, 'Desire' and 'Motherhood', and materialist feminist theory in Chapter 7 'Work'. Queer theory is used in 'Desire' and in 'Between Women', Chapter 6, which also considers race and class. These chapters show how critics differ in interpretation depending on which theoretical frame they use and sometimes how feminist critics may differ even within the same theoretical frame. Chapter 3, 'Marriage', while invoking history more than any other chapter except Chapter 7, 'Work', also uses psychoanalytic, materialist and queer theory, as well as discussing feminist critiques of the justice of that institution. Chapter 5, 'Language', includes feminist issues in editing; reception and theatrical history are considered in this chapter and several others. Overall, the critics discussed follow equality feminist theory more than difference feminist theory, or combine them, but this does not mean that they necessarily find a commitment to either kind of feminism in Shakespeare.[13]

It is now hard to find new scholarship debating whether Shakespeare was a feminist. Perhaps the arguments on the larger issue have been set out sufficiently, the concept of unified authorial intent undermined and feminism itself shown to be manifold in its meanings. Many of us believe the effects of his plays are too complex, multiple and changeable to sum up in a simple way. However, feminist theory can still help analyse the dynamics of his plays and their textual, critical, cultural and performance history.

1

Likeness and difference

The early twentieth-century playwright George Bernard Shaw, often praised during his lifetime for his female characters, said: 'I always assumed that a woman was a person exactly like myself' (Watson 1975 [1927]: 114). We have no such statement from William Shakespeare. If we did, some feminist theorists would applaud him for it, but others would object because they felt it denied important differences between women and men. As Nancy Cott writes, 'Both theory and practice in feminism historically have had to deal with the fact that women are the same as and different from men' (1986: 49). One writer could often make both points, as Virginia Woolf does in *A Room of One's Own*. She both protests the economic and social limitations women have had to deal with and praises the special domestic talents and values that, she argues, women have developed. Does Shakespeare present women as like men or different? Juliet Dusinberre, whose emphasis on women's equality in Shakespeare was quoted in the Introduction, nevertheless is explicit, as are many theorists, that equality does not mean sameness (2003 [1975]: 308).[1]

What evidence and arguments can be used to consider the question of women's likeness and/or difference to men in Shakespeare's works? Do his plays show female characters as sharing qualities with male ones, including some that qualify them to go beyond their usual social limitations? Do they better support a contrasting approach by showing women as different from men and indeed better? Or a feminism that argues that often women's differences from men are the regrettable and remediable result of male dominance (Mackinnon 2006)? Do they show not a feminist attitude but one which sees women as worse than men? Or do they reveal that the distinctions of gender are fluid and unclear? Or are they inconsistent?

In its strictest sense, equality feminism (also called humanist feminism because it defines gender difference as accidental to humanity) has as its goal 'bringing women and men under a common measure, judged by the same standards ... freeing women from the confines of traditional femininity' (Young 2006: 175–6). Most famously developed by Simone de Beauvoir and Betty Friedan, equality feminism aims to open all careers and all human possibilities to women. Difference feminism (also called gynocentric) argues that 'women's oppression consists ... [in] the denial and devaluation of specifically feminine virtues and activities by an overly instrumentalized and authoritarian masculinist culture' (Young 2006: 178). This kind of feminism, or views similar to it, is associated with French feminists such as Hélène Cixous and Luce Irigaray, as well as with psychologists such as Carol Gilligan (1982) and ecofeminists such as Susan Griffin (1978). However, as later discussion of her view of *Antony and Cleopatra* shows, Cixous does not believe that only women can show qualities that she considers both feminine and valuable. In this book, I use both 'difference' and 'gynocentric', both 'equality' and 'humanist', in alluding to the contrast between these emphases, but readers should note that the term 'humanist' is used with many other connotations in other contexts.

More than those of many other writers, Shakespeare's plays raise questions about the similarity or difference between men and women because many of his female characters disguise their sex or protest against the limitations attributed to it. While a number of characters either generalize explicitly about women or men or use metaphors about the woman- or man-like quality of their own or another's behaviour, often characters' behaviour challenges these generalizations. Furthermore, feminist criticism of his as well as of other early modern plays from England needs to evaluate the relevance of their original use of boy actors to play female characters as well as their subsequent history. Studying this question takes us more deeply into the question of what were the ideas about gender and sex in Shakespeare's society.

Boy actors

Feminist critics and others have hypothesized various consequences of the fact that boy actors originally performed women on Shakespeare's stage. One position is that casting boy actors as women was simply accepted as a convention (Jensen 1975). The opposite view emphasizes the exclusion of biological women from the stage. As developed by the influential historian Lisa Jardine, it claims that audiences responded to the plays with regard to the sex of the actor rather than the character. Thus the early interest in these plays should be largely attributed to the homoeroticism of the men in the audience, as Jardine (1989) and Callaghan (2000a) suggest. This view of the audience also appeared in the anti-theatrical tracts of the sixteenth and seventeenth centuries. These tracts assume that any man could be tempted by a good-looking boy. Most modern historians of sexuality agree that that was a prevalent assumption of the time, as opposed to the view developed mainly in the late nineteenth century that same-sex attraction is experienced only by a distinct minority (DiGangi 1997).

Stephen Greenblatt (1988) has argued that England's use of boy actors to play women is a result of the early modern belief in a one-sex model of human biology – a model postulated by historian Thomas Laqueur on the basis of the classical physician Galen's explanation of the similarities between male and female reproductive biology and anecdotes of women turning into men as a result of increasing their body heat (1990).[2] Laqueur calls the Galenic view a one-sex model, in which women were colder, incomplete versions of men. Janet Adelman, however, has shown that there is little evidence for English belief in the one-sex model at the time (1999). Nevertheless, in addition to a model of the two sexes as different, the culture also included a belief (related perhaps to Laqueur's suggestion that women were seen as incomplete men) that women and boys were similar – both groups being seen as changeable, vulnerable and attractive to men (Orgel 1997: 70; Jardine 1983; Howard 1994). This belief, not the same as the belief in the potential likeness of the sexes associated with the equality emphasis developed near the beginning of this chapter, is part of what made the performance of women's roles by boys believable onstage.

Kathleen McLuskie argues that costumes and the boys' unbroken voices also helped to make them acceptable when performing as women. 'The fictions of Elizabethan drama would have been rendered nonsensical if at every appearance of a female character ... their gender was called into question' (1989: 102). Most early modern representations of female characters on the English stage showed them as clearly female. However, many plays are theatrically self-conscious enough that there are moments that call attention to the sex of the actors. And most probably spectators differed in their interest and productions also differed in their emphasis.

Some feminist critics have suggested that the theatrical practice of training boys to play female characters could have heightened Shakespeare's sensitivity to the idea that gender is a role (Novy 1984: 20; Shapiro 1994: 37). This view can also accompany an emphasis on how women in Shakespeare's plays, whether disguised as boys or not, often show greater abilities than social convention usually recognizes (a view associated with equality feminism), and/or with a comparison between their skill at role-playing/masquerade and that of the boy actor of female characters. The early modern association of boys with women, combined with the later history of performance and interpretation, means that the use of boy actors for female characters is too complicated to be accounted for by, or to reinforce, a simple belief in either the difference or the similarity of the sexes (Callaghan 2000a). The last chapter, 'Work', returns to the issue of boy actors and the exclusion of women from some more recent perspectives.

Male rule and female responses

The worldview opposed to all kinds of feminism – the rightness of the rule of men over women – was a more explicit belief in early modern English society than is the case in much of the world today. That rule might be justified by the Bible, as it then often was, by belief in man's superior rationality or simply by biology (Howard 1994: 98–9). Katherine's long speech near the end of *The Taming of the Shrew* invokes the latter rationale, among others, when she argues from 'bodies soft, and weak, and smooth' (5.2.166) to accepting subordination.[3] But not everybody living in the same country at the same time shares the same beliefs: Raymond Williams' differentiation between dominant, residual, and emergent ideologies is helpful (1977). In many countries today, male supremacy varies between dominant and residual – in Shakespeare's time and society it was certainly dominant, though some women found loopholes.[4] However, in early modern England, emergent ideals of partnership in marriage and even the equality of the sexes could be imagined and believed in by some, and those people might have found support for their views in Shakespeare's comedies. On the other hand, those who believed in male dominance would probably have been reassured by the anticipation of marriage that concludes most of these plays.

But tragedies and histories, while they may show women attempting more than social custom allows them, often present those attempts as ending in disaster. Lady Macbeth and Cleopatra, for example, both try to function as partners in realms of violence they or others at their time consider unfeminine, the first by plotting murder and the second by leading her men in a sea battle. The former eventually suffers guilt-related insanity, the latter makes a fear-related flight. Both women kill themselves and are often considered largely responsible for the hero's downfall and death. These and most others of Shakespeare's tragedies can be seen as dramatizing a fear common in Shakespeare's time – that the influence of a woman might make a man effeminate – more like a woman, therefore cowardly and emotional. While many today may welcome the idea of fluid gender boundaries, in the early modern period (as to others today) they were often seen as threatening.

Female characters and the difference question in comedy

There are many examples of female intelligence and skill in Shakespeare's comedies. In *Twelfth Night*, Viola fills the role of Orsino's courtly attendant so well that as Cesario, s/he is preferred to all the others. Similarly, in *The Merchant of Venice*, Portia in her disguise as the young lawyer Balthasar solves Venice's legal problem with Shylock. Both Portia and Rosalind compare their own behaviour in disguise as men to those of swashbuckling, bragging men who hide the fear in their hearts or their real intentions. Like Judith Butler in *Gender Trouble*, they suggest that performing one's expected gender is no less a construction than performing a different gender (1990). Rosalind as Ganymede protects her companion Celia, still in female disguise, buys a house and charms and manages all the other characters, so she is a favourite of those who emphasize similarity and role-playing, but on the other hand she faints at the sight of blood from an injury to her beloved Orlando, which can be taken as exposure of feminine vulnerability – or affirmation of feminine sympathy (Howard 1994: 118).[5]

What about the issue of female difference or similarity in plays where cross-gender disguise is not part of the plot, such as *Much Ado about Nothing*? Does Beatrice show that Shakespeare can imagine a relationship of equals? *Much Ado* juxtaposes two characters, Beatrice and Benedick, who have much in common, and contrasts their relationship with that of the couple Hero and Claudio who are very different from each other. Beatrice and Benedick are both witty and sceptical about marriage and seem mutually hostile – in the first part of the play they have many scenes of dialogue that consist mainly of mirrored insults. Having observed their wit-combats, Don Pedro says of Beatrice, 'She were an excellent wife for Benedick' (2.1.331). He does not speak of the likelihood that, as many readers and audiences conclude, they are already interested in each other, but rather calls bringing them together 'one of Hercules' labours' (333–4). Nevertheless, this plot coincides with the frequent advice in marriage sermons at the time that husband and wife should be similar.[6]

To a large degree the play is symmetrical in its treatment of Benedick and Beatrice, showing each falling for the story that the other's insulting behaviour is really a mask for love. It is easy to imagine this fiction as representing psychological truth, though some critics see it as principally enacting Messina's social pressure towards marriage.[7] By contrast, Hero and Claudio don't start out insulting each other – they hardly ever talk to each other onstage. And Hero contrasts markedly with Beatrice, most obviously because Hero says almost nothing at all, except in two all-female scenes. Beatrice is an advocate of women's freedom, while Hero's longest speech criticizes Beatrice for her lack of respect for men.

However, responses to Beatrice show how various kinds of feminists can disagree. Her wit-combats with Benedick might seem to make this couple an example of the potential similarity of women and men. But three different arguments oppose this view. One is the claim of Barbara Everett that Beatrice exemplifies the greater maturity of the 'women's world' in Shakespeare's comedies – a loyalty and sense of values that wins Benedick over. Everett sounds like a difference feminist at this point, though she is explicitly not claiming Shakespeare as a feminist (1970 [1961]: 290). Equality feminists, however, see differences that are not in Beatrice's favour: when she gives in to love, she promises that she will humble herself to Benedick and she allows him to have the last word at the end (Park 1980: 105–6). A third view is Carol Cook's, that Beatrice's similarity to Benedick is not a good thing: 'instead of challenging Messina's masculine ethos, she participates in its assumptions and values' and this is particularly clear in her desire for revenge on Claudio (1995 [1986]: 83). Cook asserts that a gynocentric feminist position, celebrating female difference, is impossible in the world of *Much Ado*:

> the construction of femininity within an economy of representation governed by the phallus – a construction in which women mirror masculine identity by their own lack – obviates the possibility of 'feminine values' or of a feminine alternative to the 'predominately masculine ethos' (1995 [1986]: 82).

In other words, the similarity in values of Beatrice and Benedick makes the play's world one ruled by violence.

Cook is right about the oddness of identifying Beatrice with an ethic of charity, given her insistence on revenge. On the other hand, Cook's structuralist/psychoanalytic approach seems somewhat rigid, as Valerie Traub has argued (1992: 46–7). Though Beatrice wants revenge for Claudio's denunciation of Hero, urging Benedick to kill him in a duel can be seen as a moment in her behaviour in the play in which, like almost everyone in it, she goes too far, rather than as the key to her character. Another interpretation would associate her, because of her wit, more with the fool than with the phallus.[8]

Arguably, the double plot of *Much Ado* invites thought about whether a relationship based on similarity (Beatrice and Benedick) or one based on difference (Hero and Claudio) is preferable – modernity mostly chooses the first; but Beatrice and Benedick long seem to have been the audience favourites. The play seems to have been occasionally referred to as 'Benedick and Beatrice' as early as 1613, as Claire McEachern notes, so this view may not be simply a modern one (2006: 109).

Characters and the difference question in other genres

The issue of female difference or similarity is also explicitly evoked in *Macbeth*, and what Cook says about Beatrice's imitation of masculine aggression could with more truth describe Lady Macbeth. Macbeth encourages her, paradoxically: 'Bring forth men-children only! / For thy undaunted mettle should compose / Nothing but males' (1.6.73–5). Lady Macbeth wishes that both of them could collaborate, using masculine traits that would promote their success. She criticizes him for being 'too full o' th' milk of human kindness' (1.5.16), and prays to the spirits of darkness to be unsexed (40) and to have her milk replaced with gall or turned into gall (47).

But she is the 'dearest partner of greatness' (1.5.10) only briefly. Later, she is reduced to trying to comfort him in ignorance, acting out guilt as he never does, and finally to killing herself. This is the opposite of Macbeth's continued commissioning and acting out of violence against others. In the banquet scene, as in the scene just discussed, both use imagery of manhood to describe the behaviour they admire and imagery of womanhood to describe the behaviour they scorn. As the play develops, however, these similarities in how they speak coexist with the contrast in what they do. Traditionalists often analyse the play in conservatively gendered terms: they blame Lady Macbeth for forswearing the female quality of mercy and Macbeth for letting a woman overrule his better judgement

[handwritten annotation: Lady Macbeth and witches]

and also associate Lady Macbeth with the mixed-gender witches who deceive Macbeth, as women were frequently thought to deceive men. The implication becomes that a woman with masculine values will destroy and be destroyed. However, with the militarism, violence and denigration of women everywhere in the world of this play, it is also open to a reading interpreting these values, coming from patriarchal society, as themselves the problem, whether they are seen as anti-human or as opposed specifically to the more compassionate values traditionally associated with women though rejected by Lady Macbeth (Kahn 1981: 151–2).

Lady Macbeth's destruction in a military world is not unique in Shakespeare's plays. The Roman plays – *Titus Andronicus*, *Julius Caesar*, *Timon of Athens*, *Anthony and Cleopatra* and *Coriolanus* – and the English history plays include events that dramatize tensions around the women characters' relation to violence more emphatically than plays set in a mixed gender court or a peacetime household, such as the comedies. The early history plays include several aspiring women, such as Eleanor Cobham and Joan of Arc, but the best fate any of them has onstage is to survive to curse after suffering the loss of many sons, like Queen Margaret. In the second tetralogy, women have even less of a voice. *Julius Caesar* also shows a predominantly male political world and accents women's exclusion: Brutus is reluctant to tell Portia, his wife, of the conspiracy to kill Caesar, because of his belief in women's lack of self-control.

Feminist critics can interpret these plays as showing a limited view of women – or, conversely, as protesting the worlds that limit them. Coppélia Kahn, taking the second position, argues that the Roman plays 'articulate a critique of the ideology of gender on which the Renaissance understanding of Rome was based' (1997: 1). Calphurnia, Caesar's wife, tells him not to go to the Senate building on the Ides of March because of her dream; while Caesar at first listens with concern, he then concurs with Decius' mockery of this superstition. Of course, Calphurnia turns out to be right. Characters associate female difference with irrationality, but the knowledge coming from dreams and other irrational sources (augurers, presumably male) is vindicated.

An even stronger critique of the Roman ideology of gender has been seen in *Antony and Cleopatra*. The Romans generally look down on Cleopatra, as a woman as well as an Egyptian, and apply to her stereotypes of women such as lustful and fickle, but finally, even such quintessential Romans as Enobarbus and Octavius pay tribute to her personal power. The French feminist Hélène Cixous praises her for showing 'at every instant another face, at each breath a passion', so that her eventual desire to be 'marble-constant' (5.2.239) becomes just another side of her 'infinite variety' (2.2.246) (1986: 123). Cixous finds *Antony and Cleopatra* a great example of Shakespeare's ability to write in a feminine way, imagining qualities associated with both sexes, in both of his main characters; in his worlds, she says, 'man turns back into woman, woman into man' (1986: 98). American feminist critics make similar observations about this play: Peter Erickson, for example, writes that the play shows the two 'crossing back and forth over a boundary no longer seen as a rigid barrier dividing the two sexes into two absolutely separate groups' (1985: 133).

The romances mostly focus on the family life of a male ruler, involving his relation to women, rather than his identity as a warrior, to an even larger extent than the tragedies and histories. Their titular heroes sometimes compare themselves to women, and not always negatively. For example, Cymbeline, on finding his lost children, says, 'O, what am I? / A mother to the birth of three?' (5.5.369–70). Pericles sees that endurance, on which he prides himself, is a quality that crosses gender boundaries. Before he recognizes his long-lost daughter, he says to her,

> Tell thy story;
> If thine consider'd prove the thousandth part
> Of my endurance, thou art a man, and I
> Have suffer'd like a girl.
>
> (5.1.135–8)

In the fantasy world of *The Tempest's* island, Miranda can be brought up without expected gender socialization, so that she proposes to Ferdinand – and the emphasis on a shared endurance repeats when she offers to help him carry logs. In general, women are freer to act like men, or at least boys, in the comedies and the romances. In the tragedies and histories their deviations from expected behaviour are likely to end in death – but so also is their compliance with expected behaviour.

Characters' language

Today, feminist critics are less likely to discuss likeness and difference between the sexes in blanket terms, but nevertheless this issue is part of critical history, still comes up in the classroom (students have frequently mentioned to me generalizations about Shakespeare's women made by previous instructors) and is certainly a matter of discussion within the plays themselves. Many of Shakespeare's characters, whether male or female, generalize about women. Often their generalizations imply women's difference. However, many speeches describe male characters as resembling women. And, occasionally, female characters generalize about what they have in common with men. An eighteenth- and nineteenth-century tradition still with us takes characters' words out of context as direct expression of Shakespeare's own attitudes. But citation of even a few speeches shows how full of contradictions the plays are on this issue.

The Shakespeare passage in which a character makes the longest explicit argument for similarity between the sexes is a speech by Emilia, near the end of *Othello*. Its point was less unusual at the time than its specific strategy. In Castiglione's then well-known dialogue about court life, *The Courtier*, one of the speakers, the Magnifico, argues that women are intellectually equal to men.[9] Cornelius Agrippa, whose work was also translated into English around 1540, and includes a reading of the Biblical creation story that resembles Beatrice's feminist rhetoric, writes, 'the woman hath the same mind that a man hath, the same reason and speech'.[10] One of the characters in another dialogue, *The Flower of Friendship*, says, 'Women have souls as well as men, they have wit as well as men. What reason is it, then, that they should be bound whom nature has made free?' (Tilney 1992 [1568]: 133). However, Emilia declares:

> Let husbands know
> Their wives have sense like them: they see, and smell,
> And have their palates both for sweet and sour
> As husbands have. What is it that they do
> When they change us for others? Is it sport?
> I think it is. And doth affection breed it?
> I think it doth. Is't frailty that thus errs?
> It is so too. And have not we affections?
> Desires for sport? and frailty, as men have?
> Then let them use us well; else let them know.
> The ills we do, their ills instruct us so
>
> (4.3.92–102)

This speech argues for women's likeness to men on the grounds not of souls, wit or reason, but rather on the grounds of feelings not generally regarded as praiseworthy. Emilia turns around the stereotyped association of women with changeable emotions by starting with the observation that they account for men's behaviour. No idealization here – equality comes on the grounds that we are all flawed.

The status of this passage in the text is controversial. Among early versions of the play, it is found in the First Folio (F, 1623, which included almost all his plays), and not the First Quarto (Q, 1622, *Othello* only). Scholars argue about whether Shakespeare added it or cut it. Did he want to make its point explicit? Or did the boy playing Emilia have trouble saying it convincingly? Did the audience laugh?[11] Editors and directors have sometimes cut the speech because they found it shocking, and from 1755 through most of the nineteenth century, most English and American productions dropped almost the whole scene (Hankey 2005: 255, 259). But since the 1970s this speech has been recognized as one of Emilia's great moments. Briefer passages from other characters plus those from other writers just cited show that similarity between the sexes as an argument for women's rights was not impossible to contemplate at the time.

On the other hand, consider the framing of several Shakespearean passages that assert the weakness of women, because of fearfulness or changeability. Hamlet says 'Frailty, thy name is woman' (1.2.146), thinking of his mother's lack of faithfulness to his father. Orsino also sees women as frail when he insists

> There is no woman's sides
> Can bide the beating of so strong a passion
> As love doth give my heart; no woman's heart
> So big, to hold so much.
>
> (2.4.94–7)

Though she disagrees with him about women's love, Viola too believes in women's weakness. She explains Olivia's sudden love of her in her disguise by saying, 'How easy is it for the proper false / In women's waxen hearts to set their forms! / Alas, our frailty is the cause, not we, / For such as we are made of, such we be' (2.2.29–32).

How do the plays bear out or challenge the assertions about gender in these lines? In context, do *Twelfth Night* and *Hamlet* show their female characters as frail, more changeable than men? Olivia does change, from her determined celibacy to her love of Cesario to her acceptance of Viola's twin Sebastian. But so does Orsino, from his love of Olivia to his proposal to Viola. In 2.4 he insists both that he and other men are more changeable than women and that he and other men are more constant.

Viola has changed her appearance when she disguises herself as Cesario, but in that disguise she defends women against Orsino's charge of their changeability: 'In faith, they are as true of heart as we' (2.5.107). On a deeper level her character, faithful to Orsino, exemplifies this constancy. So does Maria, who is giving advice to Sir Toby Belch from her first appearance until the last.

Changeability and constancy do not easily break down by gender category in *Twelfth Night*. Sir Andrew Aguecheek is weak and frail by most definitions, Antonio apparently stable in his devotion to Sebastian. The same characters may often show signs of both. Malvolio's changeability from his initial sternness to wooing Olivia is one of the big jokes of the play, though at the end he changes back to sternness. Is the prevalence of some kind of change just because this play is a comedy? How about *Hamlet*? Does that play bear out Hamlet's charge that women are frail and insincere? Hamlet makes a number of similar charges to Ophelia, e.g. 'God hath given you one face and you make yourselves another' (3.1.144–5). Ophelia can be seen as weak because she obeys her father, Polonius, in breaking up with Hamlet at one point and then returning to talk to him when Polonius asks her; but on the other hand does it prove the sincerity and strength of her love for Hamlet that she goes mad after he kills Polonius?

Hamlet himself acknowledges his own deceptiveness or changeability in this scene when he says in successive speeches, 'I did love you once' and 'I loved you not' (3.1.115, 119). If he is pretending to be mad, he is deceptive on a larger scale; if he is really mad, then he is changeable on a larger scale. Hamlet compares his emotional language about his situation to that of 'a whore ..., a very drab, a scullion' (2.2.587–9). These suggestions of his own fear of being too feminine himself are other ways in which the play challenges the idea that men and women have distinctly contrasting characters. Gertrude may indeed be as insincere as Hamlet thinks, though we never know for sure; but Claudius, Polonius, Rosencrantz and Guildenstern are insincere also.

Hamlet's own attack on Ophelia and Gertrude for changeability can be seen as projection – he attacks them for what he hates in himself. This dynamic is often the context of words that attack female 'difference' in Shakespeare's tragedies. Iago accuses Desdemona of being deceptive, as he says all Venetian women are: 'their best conscience / Is not to leave't undone, but keep't unknown' (3.3.206–7). But he himself is deceptive. Lear in mid-play attacks tears as 'women's weapons' (2.2.469) when he feels he might weep; later, in his madness, he rails at women's lust – 'The fitchew nor the soiled horse, goes to't with a more riotous appetite' (4.6.120–1) – but he himself just a few lines later identifies the projection in a policeman's violence: 'Why dost thou lash that whore? Strip thine own back, / Thou hotly lusts to use her in that kind / For which thou whipp'st her' (157–9). Repeatedly the plays show men's attacks on women as projection.

Different, similar or equal?

Do any of the plays show women as different and actually superior to men? Many audience members, readers, and critics have said that Shakespeare's women are often more intelligent than his men, and in particular that the disguised women in comedies are more intelligent than the men they marry. This effect comes partly from the men's failure to recognize the women, but it also results from, for example, Portia's ability to deal with Shylock better than the men, and the critical attitude both Rosalind and Viola take towards the clichés about love uttered by Orlando and especially the self-centred Orsino. These plays can be seen as showing the value of female difference, without necessarily taking a stand on whether this comes from biology or experience, or for that matter whether it extends to other women than the superior heroine.

In other plays, the foolishness of men who don't see through masks of masculine clothing is multiplied in the foolishness of male characters who are deceived into believing in a woman's faithlessness – Claudio, Leonato, Othello, Leontes,

Posthumus, Ford. By contrast, loyal Beatrice and Paulina seem wise. However, these plays do contain an occasional wise man (such as the Friar, in *Much Ado*, though his plot to arouse Claudio's conscience doesn't work), and other comedies include women whose intelligence is not superior, for example Audrey, whose class position is lower than the central female characters.

The plays do not show that all women are superior to all men, although some women in them are equal to some men and superior to many. The plays do not give us easy generalizations about whether women are like men/equal to men or different. Many female characters are changeable in some ways, but so are many male characters. And some of those characters can be seen also as remaining themselves through all the changes. Beatrice says she will tame herself to Benedick, but close to the end of the play she is still teasing him.

Men and women in the plays are both flawed. Perhaps Camille Slights is right that the plays present male authority as 'an arbitrary human authority unjustified by natural superiority' (1991: 241). 'Why should their liberty than ours be more?' (2.1.10) asks Adriana in *The Comedy of Errors*. 'Would it not grieve a woman to be overmastered with a piece of valiant dust!' (2.1.55–6) exclaims Beatrice. Such questioning is not only a modern phenomenon: the idea of women's rightful equality to men as a critique of the social structure could be articulated in Shakespeare's time. In *Salve Deus Rex Judaeorum* (1611), Aemilia Lanyer's narrator, or Pilate's wife as her surrogate, says to men, 'Why should you disdain / Our being your equals, free from tyranny?' (1993 [1611]).[12]

The Shakespearean characters who raise similar questions don't name the alternative to equality as tyranny, nor does any play as a whole make an argument for women's equality emphatic enough to offend or convince a male supremacist. No characters discuss the distinction between equality and sameness. Nor does any argue that some differences between the sexes come from education or socialization.[13] But as the idea of equality of the sexes has become more widely held and the belief in their polar opposition less so, many critics have found gender equality or convergence in the plays or, more recently, have pointed out the limitations in how far the plays go towards this ideal.

2

Desire

Many of Shakespeare's tragedies and comedies are notable in their portrayal of female desire – female characters who speak of their attraction to another character and pursue that attraction. Most often it is attraction to a male character, but in *Twelfth Night* and *As You Like It*, female characters are drawn to women dressing as men and their language shows an interest that could be interpreted as homoerotic and, in *Two Noble Kinsmen*, Emilia speaks passionately about her love for a female friend who is now dead.

Is the portrayal of women's erotic desire in Shakespeare liberating? These features of Shakespeare's plays have drawn conflicting responses from feminists and earlier women with feminist leanings. In the Victorian period, George Eliot praised the initiative of Shakespeare's women in love, by contrast to the reticent, discreet female ideal of her time (1981 [1855]: 255). Since the feminist wave of the 1970s, however, some readers have regretted that Shakespearean women's desires are mostly channelled into marriage. Even as early as 1897, Mrs Lauch Mcluarin could write of these characters: 'Alas, poor girls, there was no business for them but love-making, no bargain but the world-without-end bargain' (Thompson and Roberts 1997: 245). Some recent critics make the point in a more serious and sophisticated way.[1] And while some stress what Adrienne Rich called 'compulsory heterosexuality' (1986 [1980]) in Shakespeare's comic plots, Valerie Traub and others have emphasized the importance of the moments when the plays do show homoerotic attraction between women (1992). Here as at many other places, critics' emphases will vary according to whether they take a structuralist approach, seeing a play as unified by the social hierarchies emphasized at the end, or a post-structuralist one that stresses the conflicting energies and fantasies within it.² Traub especially has argued that rather than showing female desire channelled, Shakespeare frequently presents it as multiple, ambivalent, sometimes combining homoerotic and heteroerotic elements as it circulates. Shakespeare does not stage adulterous desire as often as other playwrights of his time, such as Thomas Middleton. But when he does stage it, sometimes the play breaks down another central cultural opposition – that between extramarital and marital love.

Shakespeare's women and literary traditions of love

Shakespeare's interest in female initiative in love began early in his career. In the 1590s, he imagines Venus trying to seduce Adonis and Julia pursuing Proteus. Juliet thinks she is soliloquizing about her love for Romeo, whom she has just met, he is present and hears her, and she never turns back. Portia gives Bassanio hints about the right casket in conversation and in a song, Rosalind gives Orlando a chain and, when she meets him in disguise, strikes up a conversation.

In Shakespeare's culture, by contrast, the most prestigious analyses of desire were in the form of Petrarchan poetry, in which a male speaker explores his feelings of love and torment at being rejected by a distant, usually exalted woman. Her beauty and his suffering are typically portrayed in stock images: comparisons of her face to heavenly or floral beauty, paradoxes about pleasing pain, icy fire.³ In school, he (and other boys) read ancient Roman comedies, in which marriages at the conclusions were prizes for a man's triumph over obstacles to claim a woman. However, the English tradition of romance narrative, told both in poetry and in prose, provided many plots in which a woman actively pursues a man she loves. Helen Cooper has shown the importance of the choosing and desiring woman in this literary tradition, lesser known today but very popular from the twelfth century through the early seventeenth (2004: 218–68). Like the now mostly forgotten women of romance narrative, Shakespeare's female characters step out of the objectifying frames of Petrarchan discourse and show their agency.

Not only do most of Shakespeare's central female characters pursue a husband they have chosen, but they also speak of their interest in sex with him in terms that often got censored for the more conservative audiences of the eighteenth and nineteenth centuries. Juliet anticipates her wedding night with Romeo in an eager and sensuous soliloquy, Desdemona speaks to the Venetian senate of not wanting a separation that will keep her from her 'rites' and/or 'rights' (both words capable of a sexual interpretation) with Othello (1.3.259). Cleopatra, away from her lover, exclaims, 'O happy horse, to bear the weight of Anthony!' (1.5.22). Perdita imagines herself strewing Florizel with flowers 'like a bank, for love to lie and play on' (*WT* 4.4.130) or as if she is burying him alive in her arms.

A woman's interest in sex is unexpected in the Petrarchan language of love. Few of Shakespeare's women in love use Petrarchan language and images about their feelings without transforming them. Juliet at her first meeting with Romeo accepts his image of himself as a pilgrim and her as a saint, but the mutual kisses that cap this dialogue are transgressions of the Petrarchan pattern, in which the woman stays distant. Women's language about the men they love is often simply matter of fact, as in Viola's 'Whoe'er I woo, myself would be his wife' (1.4.42). In Shakespeare's late romance, *The Tempest*, Miranda on first seeing Ferdinand is Petrarchan: 'I might call him / A thing divine, for nothing natural / I ever saw so noble' (1.2.417–19), but she woos him with very un-Petrarchan directness: 'I am your wife, if you will marry me' (3.1.83).

In the tragedies, women may praise their beloved eloquently and lengthily, but again their words are usually of his actions and character, not of his beauty, as is usual in Petrarchan poetry (even in praise of men, often in Shakespeare's sonnets). Not only do his female characters escape Petrarchan clichés about women, but when expressing love for men they are much too vital to use a Petrarchan approach with the sexes reversed. For example, Cleopatra says of Antony, 'For his bounty, / There was no winter in't; an autumn it was / That grew the more by reaping' (5.2.85–7). Juliet's language also exemplifies the generosity several of Shakespeare's women delight in as they talk about their love, when she pledges, 'My bounty is as boundless as the sea, / My love as deep: the more I give to thee / The more I have, / For both are infinite' (2.2.133–5).

Mary Beth Rose and Valerie Wayne have analysed the mixture of different attitudes towards women, love and marriage in England at this time (Rose 1988; Wayne 1991). Women were traditionally associated with the body and sex, and thought to be more lustful than men – unless they were the idealized Virgin or other exalted figures. In Catholic tradition marriage was officially thought to be inferior to virginity for both males and females; the Reformation declared marriage better, and sermons praised the virtues of marital sexuality. Furthermore, companionship was increasingly seen as important in marriage, rather than the economic or social improvement that upper-class parents, especially, often had as a goal for their children.

The idea of women as being purer than men, less sexual, passionless, might be attached at this point to Queen Elizabeth or to a beloved in Petrarchan poetry, but it was not yet thoroughly developed as it would later be, especially in its most culturally dominant position, the Victorian era. In Shakespeare's time, women's interest in sex could be accepted, as it often was in the romance, assuming it was sex in marriage, or it could be part of their degradation in a man's misogynistic worldview. Joseph Swetnam's *Arraignment of Women* sold stunningly and was reprinted many times, but defences of women quickly responded (Woodbridge 1984). Antifeminism was seen as old-fashioned – perhaps part of the audience read Swetnam for laughs somewhat the way many 1970s Americans watched Archie Bunker in the television show *All in the Family,* assuming his prejudices were on the way out. Desdemona's response to Iago's doggerel dismissing all women as lustful suggests this: 'These are old fond paradoxes to make fools laugh i'th'alehouse' (2.1.138–9).

An old-fashioned view of women went along with an old-fashioned hostility to marriages made by the couple themselves against parental wishes. Thus in the sources of *Romeo and Juliet* and *Othello,* for example, the narrators speak with more condemnation of the couple for choosing rashly; Brooke describes Romeo and Juliet as 'thralling themselves to unhonest desire, neglecting the authoritie and advice of parents and frendes' (Shakespeare 1980: 239). Shakespeare presents the authority of parents much more critically. The sympathy of his audience for the lovers might also have increased because both plays are set in Italy, both plots came ultimately from Italian novellas, and Italy was known as a place where women were given less freedom than in England (they did not have the benefit of the revaluation of marriage emphasized by the Reformation).[4]

Cultural historians such as Denis de Rougemont and C. S. Lewis have long noted that the Petrarchan tradition made poetry out of adulterous love, in a court society where love often was not present in marriage (de Rougemont 1956 [1940]; Lewis 1958 [1936]).[5] In many of Shakespeare's plays, Petrarchan language – frequent among male characters in love – is symptomatic of their self-deception and/or immaturity. A reader who paid attention only to the male characters' language or set women's responses down to lack of understanding of poetic simile might miss this critique.

Though some are sceptical of men's words of love, others of Shakespeare's women find that their own love gives them power to say and do things they otherwise would not. Dympna Callaghan has noted how different Juliet's agency is from the usual portrayal of women in Petrarchan tradition (2003: 18). She amazes the friar with what she is willing to risk to maintain her love for Romeo. In *A Midsummer Night's Dream*, Hermia says, 'I know not by what power I am made bold' (1.1.59), when she questions her father's decree about whom she should marry.

Desire may appear to liberate Shakespeare's women from the idealized but static position of the Petrarchan heroine. But do his plots actually confine them? Do his tragedies, for example, release women's energies only to trap them in the tradition discussed by de Rougemont, the link between passionate love and death? Critics have different answers to these questions. Julia Kristeva, whose approach develops from the psychoanalytic theories of Freud, Melanie Klein, and Lacan, argues that the feud in *Romeo and Juliet* plays the same role that the opposition of the law plays in the case of the adulterous love of Tristan and Isolde. Recalling that 'die' was early modern slang for sexual orgasm, she says that in both stories 'death ... rules at the core of amatory jouissance' (Kristeva 1987: 220).[6] She even writes of 'the unconscious hatred of the lovers for each other' (221), using as evidence Juliet's fantasy that Night would, upon Romeo's death, 'take him and cut him out in little stars' (3.2.22), and her nightmare premonition of him 'as one dead in the bottom of a tomb' (3.5.56).[7] For Kristeva, the death of the lovers is inevitable because intense passion cannot survive ordinary marriage. 'Whose fault is it? The parents? Feudal society? The Church, for it is true that Friar Laurence departs in shame? Or love itself, two-faced, sun and night, delightful, tragic tenseness between two sexes?' (216). Kristeva's rhetoric and the rest of the essay make clear that the last is her answer. Her variety of feminism appears when she writes that in a clandestine relationship such as that of Juliet 'the woman recaptures with her secret lover the unsuspected jouissances of maternal fusion', though given the coldness of Juliet's actual mother in the play, the Nurse may be a more likely source of such memories (211, 224).

Coppélia Kahn, a psychoanalytic feminist critic in the American tradition, takes a different approach. The deaths in *Romeo and Juliet*, she argues, occur because the play's society links masculinity with violence, because 'the two families have established a state of affairs whereby their children are bound, for the sake of family honor, to kill each other' (1981: 99). Romeo's submission to the cultural and internal pressure to show his manhood by killing Tybalt in revenge for Mercutio's death is arguably the crucial moment in the play. The lovers are 'impelled to seek consummation in death only because the feud makes it impossible in life' but still the love–death 'is the lovers' triumphant assertion over the impoverished and destructive world that has kept them apart' (1981: 98 n.103).

Catherine Belsey, who uses psychoanalysis among her approaches to the play, disagrees with Kristeva about the presence of violence in the 'cut him out in little stars' image. She sees these lines as a tribute to Romeo, such as occurs in Ovid's *Metamorphoses*, much read in Shakespeare's time, narrating transformations of humans into flowers, animals, stars, and trees: he is to be made into a constellation, a 'fretwork of stars' (Belsey 2014: 62). Like Kristeva she finds relevant to the play Lacan's theory that love and death are 'a single drive that might issue in either passionate love or deadly hate, the two sometimes inextricably entwined' (58). But she also includes gender analyses more like Kahn's. 'In the end, it is (effeminating) love that resolves the feud, but not before (manly) violence has done a good deal more harm' (32–3). Belsey also notices how active Juliet is and how the play presents a parity as well as reciprocity between the lovers.

Do Romeo and Juliet die because of an aspect of intense love itself or because they are living in a violent society and the link between manhood and violence is something that even Romeo accepts? Because they are in a tragedy? Or all of the above? Why is it that all of Shakespeare's tragedies of erotic love – *Romeo and Juliet*, *Othello*, *Antony and Cleopatra* – are set in worlds where the relationship between manhood and violence is culturally emphasized, because of the role of warfare and the family feud, but also have female characters who love outside the bounds of what is expected, transcending the other loyalties expected of them?[8] Tragedy takes everything to its most painful extreme – love of the outsider in a violent world may be the most painful kind of love, and its most painful outcome is death. Ironically, because these women behave so unlike the Petrarchan heroine, this can all be seen as an unmetaphoring of Petrarchan tradition, in which love is frequently described as a war, and the beloved is addressed as an enemy.[9]

Desire and disguise

Lysander says in *A Midsummer Night's Dream*, 'The course of true love never did run smooth' (1.1.134). Even in comedies there have to be obstacles to love or else there would be no five-act plot. But in the comedies nobody dies for love and there are ways of getting around obstacles. One of the most frequent is a plot in which women in love wear masculine disguise. Julia in *The Two Gentlemen of Verona* and Jessica in *The Merchant of Venice* take on disguise to be with the men they love. Rosalind doesn't expect to meet Orlando during her masquerade, but makes the most of the opportunity to speak with him. Viola may already be interested in Orsino when she disguises herself; as an apparent boy she has a chance of getting a place in his court, and like Rosalind's the disguise permits her to educate him. These disguises act out the traditional power of love to perform metamorphoses (Ovid's stories are frequently recalled).[10] They permit the characters to travel and act more freely even though keeping the disguise, in other ways, sets limits on their freedom of speech. Though they are assuming a false identity, in disguise characters may get to know each other better than if they were following traditional codes of male/female speech in courtship (Dusinberre 2003 [1975]: 251). And there is dramatic tension when the spectators guess the real feelings of the character in disguise and wonder when the real identity will be revealed.

Feminist critics have often found the disguises of these characters making a point supportive of equality feminism. Germaine Greer writes that 'transvestism' is a 'mode of revelation', when in *As You Like It*, Rosalind in disguise teaches Orlando 'about women and time, discovering her own role as she teaches him his, thereby leaping the bonds of femininity and tutelage' (1971 [1970]: 219). Catherine Belsey suggests that these comedies and earlier narrative romances use masculine disguise 'to find a way of identifying women as partners for men, draw [ing] on the old heroic and chivalric tradition of friendship between men' (1985b: 179). Mihoko Suzuki (2000: 141) observes that Viola, in her disguise, tries to educate Orsino to take women's feelings seriously: 'But if she cannot love you, sir? ... In faith, they [women] are as true of heart as we' (2.5.88, 107). Jean Howard discriminates among the comedies; she finds that Viola's disguise still leaves her a 'properly feminine subjectivity' but says that Rosalind's 'masquerade ... reveals the constructed nature of patriarchy's representations of the feminine and shows a woman ... theatricalizing for her own purposes what is assumed to be innate, teaching her future mate how to get beyond certain ideologies of gender to more enabling ones' (1994: 119).

Much Ado About Nothing does not clearly show a woman pursuing her desire, but raises questions about how much Beatrice's behaviour (and Benedick's) involves conscious (or even unconscious) disguise of desire. In *Much Ado*, Beatrice recalls Benedick having previously won her heart, and near the beginning of the play is the first to ask the messenger from the war about him. Her uncle speaks of their 'merry war ... they never meet but there's a skirmish of wit between them' (1.1.59–61). Many critics and spectators have seen mutual attraction on some level behind what looks like hostility. This dynamic is imagined for both Beatrice and Benedick in the scenes staged for them to eavesdrop: 'if she should make tender of her love, 'tis very possible he'll scorn it, for the man, as you know all, hath a contemptible spirit' (2.3.175–7; see also 3.1.77–80). Part of the appeal may be that an audience can imagine that the characters already have unexpressed, even unconscious, feelings for each other.

However, Don Pedro, when he invents the eavesdropping plot, calls it 'one of Hercules' labours' (2.1.343); he either doesn't consciously think that they are already attracted or else doesn't want to admit it. And some recent critics have presented highly anti-romantic readings: Jean Howard argues that the eavesdropping plot succeeds because of the high rank of Don Pedro (1994: 65), and Stephen Greenblatt floats the possibility, developed earlier by Harry Berger, that 'it would not at all be clear that they love each other, entirely independent of social manipulation, at the close' (Greenblatt 2007: 1412; Berger 1982).

Many viewers and readers have found the comic heroines' assumption of male disguise liberating during the section of the play where they wear it, and some also enjoy the untamed language of Beatrice, whether or not it is seen as disguising her attraction to Benedick. The treatment of disguise at the ends of the plays complicates the issue. The key question is how much we take the ending as giving the play a definite meaning that structures it all in a unified way. The alternative is to emphasize tensions in the play, to consider that it might have liberating moments not cancelled out by the conclusion (Belsey 1985b: 188).

Homoerotic desire

Shakespeare's comedies are unusual in English theatre of their time in the extent to which they portray not only female friendship and emotional appeals to its memories, but also women who fall in love with boys who turn out to be women in disguise. The women who love women in these plays always marry men at the end, and so to some critics this is a clear indication that their plots of compulsory heterosexuality confine women's desires (Rich 1986 [1980]). The key question here again is how much we see the play as unified by the ending – a structuralist view – rather than take a post-structuralist approach and acknowledge tensions. After all, finding women desiring women in a canonical text is not such a common experience, so portraying such desire at all makes it less unmentionable and invisible. Valerie Traub's criticism has been the most influential guide to approaches to female homoeroticism that go beyond its denial in comic conclusions (1992: 105). She finds it important to escape the false binary of seeing Shakespeare's portrayal of homoeroticism as either phobic or celebratory, and the other false binaries of assuming that because the boy actors could have a homoerotic appeal to male spectators, their characters could not also have had a heteroerotic appeal to them, and that they could not also have had an appeal to female spectators in which homoeroticism and heteroeroticism were mixed.

The best-known examples of female homoerotic desire in Shakespeare are Phebe's attraction to Rosalind in her disguise as Ganymede and Olivia's to Viola in her disguise as Cesario. Phebe's especially is as quick as a lightning strike; she quotes Christopher Marlowe's line: 'Dead shepherd, now I find thy saw of might, / "Who ever lov'd that lov'd not at first sight?"' (3.5.81–2). More than any other female character in Shakespeare's plays, she expresses her love partly by admiring physical description, indeed later in this scene closely echoing descriptions of women in Petrarchan poetry.

> There was a pretty redness in his lip,
> A little riper and more lusty red
> Than that mix'd in his cheek; 'twas just the difference
> Betwixt the constant red and mingled damask.
>
> (120–3)

These images were so familiar that Shakespeare mocks them in his anti-Petrarchan Sonnet 130: 'I have seen roses damasked, red and white, / But no such roses see I in her cheeks'. Phebe's lines can suggest that she is attracted to the woman (fictionally) beneath the masculine disguise – but they could also indicate an attraction to a teenage boy young enough to play a woman on the Elizabeth stage.

Phebe and Silvius both frequently speak in Petrarchan images, although Phebe also makes fun of Silvius's uses of such images, telling him to 'Lie not, to say mine eyes are murderers' (3.5.19). By giving other characters such conventional language, the play makes Rosalind seem more unconventional. But perhaps Phebe's Petrarchan language is also supposed to be more ridiculous because she is a shepherdess. Phebe's class as a shepherdess is known to the audience to be lower than that of Rosalind as a duke's daughter, and Rosalind/Ganymede suggests this in speaking of Phebe's 'leathern hand' (4.3.24) (Sale 2011).[11]

But if Phebe differs from most of Shakespeare's women in love in using more Petrarchan language, she shows an ambivalence or wish to disguise her feelings that could be compared to the ambiguous language of Beatrice. Phebe is as preoccupied with Ganymede as Beatrice is with Benedick, but Phebe's language, when talking to Silvius, is more fractured by her conflict of feelings. In the first part of her speech, Phebe takes back almost everything positive she says about Ganymede, and then returns to it – 'he talks well – / But what care I for words? Yet words do well / When he that speaks them pleases those that hear' (3.5.110–12). She is either unsure of her feelings or dissembling when she says to Silvius, 'I love him not, nor hate him not' (127), but the description gives a clear sense of her fascination. Traub notes that she is ambivalent when considering him in terms of conventional male attributes such as height, but when she falls into the Petrarchan praise of Ganymede's feminine or boyish complexion quoted earlier, 'she capitulates to her desire altogether' (1992: 125). Nevertheless, after this she returns to ambivalence and eventually voices hostility in her speech: 'I have more cause to hate him than to love him ... I'll write to him a very taunting letter' (128, 134).

The letter is another Petrarchan effort, writing of *'the scorn of your bright eyne'* and threatening to *'study how to die'* if rejected (4.3. 50, 63), but two lines are particularly interesting in this context: *'Whiles the eye of man did woo me, / That could do no vengeance to me'* (47–8). Ganymede comments, 'Meaning me a beast' (49), but not only does the poem speak of godhead – the mythological Ganymede was made immortal by Jupiter after being abducted into heaven (hence strong associations with homoeroticism) and was sometimes spoken of as having become divine – but the contrast could also be with the eye of man, i.e. adult male, not boy or female.

In *Twelfth Night,* Olivia, a countess rather than a shepherd, makes an inventory of Cesario's virtues, using the word 'blazon', frequently used to describe the list of beauties of the beloved found in Petrarchan poetry: 'Thy tongue, thy face, thy limbs, actions, and spirit / Do give thee five-fold blazon' (1.5.286–7). The word 'blazon' itself expresses Cesario's androgynous appeal, for it can refer both to a coat of arms and to descriptions of female beauty. Furthermore, the inclusion of attributes beyond physical features – actions and spirit – also breaks the convention of typical Petrarchan praise.

Both Phebe and Olivia are affected by their beloved's speaking abilities, seldom found among the usual Petrarchan woman's accomplishments. It is comic that both Phebe and Olivia fall in love so quickly after refusing another wooer; both Ganymede and Cesario are forceful personalities who throw their interlocutors off balance by their energy. The words that strike Olivia most are a fantasy of persistent and poetic wooing with 'loyal cantons of contemned love' (264) she would hear even in the dead of night. Olivia, unlike Phebe, is given a soliloquy which shows that she is totally aware of her new feelings of desire, and, after calling it a 'plague', gives in – 'let it be' (289, 292).

Historical evidence suggests that many spectators also found Viola and Rosalind fascinating in their masculine disguise. Some boy actors, at any rate, became famous, and their erotic appeal to the spectators was a commonplace of attacks on the theatre (Jardine 1989 [1983]; Orgel 1997: 27–82). It was usually framed in terms of an appeal that would lead the male spectator astray, but, as Rosalind's epilogue notes very explicitly, there were women in the audience, and not only prostitutes, as the anti-theatricalists charged. Quite likely some of both sexes identified with Phebe as they figured out how she felt about Ganymede, and also with Olivia as she praised Cesario.

Do Rosalind and Viola reciprocate the desire that Phebe and Olivia feel for them in their male costumes? Traub argues that they do; at least they speak flirtatiously to the other women while in their disguises, enjoying their interest: 'Is there not a sense in which Rosalind/Ganymede elicits Phebe's desire, constructing it even as she refuses it?' (1992: 126). Viola/Cesario, she points out, uses hypothetical clauses that provoke in both Orsino and Olivia the fantasy of being the object of love: to Olivia, 'If I did love you in my master's flame ... In your denial I would find no sense' (1.5.258, 260), and to Orsino, 'My father had a daughter lov'd a man, / As it might be perhaps, were I a woman, I should your lordship' (2.5.108–10). Traub argues, 'What predisposes us to credit the second comment as truth but the first as false, a suspect performance, is, I suggest, largely our assumption of universal heterosexuality' (1992: 132). However, for the spectator or the reader, the belief in the second comment and not the first is over-determined: the heterosexual norm is reinforced because the text is emphatic that Viola, though in male disguise, is a woman and wants to marry Orsino. But Olivia, without the knowledge the audience has, is at least as likely as Orsino to believe in the page's possible love.

Still, whether Viola and Rosalind enjoy finding the other women attracted to them in disguise and whether they reciprocate that attraction are two different issues. There is no proof that they do reciprocate it on some level and no proof, even in Viola's words of discomfort about the triangle, that they don't. Traub gives us a more complex picture of how desire may circulate in the play, imagining a subtext in which more characters than make it explicit might 'temporarily inhabit a homoerotic position of desire' (1992: 128).

Traub also finds erotic desire in several passages in which a female character speaks of a past relationship with another woman, which usually could equally be called friendship or love. The clearest example of this is in Shakespeare's *Two Noble Kinsmen*, co-authored with John Fletcher. This play's Emilia speaks of her love for Flavina, dead when only eleven, and concludes from her experience 'that the true love 'tween maid and maid may be / More than in sex dividual' (1.3.81–2). This is the place in the language of a Shakespearean female character where love between women is most explicitly put in hypothetical competition with heterosexual love.[12]

Many historians of sexuality and Shakespeare scholars believe that for the most part people in early modern England did not have the concept of a sexual identity, did not define themselves according to which sex attracted them, and thus might, as several characters in Shakespeare's comedies do, experience both same-sex and opposite-sex attraction, sometimes even at the same time (for example, to Rosalind/Ganymede or Viola/Cesario) (Bray 1994; Smith 1995; DiGangi 1997). However, Emilia finishes the conversation with her sister Hippolyta (here as in *A Midsummer Night's Dream* an Amazon, but about to be married to Theseus), in which the phrase just quoted appears, with a sentence suggesting that her love of women is as strong a part of her identity as religion, which definitely was an identity category at the time: 'I am not / Against your faith, yet I continue mine' (1.3.96–7).

The fact that Flavina and she were both eleven when Flavina died makes it possible for audiences to place Emilia's commitment to love of women as dependent on her not having reached puberty at that time. But Emilia's unhappiness is not just from the loss of her greatest love; it is also from a plot that makes her, more than most of the female characters we have discussed, an object, a prize to be given to one of the kinsmen of the title, forced into marriage, first with a choice only between those two, and later with no choice. Given this framing, she does briefly show interest in each of the men in turn, but without much enthusiasm. On the other hand, when those two gentlemen first see her, she says she is 'merry-hearted' and accompanies her servant woman to 'lie down' (2.2.151, 152). Even if not the perfect love she had with Flavina, erotic enjoyment with women apparently is part of her life before she falls prey to the customs of male friendship and chivalry.

Helen and Hermia, in *A Midsummer Night's Dream*, Marina and Philoten, in *Pericles,* and Rosalind and Celia, in *As You Like It*, are also given close female friendships, though Marina's is just described by the narrator. Helena's description of her friendship with Hermia is in the past tense, told to arouse Hermia's guilt at her supposed collusion with men in mocking Helena (3.2.198–216). These friendships, like Emilia's, are presented to a large extent as in the elegiac mode – a memory of something lost, as in the poems James Holstun discusses (1988). It may be significant that Celia, not Rosalind, is the one who describes their friendship, not just because she is trying to persuade her father not to banish Rosalind, but also because from their first appearance Celia feels that she is more involved in the friendship than is Rosalind: 'I see thou lov'st me not with the full weight that I love thee' (1.2.7–8). Traub sees these relationships as being more erotic than the description of them as friendship would usually suggest. However, unlike Emilia's, none of these relationships is a serious obstacle to heterosexuality. As Julie Crawford has argued, they may well be imagined as continuing after the final marriages.[13]

Still, Phebe and Olivia, in their attraction to Rosalind/Ganymede and Viola/Cesario, follow a narrative of falling in love and speaking about it that is parallel and somewhat comparable to heterosexual relations as presented in comedies and in love tragedies. This parallel may support Traub's argument that the plays often break down the dichotomy between homoeroticism and heteroeroticism.

Adulterous desire

Shakespeare's plays show much less adulterous desire than those of his contemporaries; This was reason to praise him in the eighteenth and nineteenth centuries and part of the twentieth, but more recently it has sometimes been seen as part of a limiting idealization of women. However, in addition to Cleopatra, Shakespeare presents adulterous desire in Margaret, who first appears as a captive French queen, then is married to Henry VI and appears in all three plays named for him; Tamora, the Goth queen in *Titus Andronicus* who also first appears as a captive; Titania, in *A Midsummer Night's Dream*; and Goneril, in *King Lear*. All of these women are married to rulers; two of them, by their captivity, have their marriage choices constrained, which could provide some sympathy for their erotic interest in others. Lear's behaviour with Cordelia's suitors suggests Goneril's marriage to Albany may also have been constrained. Titania is in a different category since she and Oberon preside in fairyland and in a comedy; she can be relieved of responsibility for her transgression with Bottom, since it was imposed upon her by Oberon.

Some might argue that the presentation of these women, like the presentation of Phebe and Olivia, also moves towards breaking down a strict dichotomy between transgressive and acceptable desire. Margaret's mourning of the exile of the Earl of Suffolk, who hoped for her love when he made the marriage between her and Henry, and her reluctance to part with him, when Henry banishes him, is close to passages in *Romeo and Juliet*.

> O, go not yet. Even thus, two friends condemned
> Embrace, and kiss, and take ten thousand leaves,
> Loather a hundred times to part than die.
>
> (*2H6* 3.2.353–5)

The intensity drawn from secrecy in a secret marriage has much in common with the intensity drawn from secrecy in an affair outside marriage, as Kristeva has noted (1987: 211). However, while Romeo's banishment is for an impulsive retributory killing of a clearly dangerous Tybalt, Suffolk's banishment is for arranging the death of the good Duke Humphrey and thus Margaret's love of him, like Goneril's love of Edmund, adds to the sense of her immorality even though both women's wish for a love outside a loveless marriage might be understandable.

The adultery in Margaret's relationship with Suffolk is Shakespeare's addition to his historical sources, where it is just a rumour (Howard and Rackin 1997: 72). Shakespeare also adds her participation in the plot against Humphrey and his wife. These additions, as well as her adultery, are unnecessary to the plot; they add to her demonization as a woman who is cruel and sexually and politically aggressive (Howard and Rackin 1997: 94). Still, when we first meet her, she is Suffolk's prisoner, unaware of his designs on her and believing in his honour.

Similarly, Tamora first appears as a sympathetic character, a mother, captured in battle, fruitlessly begging Titus Andronicus not to kill her son. Saturninus, who has just become Emperor, claims her as wife, and she accepts, seeming to define wifehood in terms of service: 'She will a handmaid be to his desires, / A loving nurse, a mother to his youth' (1.1.336–7). But soon she is duplicitously advising him to appear to pardon Titus for his son's offenses while secretly advising him 'I'll find a day to massacre them all' (1.1.455).

Goneril, Tamora and Margaret are all in love with men guilty of cruel violence, share with them in that violence and urge and/or commit violence in other scenes independently of those men. Though at the beginning they are in victimized positions, or, in Goneril's case, relative subordination as a king's daughter, their later violence and adultery contaminate each other and they all become demonized. This is quite different from the way women whose desires are not adulterous are portrayed.

Shakespeare's plays also include women who commit adultery and are not demonized – but somewhat like Titania, they are protected from clear responsibility for adulterous desire. In *King John*, Lady Faulconbridge confesses her adultery with the deceased King Richard Coeur-de-lion, which produced the character first known in the play as Philip Faulconbridge and then as Bastard (though his name has now officially become Richard Plantagenet). She describes his conception thus: 'By long and vehement suit I was seduc'd / To make room for him in my husband's bed' (1.1.254–5). Having clarified her son's paternity, she never appears again in the play. A better known historical figure, Ann Bullen [Boleyn], speaks in one scene of *Henry VIII*, mainly to express sympathy with Henry's rejected queen Katherine and to deny ambition to replace her. The historical Ann was suspected of having sex with Henry while he was married to Katherine, but there is a tradition that she held out for marriage (and queenship). In the play, she appears once more, silently, at her coronation. In any event, if her transgression, like that of Lady Faulconbridge, comes from a king's pressure, rather than from her own acknowledged desire, the play does not make her a threat. These cases may break down the dichotomy between acceptable and unacceptable desire – but on the other hand these women do not articulate their desire at all.

What is desire?

There is, however, at least one Shakespearean character who does break down this dichotomy – Emilia in *Othello*. 'Have not we affections? / Desires for sport? and frailty, as men have?' (4.3.99–100). For her, desire is simply part of being human. It is not a specifically female characteristic, but a parallel with male desire rather than a contrast with male control. Yet, how different desire here is from the desires of Juliet, Cleopatra and Desdemona, and even from the Rosalind who says, 'My affection hath an unknown bottom, like the bay of Portugal' (4.1.199–200). If sexual desire is just desire for sport, it is not enough for Shakespeare to build a tragedy or his greatest comedy around. But that view gives a whole new perspective to a play that has dramatized what desire means to Desdemona and Othello. On the other hand, some difference feminists, though not all (and I know of no Shakespeare critic who has written this), might say that in arguing that women should avenge themselves on jealous husbands by making desire a sport, Emilia is giving up an important female quality of sincere passion.

Which portrayal of desire is liberating? A human quirk or a transforming but possibly fatal power? Or is the most liberating viewpoint the ability to keep all these possibilities in mind at once? Equality/humanist feminist theory suggests that it can be liberating only if it involves similar possibilities for all, not just for men. But since desire in Shakespeare so often is oriented towards marriage, to consider the question thoroughly we must examine his portrayals of marriage.

.

3

Marriage

Many literary critics have been struck by the number of Shakespeare's plays in which marriage figures, not only comedies where it would be generically expected at the conclusion. Feminist critics take different positions with regard to how Shakespeare portrays marriage. Juliet Dusinberre, for example, emphasizes the importance of women's free choice of a husband in his plays, and finds the marriages suggesting movement towards equality (2003 [1975]; Rose 1988). On the other hand, critics such as Lisa Jardine (1989 [1983]) Peter Erickson (1985) and Frances Dolan (2008) have emphasized the patriarchal structures and violence in these marriages. Shakespeare's plays portray more marriages than do his contemporaries or his classical models, observes Lisa Hopkins, but this is not because he romanticizes the institution: she argues that he is interested in both marriage's 'usefulness as social glue and its arbitrariness and psychological cost' (1998: 9).

Do Shakespeare's plays primarily idealize marriage or show its problems? Does their presentation change according to genre or chronology? Or are they too various to support such generalizations? This chapter will examine some of the ways in which critics answer these questions.

Early modern marriage

Juliet Dusinberre, Mary Beth Rose and other critics have contextualized Shakespeare's plays within Protestantism's increased emphasis on marriage, and in particular the recommendation sermons give of marriage as a freely chosen relationship of companionship and love between compatible partners (Haller and Haller 1942).[1] Among the aristocracy especially, marriages had often been made for the financial and social advantages of the whole clan, and preachers saw connections between parental pressure and the large number of notorious marital quarrels and separations at the time (Macfarlane 1986: 131–6).[2] They urged, instead, a union of hearts in marriage, and advised marrying someone with similar interests – emphasis on the relationship between two individuals had different requirements than the goal that the marriage should produce children and raise the extended family's wealth and position.

However, Catherine Belsey (1985a: 145–8) and Lisa Jardine (1989 [1983]) maintain that emphasis on love in a patriarchal marriage could lead to a more oppressive tyranny because the husband in such a marriage has more power over his wife's emotions. Frances Dolan argues that the three most common early figures for marriage all suggest an economy of scarcity and violence: the Christian image of marriage as the creation of 'one flesh', the common law legal fiction that 'husband and wife are one, and that one is the husband' and the comic tradition of portraying marriage as a war for mastery (2008: 3).[3] In their emphasis on inequality, these critics would have support from feminist theorists such as Carole Pateman, who has pointed out the history of inherent inequality in what she calls 'the sexual contract' (1988), and Gayle Rubin (1975) and Eve Sedgwick (1985), who have emphasized the role of marriage – even one apparently freely chosen – as using women to form bonds between men.

Still, a recent historian, Mary S. Hartman, argues that marriage in England and the rest of northwestern Europe was more nearly equal than elsewhere because of the later average marriage age for women, closer to that of their husbands (2004).[4] Decisions to send daughters into service in other households resulted in those daughters having both increased self-confidence and bargaining power when they married. This pattern began among medieval peasants and eventually spread upwards. Such a dynamic would provide a demographic explanation for English interest in plays about marriages of comparative equality. <u>Hartman asserts that husbands were uncomfortable about how dependent they were on their wives.</u> Other historians, such as Anthony Fletcher (1999) and Bernard Capp (2004), have written some of the history of early modern women's struggles for power; Don Herzog has noted writers' sympathetic portrayals of wives' rebellions (2013).

How do Shakespeare's plays relate to these historical and theoretical analyses? Plays do not literally reflect their societies, but they often dramatize their tensions, in this case tensions resulting from different beliefs about marriage. For example, there was a tension, suggested above, between the belief that marriage was a matter of the couple's decision – as a relationship of individualized reciprocal love – and the belief that it ought to be acceptable to the couple's parents – as a hierarchical social and familial institution. In *Romeo and Juliet*, *A Midsummer Night's Dream*, *Othello* and *The Merchant of Venice*, a woman chooses marriage against the wish of her father and all give, to some degree, a picture of the father's suffering at the loss of his daughter.

Marriage and the endings of comedies and romances

The plots in many of Shakespeare's comedies and romances, resolving some of these tensions, show a woman who chooses a husband but also confirms a bond with her father at the same time. Portia manages to help the man she wants pass her father's casket test. Rosalind falls for Orlando knowing their fathers were friends. Prospero sets up Miranda's meeting with Ferdinand and strengthens their love by seeming to oppose it. Erickson (1985) and Louis Montrose (1981) see *As You Like It* as emphasizing the way marriage serves patriarchal structures by making women objects of exchange, and since that play has the strongest heroine, it is easy to extend this argument to the others. However, some argue that the plays give such structures lip service but allow their heroines more freedom to maneuver – with regard to both father and husband – by their specific nuances.

For example, *Twelfth Night* does not give Viola's dead father much power and when Viola maintains a boy's costume at the end of the play, that garb adds to the sense of her companionship with Orsino (Belsey 1985b). Portia's father's test gets rid of the men she does not want and allows her to successfully give Bassanio a hint. Her own test of how seriously Bassanio will keep his promise to keep her ring teaches him a lesson – he must anxiously apologize while she jokes about how she will repay him. Rosalind gives herself in marriage to Orlando without waiting to be given by her father (the need for someone to give the bride away is specifically emphasized at two earlier places in the play), she pays little attention to her father while she is in her disguise, and she speaks the epilogue, traditionally the prerogative of the highest ranking character. And Prospero's plot to unite Miranda and Ferdinand works only if she is willing to rebel against him.

Contemporary sermons and advice books often urged silence on women as an important virtue (Stallybrass 1986: 126–7). Are women silenced by the marriages and proposals at the end of the comedies? Erickson argues that the epilogue in *As You Like It* is not a counter-example, but rather a proof of women's subordination: Rosalind, though given the epilogue, becomes not the character but the boy actor who performs her by its conclusion (1985: 34).

But the claim that Shakespeare's comic women are silenced does not fit equally with every comedy – and some it does not fit at all. Hermia and Helena don't speak in the last scene of *A Midsummer Night's Dream*, but Hippolyta and Titania have some important lines. Though Viola says nothing in the last 125 lines of *Twelfth Night* while the other characters' outcomes are being sorted as hers has been, Olivia has three important speeches during this period. She exclaims 'Most wonderful!' (5.1.221) on realizing that she has been married to Sebastian and she deals with Malvolio succinctly and graciously. Marriage – before she goes to Venice – does not silence Portia; in the last scene no one but Gratiano speaks after her, and the joke about him from the beginning is that he talks too much. The main textual basis for this image of female silence at the end of comedies may be Benedick's speech to Beatrice in *Much Ado*, 'Peace! I will stop your mouth' (5.4.97).[5] And, indeed, Beatrice is silent for the remaining twenty-five lines, but this is just after she has jokingly maintained that she is marrying him because he is dying of a consumption. Leonato predicted earlier, 'If they were but a week married, they would talk themselves mad' (2.1.332–3), not 'he would talk her mad'.

The most interesting female silence about a final marriage is in *Measure for Measure*. This play, the first to be identified as a problem play (a term first used for Shaw's and Ibsen's and applied to it soon after their plays were first performed) has, close to the end, one of the most textually unprepared proposals ever, from a Duke who has been in disguise as a friar, to Isabella, whom he has been counseling, and who began the play entering a convent. Isabella is given no answering line. Until 1970, it was generally assumed that the play should be staged with her clearly accepting the proposal, whether because of the pressure that comes from the desires of a high-ranking man or because the play could be interpreted allegorically, with their wedding the union of mercy and justice or Christ's bride with Christ's representative on earth. But at the Royal Shakespeare Company (RSC) production in

1972, directed by John Barton, Isabella refused. Since then, Isabella usually has a choice.

Measure for Measure is the Shakespearean comedy which presents the most marriages lacking reciprocal desire, emphasizing the tensions in the institution of marriage, with romantic love, if any, coming only from the ideology the reader or audience, or possibly the director, supplies. There is no real courtship, though the Duke praises Isabella for her beauty and goodness. He commands marriage at the end to her brother and his secretly betrothed wife, who may already be married according to one set of laws of the time – and their desire for marriage is mutual. But the Duke also commands that Angelo marry his betrothed Mariana, whom he has jilted, and that another character, Lucio, marry the prostitute who has borne his child, though Lucio considers this a fate worse than death. For these last two couples, marriage is clearly punishment. The Duke has much earlier claimed to have a 'complete bosom' (1.3.3), in other words, to be above love, and his proposal to Isabella presumably shows that he has learned that he is not – so this may dramatize the view of marriage as necessary social glue which keeps sexuality from being disruptive. Chapter 5 of this volume, however, presents a range in the way this ending has been performed in the years since Barton's Isabella's refusal.

Most of Shakespeare's other comedies also end with the promise of marriages of three or four couples or marriages of some and reunion, reconciliation and/or consummation of others. All are entering into the same institution, and yet they inhabit it differently. These plays contrast one kind of marriage, usually involving more mutual understanding and less male dominance, with other kinds, and could be understood to affirm the first and to critique the others. *As You Like It* is the most self-conscious about the multiplicity of the marriages and the contrasts among them, because of the final, varying messages to the couples from Hymen and Jaques. Rosalind and Orlando have a relationship tested by acquaintance and conversation (though with Rosalind in disguise), Celia and Oliver apparently a sudden mutual passion, Silvius and Phebe romance on one side and acceptance on the other and Touchstone and Audrey a reciprocal sexual interest not likely to last or to overcome the difficulties of living together. *Much Ado about Nothing* has only two engaged couples at the end, and a contrast is sharply drawn between the many conversations – though sometimes antagonistic – of Beatrice and Benedick and the lack of them between Claudio and Hero, the establishment of trust between the first couple at the same time as the break of trust in the other, the similarity of roles in the first couple and the differentiation in the second, in which Claudio is much more verbal and aggressive than Hero. If we supply a belief in repentance or character improvement after adolescence, the Claudio/Hero plot has a happy ending, but without those beliefs Hero's fate looks grim. Some feminists also doubt that Beatrice and Benedick can have a different kind of marriage: Lynne Magnusson, for example, calls it 'very much a play in which existing social relations are reproduced' as Beatrice and Benedick fall into conventional roles (1999: 157).

In *The Taming of the Shrew*, the comparison among the marriages becomes explicit with the contest that Petruchio sets up to see whose wife is the most obedient. The play can be read as like *Much Ado* in contrasting an unconventional couple who get to know each other antagonistically with a more conventional one, though Bianca and Lucentio speak to each other a little more than Claudio and Hero, and Bianca, unlike Hero, refuses to subordinate herself. In his last line, Petruchio calls himself 'winner' (5.2.188), by contrast to Lucentio, and many spectators have felt that he is justified in this. While in *Much Ado* the marriage between Beatrice and Benedick can easily look promising, even if it is accomplished partly by social pressure, the relationship between Katherine and Petruchio is more troubling to an audience today. Even in, or close to, Shakespeare's own time (probably between 1609 and 1622) his occasional collaborator John Fletcher wrote a sequel, *The Woman's Prize, or The Tamer Tamed*, which imagines Katherine dead from her struggles with Petruchio and a second wife taming him and explicitly invoking the idea of equality in marriage. Although Shakespeare's Petruchio does not actually inflict the violence upon Katherine that was accepted in the punishment of scolds, as documented by Lynda Boose (1991), and although Petruchio is not just a boor but rather imaginative, nevertheless the resolution of this play depends on female submission to male authority backed up by physical strength. Petruchio's frequent beating of his servants is a lesson about his willingness to use his strength to dominate if necessary. Against Katherine herself, he uses more psychological violence than physical.[6] And in addition, she may learn from Petruchio that if she is subordinate to him she can be violent to servants and other women (Dolan 2008: 121–7).

In spite of the emphasis on male authority, Katherine's last speech presents a picture of marriage as a contract, if a hierarchical one – the wife's 'love, fair looks, and true obedience' (5.2.154) are payment for the husband's 'painful labour both by sea and land' (150). However, feminist critics have noted that the play doesn't show Petruchio at any of this 'painful labour'. Natasha Korda (2002) has added that Katherine's image of marriage doesn't include her own household work, picturing her as just lying 'warm at home, secure and safe' (152). Dolan most recently argues that it leaves out the prominent domestic roles of the 'large cast of servants', who experience beatings from Katherine as well as Petruchio: this play suggests that 'marital harmony depends upon rather than standing distinct from carefully managed domestic violence' (2008: 122, 127). Detmer, further, puts Katherine's harmonious picture of marriage here in the context of recent real world battered wives and the hostages whose affection for their captors gave rise to the term 'Stockholm syndrome' (1997). Although many directors and performers suggest that Katherine is in love with Petruchio, even when fighting with him, the three different marriages that this play presents at the end are all problematic.

The difficulties that this play's treatment of marriage poses in a time of more public recognition of women's rights, with a woman rationalizing patriarchal ideology at length as the culmination of her husband's attempts to change her, are obvious in the many different performance versions of Katherine's speech and directorial adaptations of its framing and aftermath. At least since 1908, occasional Kates have delivered it with a tone of mockery: in the 1929 film, Mary Pickford winked at the audience (Oliver 1984: 72; Thompson 1984: 22).

Since the late 1960s, many directors have staged the play in more dialogue with feminist ideas in wide circulation. Some want to shock the audience by dramatizing how marriage can involve a woman's loss of power. In 1974, Charles Marowitz turned the play into 'a Gothic tragedy' which ends with 'a mesmerized or drugged victim droning the words her tormentors could not make her speak voluntarily' (1978: 15, 19) In Michael Bogdanov's 1978 RSC production, a more subtle refusal of a happy ending, Paola Dionisotti saw Petruchio's challenge as a betrayal and delivered her speech as a mockery of his ideals. When she started to kiss his foot, 'he gasped, recoiled, jumped back' and the last image of them was as 'two very lonely people' (Rutter 1988: 23). Drastic shock recurred in Turkey, in 1986, when the director Yücel Erten had his Katherine reveal after her speech that she had slit her wrists (Elsom 1989: 75).

Many productions, however, have tried to make the ending happier by having Petruchio apologize or kneel with Katherine, or, before she can kneel, sweep her 'into his arms for a big romantic kiss', and/or by emphasizing that Katherine's lines don't reflect her belief and she retains some freedom.[7] Another alternative is to take a metatheatrical approach, end the Katherine/Petruchio plot with reconciliation but present it as a fantasy, as Di Trevis did with a 1985 RSC production. Here, the actress who played Katherine reappeared at the end, looking downtrodden, and made an alliance with the tinker Christopher Sly from Shakespeare's induction (Holderness 1989: 46–8). Like the variety of critical views of the text, these performances show that interpretations of feminist possibilities in a Shakespeare play depend on many variables, including the particular historical situation at the time of analysis.

No Shakespearean comedy or romance unambiguously ends patriarchal order, though no other ends with as many words praising it as does *The Taming of the Shrew*. But all of them include a heroine with a sense of her agency, and in *As You Like It*, *The Merchant of Venice* and *Twelfth Night*, that agency has been important throughout the play in making the marriage. Some critics would argue that this is ironic given that marriage will result in giving up her agency, but others maintain that this is too monolithic a picture.

Histories: A male-dominated world and one comic ending

In general, women have more power in the marriages of Shakespeare's comic worlds than in the marriages of other genres. The history plays have the least room for women, and where they do appear the marriages often have little love. As Jean Howard and Phyllis Rackin write, 'the first tetralogy [the three *Henry VI* plays and *Richard III*] and *King John* imagine the past as a world where marriages are dynastic' (Howard and Rackin 1997: 29). Margaret, from the royal family of Anjou, engaged to King Henry VI without even seeing him, is disappointed in his meekness and piety, and remains more allied with Suffolk, her lover, who made the marriage partly so she would be available to him.

The second tetralogy (*Richard II*, *1* and *2 Henry IV* and *Henry V*) shows an even more male-dominated world than the other histories. Isabella, Richard's queen, has a minuscule role.[8] The main plots of *1* and *2 Henry IV* are mostly developed without any women present – the important relationships are those between Hal and his father, on one hand, and Falstaff, on the other. However, in one scene of *1 Henry IV*, Mortimer's Welsh wife and Hotspur's Kate appear, presenting a miniature contrast of two marriages. In one, the two spouses have no common language, though Mortimer appreciates her singing in Welsh, and in the other, their language is generally antagonistic, suggesting that of Beatrice and Benedick or perhaps Petruchio and Katherine, for whom this Kate may have been named (the historical figure married to Hotspur was Elizabeth Percy). Nevertheless, this Kate invokes an ideal of partnership in marriage as she feels entitled to question Hotspur about his worries, and in *2 Henry IV* she has one of the most moving speeches, mourning him after his death.

By contrast to marriage's relative unimportance in the other history plays, *Henry V*, and therefore the second tetralogy, ends with Henry's negotiation of marriage to Katherine of France. Henry and England have won the war against France, so Katherine is on one level a spoil of war or, as Henry calls her, a 'capital demand' (5.2.96). Henry's speech before the Battle of Harfleur portrays his soldiers as potential rapists and, like a rapist, Henry, on one level, uses violence to obtain Katherine – as he says, 'I get thee with scambling [fighting]' (5.2.201).

However, Shakespeare gives Henry not only this acknowledgement of his violence but also a gracious humility and wish for Katherine's explicit consent. As Hopkins writes, 'the entire episode hinges on a sustained mystification of political reality as personal choice, and yet, especially in the theater, ... it is also a very charming scene, and one which offers its audience profound gratification' (1998: 92). After much violence and pain, interspersed with celebration of military victories, the play moves to a lighter mood. Henry woos her with a bit of Petrarchan language – 'an angel is like you, Kate, and you are like an angel' (109–10) – but mostly with plain words, 'I know no ways to mince it in love, but directly to say, "I love you"' (126–7), and with deprecating jokes about his appearance, 'My comfort is that old age, an ill layer-up of beauty, can do no more spoil upon my face' (226–8). This image of himself as the plain, blunt soldier incorporates the persona of Hotspur earlier in the tetralogy and his modesty also echoes that of Petruchio, whose words, 'Could I repair what she will wear in me / As I can change these poor accoutrements, / 'Twere well for Kate and better for myself' (5.2.118–20), echo when Henry says, 'Thou hast me, if thou hast me, at the worst, and thou shalt wear me, if thou wear me, better and better' (228–30). He is even more like Petruchio in begging for a public kiss for which his Katherine is reluctant, and his insistence that 'we are the makers of manners' (268–9) articulates the same scorn of ordinary custom that Petruchio shows.[9]

Thus Henry combines the figures of these two husbands associated in varying ways with violence but also with linguistic ability, as he repeatedly anglicizes his French queen's name to the nickname 'Kate', which she shares with both other wives, and this fits perfectly with the way his own marriage depends on violence. But unlike the other two figures, he speaks of his kiss as stopping her mouth, and she indeed, for almost ninety lines, as the other royalty and lords return, says nothing more. By contrast, Katherine the 'tamed' shrew, gives verbal consent – 'Nay, I will give thee a kiss' (5.1.138) – even though this is part of a bargain rather than given with total freedom, and has much to say after that, ultimately winning social approval and the centre of the stage.

In *Henry V*, what follows the kiss immediately with the return of the rest of the court is dialogue full of jokes about maids' blindness and winking consent, and then King Charles' verbal consent to the marriage, which Henry follows with a demand for the cities and title to the throne of France he also asks. But afterwards there are wishes expressed by King Charles, and also Queen Isabel, speaking for the first time in the play, for peace, 'neighborhood and Christian-like accord' (345) that 'God, the best maker of all marriages, / Combine your hearts in one, your realms in one!' (351–2), hoping that a peaceful spousal of kingdoms would follow 'As man and wife, being two, are one in love' (353). As was mentioned earlier in this chapter, the male dominance in this image has become increasingly obvious. The critical responses to *Henry V* have been, more than on many plays, split between seeing it as a glorification of Henry and a critique of him – the same could be said of how the play handles this final marriage (Rabkin 1967).

Tragedies and marital companionship

No tragedy ends in a literal marriage, but marriage is important in many of them, and in the cases where it is the hero's own marriage, one of the key issues is the possibility of marital companionship, advocated by preachers in Shakespeare's society. This theme is raised in tragedy for the first time in *Julius Caesar*. In a speech rather like the earlier one of Lady Hotspur, Portia demands to know what is troubling Brutus in terms of the requirements of 'the bond of marriage' (2.1.279):

> Am I your self
> But as it were in sort or limitation,
> To keep with you at meals, comfort your bed,
> And talk to you sometimes? Dwell I but in the suburbs
> Of your good pleasure? If it be no more,
> Portia is Brutus' harlot, not his wife.
>
> (281–6)

Portia tries further to gain his confidence by showing him a self-inflicted wound in her thigh and claiming strength more than women have because of her associations with him and with her father. Later, however, she has more difficulty with the secret about the conspiracy against Caesar than she expects; she feels humiliated to find 'how weak a thing the heart of woman is' (2.4.40–1). And eventually she finds Brutus' impending defeat also too hard to deal with, and, offstage, kills herself. In the male-dominated and militarist society of this play, the companionship offered in marriage cannot really go very far.

The preacher Henry Smith, in his much-reprinted *A Preparative to Marriage*, advised men to marry wives who were similar in interests to themselves: 'If thou be Martiall, choose one that loveth prowess' (1591: 25). Two of Shakespeare's tragedies, *Othello* and *Macbeth*, present men who have done so. In both plays the question of how a general's wife can be his companion is central. When Othello retells the story of his engagement to Desdemona, he remembers Desdemona saying, after hearing his history, 'she wished / That heaven had made her such a man' (1.3.163–4). She wants to go with him to Cyprus, not to be a 'moth of peace' (258). The idea of their partnership emerges again on Cyprus when he calls her 'my fair warrior' (2.1.180), though his emphasis on her fairness is problematic because of its double reference to beauty and whiteness, suggesting his internalized racism (Erickson 2014: 161).

But when she gives him advice about his treatment of his ensign Cassio, they are no longer partners. She is outside the world of military discipline, and he hears in her pleading for Cassio only infidelity. He feels he has to kill her, and when he finds out the truth of her faithfulness, he feels he has to kill himself – so they can finally be united again – 'No way but this, / Killing myself, to die upon a kiss' (5.2.358–9).

Macbeth is also a tragedy of the destruction of a marriage. Though Macbeth initially calls his wife 'my dearest partner of greatness' (1.5.10), this partnership ultimately provides only isolation. Macbeth knows they are both in the same condition, each with 'a mind diseas'd' and 'that perilous stuff / Which weighs upon the heart' (5.3.40, 44–5), but he will not acknowledge it to her or to the doctor and, apparently a suicide, like Brutus's Portia, she dies alone.[10]

Does any kind of feminist theory have an explanation of the conflicts in these marriages? And how do these plays contribute to the debate about whether Shakespeare's plays glorify or show problems in marriage? Are the causes of the disconnection between the main characters external to them, unique to them, related to problems of marriage in their society or related to problems in marriage as it has historically existed?

In terms of the plot, Iago causes Othello's jealousy and murder of Desdemona, but he is able to influence Othello for social reasons as well as reasons personal to Othello. Othello sees theirs as an idealized love – she is his 'soul's joy' (2.1.182) and is emphatic that his feelings are above appetite. He is eager to leave Venice for Cyprus without thinking there would be any conflict between his love of war and his love of Desdemona – and looks down on housewives and skillets, as opposed to helmets, without thinking that Desdemona will be a housewife (1.3.274).[11] Iago can bring out Othello's feelings of being an outsider as well as his latent distrust of women when he says, 'I know our country disposition well – / In Venice they do let God see the pranks / They dare not show their husbands' (3.3.204–5).[12] Soon Othello is saying, 'O curse of marriage / That we can call these delicate creatures ours / and not their appetites!' (272–4). He is living in a society in which the language of many characters shows racism and prejudice against women, as in the proverbial quality of Iago's anti-feminist jokes as well as in her father's own mistrust of her. At the beginning of the play Othello exalts Desdemona, but this exaltation is part of a polarized attitude towards women, and once he can imagine her as off her pedestal he cannot help seeing her as a whore. In one scene, she goes from 'sweet Desdemona ... when I love thee not / Chaos is come again' (3.3.55, 91–2) to 'lewd minx' and 'fair devil' (478, 481). Othello takes first his idealization and then his disgust to extremes, as tragic heroes generally do with everything, but they are both attitudes of his society. In a traditional pattern of male dominant culture, he sees himself as above sexual desire – 'the young affects in me defunct' (1.3.265–6) – and when he becomes jealous, accepts Iago's projection of desire onto women and to Desdemona. Related to this is his willingness to believe Iago rather than Desdemona – his greater loyalty to male friendship – which has been culturally honoured longer than marriage and is frequently seen as in conflict with it.

While Lady Macbeth is often blamed for Macbeth's crimes, this scapegoating, like that by Iago, should be qualified. In Macbeth's world, the ability to use violence, as he is initially praised for doing in killing Macdonwald, is the greatest source of value. As in *Othello*, most of the characters show bias against women, though it is more on the basis of belief in their weakness and fear rather than belief in their sexual desires, and can be expressed as a desire to protect them – for example, Macduff won't describe Duncan's dead body to Lady Macbeth because he believes 'The repetition, in a woman's ear / Would murther as it fell' (2.3.83–4). In both of these plays the central female character seems to her husband, for a while, to be a woman unlike all others. In *Macbeth*, she herself shares this belief. But their shared planning does not continue.

This change may occur because he still believes that as a woman she can't handle the terrible deeds he is planning and ordering – 'Be innocent of the knowledge, dearest chuck' (3.2.45) – or because he wants to be in control rather than executing her plan and hearing her criticism if he doesn't.[13] Lady Macbeth's sleepwalking and obsessive return to those murdered by Macbeth and his followers could be seen as a sign that she really is a weak woman after all, but feminist ethics need not deny that it is human to be disturbed after being responsible for a murder, knowing that the man you pressured to commit one murder has caused many more.

Thus, both of these plays imply a conflict between an image of marriage as partnership and stereotypes of women as weak – lustful in one case and fearful and repelled by violence in the other – though this conflict looms larger in *Othello* than in *Macbeth*. But Shakespeare wrote a third play exploring the possibility of partnership between a woman and a general: *Antony and Cleopatra*. Although Antony is never legally married to Cleopatra, but, in sequence, to two other women during the course of the play, Shakespeare shows Cleopatra as more of a companion to Antony than either Fulvia or Octavia.

Antony and Cleopatra, more than any other couple in his tragedies, are pictured as they relax together, whether walking around the city and looking at other people or trying on each other's clothes.[14] Though Cleopatra has some desire to witness Antony's military adventures and encourage his ambition, such vicarious living is less important than in *Othello* and *Macbeth*. Cleopatra has more in common with Antony because they are both, as characters, performers on a public stage, he as triumvir and general and she as reigning queen. When Cleopatra's military judgement influences Antony's, as in the Battle of Actium in which she participates (showing her discontent with merely vicarious fighting), but then flees, they are defeated. This seems to reinforce the idea that a woman's advice about warfare is dangerous. But even though Antony begins by reproaching her – 'O, whither has thou led me, Egypt?' (3.11.51) – when she asks for pardon, he says, 'Fall not a tear ... One of them rates / All that is won and lost' (69–70).

Like Othello, Antony expresses unwarranted jealousy – accusing Cleopatra of betraying him with her seemingly flirtatious courtesy towards the servant Thidias, and also nonsexually, when she forms an alliance with Octavius. But unlike Othello, he immediately expresses his anger at her, uses no physical violence and ultimately forgives her. Similarly, unlike in *Othello*, Cleopatra also expresses jealousy – of Antony's relationships with his legal wives, Fulvia and Octavia. In this way, as in others, she conveys a sense of her own rights in her relationship with Antony. Her suicide is partly motivated by her desire not to be controlled and humiliated by Caesar, but at the last she speaks more of Antony – 'Husband, I come! / Now to that name my courage prove my title!' (5.2.285–6).

In the mid-twentieth century, the traditionalist critic William Wimsatt wrote that *Antony and Cleopatra* creates an aesthetic problem because it glorifies an immoral relationship (1963). More recent critics are likely to see their relationship as preferable to Antony's legal marriage with Octavia not just because it is more passionate but also because it involves more companionship and reciprocity. Antony has only political motivation to marry Octavia, and it could be argued that his relationship with Cleopatra is a truer marriage even without the name.[15] Though the relationship between Antony and Cleopatra does not have the social function usual for marriage in Shakespeare and though Shakespeare cuts the marriage that historically took place and is mentioned in Plutarch and in other sources, their bond is public knowledge and not clandestine (Neely 1985: 145, 163). As with the speech of Emilia near the end of *Othello*, this play breaks down the dichotomy between marital and non-marital love – but here it is not because love is imagined as merely a frailty – rather it raises the question of what it is that makes a relationship a marriage. And because a woman's desiring love for a man while she cannot legally marry him is portrayed with depth and eloquence, the play breaks down the dichotomy between 'good' and 'bad' women (Erickson 1985: 124).

In this play, several of the Roman characters express the same stereotypes of women as lustful, deceitful and destructive that appear in *Othello* and *Macbeth*. Antony occasionally invokes those stereotypes too, but he always repents and ends by expressing his love for Cleopatra. Critics have long found *Antony and Cleopatra* unique in its presentation of gender – but today when the definition of marriage and its essence are being re-examined, we should notice that this play is also unique in its presentation of marriage.

Jealous men

While in *Antony and Cleopatra*, Shakespeare explores jealousy as expressed by characters of both sexes, many more of his plays portray male jealousy. Not only does Iago trick Othello into believing that Desdemona is unfaithful, but Don John induces a similar delusion in Claudio in *Much Ado* about his fiancée, Hero. Ford, in *The Merry Wives of Windsor*, has the same false belief about his wife. In one late romance, *Cymbeline*, jealousy makes Posthumus order his wife killed, and in another, *The Winter's Tale*, Leontes tries and condemns his wife for adultery. In every case, the suspicious man is wrong, it is clear to an attentive audience that he is wrong, and he learns that he is wrong near the end of the play. The woman is true and the accusations against her are false. Likewise, the suspicion of this particular woman is linked with mistrust of women in general. So, while there are many anti-feminist lines, these plays can be taken to vindicate women against male suspicion. (There are other plays that include unfaithful women, but their husband's or lover's jealousy is not the focus on the play in the same way: for example, the conflict between Goneril and Albany is motivated earlier by his recoiling from her behaviour to Lear than by her relation to Edmund.)

Women's vindication in the jealousy plays – *Much Ado About Nothing*, *The Merry Wives of Windsor*, *Othello*, *Cymbeline* and *The Winter's Tale* – goes against the grain of the culture of Shakespeare's time. Its drama, including Shakespeare's, was full of jokes about how many men were cuckolded – deceived by their wives. The audiences apparently felt that women's adultery showed how ridiculous men's claims to control their wives were. The idea that women were more lustful than men was a cliché and, nevertheless, there was a double standard according to which a woman's adultery was a serious offense, legally and morally, and a man's was not. Iago is able to draw on a prevailing mistrust of women. Perhaps some viewers returned from the plays with the conviction that only Desdemona, for example, was faithful and all other women were not. But Shakespeare's plays show the cost of such pervasive mistrust. Because of a man's murderous commission to a servant or a woman's faint, a woman's life seems to be at issue even in his jealousy plays that end without tragedy.

The one exception to this rule about endangered women is *The Merry Wives of Windsor*, which is also his only comedy in which the most important female characters are two married women, and at least one of them is old enough throughout to have a grown daughter. This is also the only play in which the wife with the jealous husband encourages her ridiculous would-be seducer to visit her for the purpose of punishing him. Since Ford, in disguise, also encourages Falstaff's visits because he wants to test his wife, Alice Ford's encouragement also punishes him and eventually the revelation of Falstaff's humiliation motivates Ford to apologize for his jealousy and to promise to reform. Ford is more ridiculous than any other jealous husband in Shakespeare, contrasting clearly with the calmer Page, Alice's friend's husband. Here jealousy has little stature when faced with female power and friendship.[16] Interestingly, the wives' power extends not only to their ability to trick Falstaff, but also includes financial power in their households, part of what Falstaff hopes to get from them.

In all Shakespeare's jealousy plays except *Othello*, whatever the danger, every woman survives. In *Cymbeline*, Posthumus even repents and dismisses the seriousness of a woman's adultery before he knows that his wife Imogen is innocent, saying to imagined husbands in the audience, 'If each of you should take this course, how many / Must murder wives much better than themselves / For wrying [going astray] but a little?' (5.1.3–5). A man at this time might think of his own adultery as 'wrying but a little'. But his wife's? No other male character in Shakespeare says anything similar. However, in lines already discussed in the chapter about likeness, and partially quoted near the end of the last chapter, in *Othello* one female character, Emilia, speaks against this double standard. This defence of women's feelings as similar to men is most specifically a defence of wives:

> Let husbands know
> Their wives have sense like them ...
> And have not we affections?
> Desires for sport? and frailty, as men have?
> Then let them use us well: else let them know,
> The ills we do, their ills instruct us so.
>
> (4.3.92–3, 99–102)

This is not the only place in Shakespeare where a woman argues against the double standard. In a very early play, *The Comedy of Errors*, Adriana makes a serious argument for higher moral expectations for both sexes – telling her husband that if her hypothetical adultery would shame him, his (which hasn't really happened) shames her. In a more comic version of Emilia's argument, in *The Merchant of Venice*, Portia teasingly argues that since Bassanio has given her ring away to someone else (actually herself in disguise), she has the right to sleep with that person.

The double standard, these three women argue, is an injustice in marriage, and at another point a character's invocation of the double standard is so gratuitous that it is hard not to see the exchange as another kind of critique: In *Measure for Measure*, the Duke, disguised as a friar, says to a woman in prison for sex with her fiancé, 'So then it seems your most offenceful act / Was mutually committed? ... / Then was your sin of heavier kind than his' (2.3.26–7, 28).

Many have explained the double standard with reference to men's desire to make sure children born within marriage are legitimate, so they deserve to inherit property, and Keith Thomas has added as cause 'the desire of men for absolute property in women', but feminist analyses provide additional explanations (1959: 216). In Western culture, women have been traditionally more identified with the body, by contrast to men's easier affiliation with the world of the mind. When polemical and proscriptive texts assert that women are more lustful than men, this belief provides a rationale for keeping women's sexual desire under a stricter social control. This is another example of the projection discussed in Chapter 1 – men have often projected their sexual desires onto women. Although reformers argued against it, men could easily think of their own adultery as a right and their wives' adultery as a degradation to both of them.

Justice and marriage

The religious reformers later referred to as puritans were, like Adriana, looking for justice, and they demanded a single higher standard for both sexes. There are other justice issues in marriage, and Emilia's whole speech has reference to some of them as well: 'say they strike us, / Or scant our former having [allowance] in despite' (4.3.89–90). In a patriarchal society, men are given some right to discipline their wives, but even in such a society, men's physical force can be seen as excessive or totally unjustified. Observers see that Othello has crossed that line when he strikes Desdemona.[17]

Feminist theorists today go even further beyond the abolition of the sexual double standard in thinking about justice in marriage (Okin 1989; Shanley 2004). In feminist theory, neither partner is hierarchically entitled to rule over and correct the other, physically or by some other form of punishment. And feminists today also think more about other kinds of justice in marriage. Statistics show that employed women with employed husbands generally still do more housework than their husbands (Hochschild and Machung 1989).[18] Money should be distributed more equitably, also. After a divorce, women typically are much poorer than men, no matter how much they have contributed to their husbands' lives and careers. This is partly because women are still paid less than men in similar occupations, and also because more women are in lower paying careers and are more likely to take some time out for child care. The marriages that apparently have the most equality, at least in terms of household work, generally have it only because they have hired female help, and Dolan parallels this fact to the importance of servants in *The Taming of the Shrew* (2008: 128–31). It is conditions such as these that have contributed to Carole Pateman's argument that the marriage contract is inherently an unequal one (1988). And in some cultures a husband might still kill his wife for adultery and receive exoneration on the basis of 'honour' or 'passion'.[19] Today, some feminists still seek to remake marriage by making it a more equal partnership accessible also to same-sex couples – while other feminists find its permanence and exclusiveness oppressive and the male dominance in its tradition beyond repair.[20] Catherine Belsey argues that an ideal combining desire with marriage makes marriage inevitably unstable: 'Marriage based on love means the conjunction of contraries, peace and anxiety, completeness and lack, companionable tranquility and danger' (1999: 82).[21] Thus it is not surprising that feminist critics would differ in their evaluation of fictional marriages (Dusinberre 2003 [1975]: xvi–xvii, xxvi–xxvii; Jankowski 2000).

Do Shakespeare's plays idealize marriage? Some of the characters do – most obviously, and ironically, Othello. There is some degree of tension in virtually every marriage shown in the body of a Shakespearean play, caused not necessarily by jealousy but alternatively by issues such as the desire to know secrets or disagreement about a daughter's planned marriage. The endings of comedies are the most likely places to find idealization, but the contrasts among the couples marrying in many of them, the ambiguity of using ritual for closure, and occasional details of language use provide other cautionary notes.

Shakespeare's plays do not deal with every kind of tension in marriage, whether to resolve it, as in most comedies, or to expose it, as in some of the tragedies. But, nevertheless, many tensions appear. The plays can also be read to comment on other issues relating marriage to justice – who is allowed to get married, how much marriage is privileged as the most important relationship in people's lives and the sign of their achieved maturity. In several of Shakespeare's plays, such as *Twelfth Night*, with Antonio and Sebastian, there are hints that the most reciprocal loving relationship might be between two people of the same sex. In *As You Like It*, as Will Fisher has pointed out, Rosalind and Celia set up an autonomous household together with economic as well as emotional bonds (2010). In many plays, characters such as Antonio, unmarried at the end, might be among those who interest the audience most. Shakespeare was writing at a time when conflicts between marriage and male friendship had customarily favoured male friendship. Our established social system now favours opposite-sex marriage, but his plays speak also to people who see them with a perspective from a newly emergent sex/gender social system which accepts same-sex marriage and, in a different way, to those who argue for a validation of the autonomous individual or for a multitude of kinds of relationships against the privileging of the permanent coupling of marriage.[22] In spite of the legal organization of his society around marriage, after all, one third of adult women in Shakespeare's society remained single all their lives (Froide 2005).

4

Motherhood

Where are the mothers in Shakespeare? Mary Beth Rose finds them mostly missing or circumscribed (1991). Shakespeare's plays include many more daughters, fathers and sons than mothers. Nevertheless, a number of mothers appear in his less famous plays, often characters he added to his source. Elsewhere, characters may refer to mothers who are not present or use imagery suggesting motherhood, sometimes to give more resonance to women (or even men) who are not literal mothers, sometimes to show men's fear of what they associate with mothers. His plays include many more lines asserting a mother's influence on a child than asserting a father's influence.

However, his characters' allusions to maternal influence are sometimes hostile and some of the mothers on stage are villainous. Feminist theory has much relevance to Shakespeare's presentations of motherhood in exploring the polarized fantasies which they often suggest, sometimes drawing on psychoanalysis. Nancy Chodorow analyses the idea of traditional masculinity as involving disidentification with and rejection of mothers (1978), and Madelon Gohlke [Sprengnether] (1980) and others show this in many of the plays. But the plays invite other kinds of feminist analysis as well. Plays Rose does not discuss provide a different view of Shakespeare's mothers.

Feminist disagreements

In Chapter 1, I mentioned disagreements between equality/humanist and difference/gynocentric traditions of feminist theory. These also appear with regard to their treatment of motherhood. Difference feminism emphasizes a mother's physical role in reproduction, through conception, pregnancy, childbearing, nursing and subsequent child care. Equality feminism presents motherhood as an option rather than a requirement, stresses the idea that a mother's identity includes other elements than motherhood, and, often argues the need to involve men in child rearing. Sara Ruddick tries to bridge contrasts between the two traditions by emphasizing 'maternal thinking' (not instinct), the mother's role as an educator, and an expansive definition of motherhood including men doing 'maternal work' (1989). Both kinds of feminism often include the idea that a mother's experience may give her sympathy for children other than her own and solidarity with bereaved and troubled parents outside her own immediate circle. Adoptive and foster motherhood could be validated by either kind of feminist, but there is often a special intensity in a gynocentric feminist's claim of biological motherhood as opposed to adoption or even to fatherhood.

Many of Shakespeare's characters stress biological aspects of motherhood, though, on the one hand, the Countess, in *All's Well that Ends Well*, speaks of her strong feelings about her adoptive daughter and, on the other, Lady Macbeth is not traditionally maternal in spite of the fact that she has borne and nursed a child. Characters as different as Margaret Page of *The Merry Wives of Windsor* and Cleopatra speak and act sometimes as mothers – and sometimes in other roles, such as friend, lover or ruler.

Feminist theories vary in their approaches to a daughter's relationship to her mother. Difference/gynocentric feminism emphasizes their bonds, while equality/humanist feminism might stress the daughter's freedom to behave differently from her mother, if her mother follows a traditional model and the daughter wants something else. As Ynestra King writes,

> Most of us in becoming feminists have rejected the self-sacrificing, altruistic, infinitely forgiving, martyred unconditionally loving mother – for this is how I saw my mother – have rejected that mother in *ourselves* as the part of ourselves that is complicitous in our own oppression. (King 1983 qtd in Ruddick 1989: 39)

The absence of their mothers may make many of the daughters in Shakespeare seem more independent, yet here is an apparent paradox: Desdemona, who makes the most daring marital choice, tries to gain her father's acceptance by arguing that she is acting like her mother in putting her duty to her husband over her duty to her father.

From the point of view of equality/humanist feminism, the difference feminist attitude to motherhood may be too close to the patriarchal tradition associating women with the body and making motherhood an all-encompassing role orienting women to service. From the point of view of difference feminism, the equality feminist attitude may be too close to the patriarchal tradition of looking down on the female body and the grubby details of birthing and rearing children.[1] However, Hélène Cixous, usually associated with difference feminism, can still reconcile motherhood and writing when she says that a woman's writing includes 'at least a little of that good mother's milk. She writes in white ink' (1980 [1976]: 251).

Equality and difference feminism concur that the dominant culture has for many centuries looked down on mothers, even though it does sometimes idealize them as well. Many feminist critics would agree that mothers are often polarized as good or evil in Shakespeare, though they disagree about how much this is mitigated. The plays have few examples of the loving and peaceful mother that difference feminism sometimes assumes as the norm; the most harmonious mother–daughter relationships occur in the reunions of Hermione (*The Winter's*

Tale) and Thaisa (*Pericles*) with daughters from whom they had been separated since shortly after childbirth. But men's language in the plays often indicates a pervasive unease about motherhood that some kinds of feminist theory also find important as an origin of psychic and social problems.

Mothers, history and Shakespearean genres

Many critics have discussed the fact that Shakespeare's plays are full of families represented as father–son or father–daughter. This could be explained by the material conditions of Shakespeare's theatre: perhaps not very many boy actors were skilled enough to play women old enough to be mothers. Or perhaps the family structure onstage represents the legal inclusion of wives into their husbands – as a Tudor legal document has it, 'the husband and wife are one and that one is the husband' (qtd in Rose 1991). It has been suggested that the high mortality rate of mothers, especially in childbirth, would make some of their absences less remarkable, but actually historical demography suggests that, as at present, women then had a longer life expectancy than men.[2] In many cases, mothers are also absent in Shakespeare's sources. Their absence may help to suggest other relationships, particularly between father and daughter, are more intense. The conflict between female subjectivity and patriarchy is dramatized more harshly in *King Lear*, for example, because there is no mother. However, surprisingly, Shakespeare's plays often add one or more mothers to their sources or give a mother more attention – sometimes she survives to play an important role after her death in the source or the historical record.

Shakespeare's genres vary in the roles they give to mothers. In Shakespeare's twelve comedies, only four mothers have speaking parts: Emilia in *The Comedy of Errors*, Mistress Page in *The Merry Wives of Windsor* and the Countess of

Rossillion and the Widow in *All's Well that Ends Well*.³ The tragedies include two plays with one mother (Tamora in *Titus*, Gertrude in *Hamlet*) and four plays with two (Ladies Capulet and Montague, Ladies Macbeth and Macduff, Cleopatra and Octavia, and Volumnia and Virgilia in *Coriolanus*). The histories include five mothers in the first trilogy, Richard II's queen, the Duchess of Gloucester, the Duchess of York and (with one line at the end of *Henry V*) the queen of France in the second trilogy, three mothers in *King John*, and Katherine of Aragon in *Henry VIII*. The romances have two evil foster or stepmothers (Dionyza in *Pericles* and the Queen in *Cymbeline*), one good foster mother (Lychorida in *Pericles*) and two good mothers who return after a long absence (Thaisa in *Pericles* and Hermione in *The Winter's Tale*).

Mothers in the comedies

The greatest disproportion, and the one most often noted, is the one in the comedies, between the absence of mothers and the presence of fathers.⁴ These are also the plays in which young women are most prominent. Probably the limited resources of Shakespeare's acting company have something to do with the absence of mothers here. If the company had only four actors who could play women and the plot involved four couples, as in *As You Like It*, there was no one left to play a mother. Five is the maximum number of speaking parts for women in Shakespeare's plays and the fifth part often has only one scene.⁵

It could be considered another sign of the male dominance of the society that a play with few women seemed a theatrically effective representation of its dynamics. Rose writes of the 'romantic comic interpretation of marriage as the institution symbolizing the ideal society, a society based upon the sacrifice of the mother's desire' (1991: 304). She finds a significant parallel to the absence of motherhood in Shakespeare's comedies in an influential book by the early modern humanist Juan Luis Vives, *The Instruction of a Christen Woman* (first translated into English c. 1528), which implies that 'separation from the mother (and consequent identification with the father) ... proves the enabling condition for a full (i.e. both public and private) adult life' (1991: 301).[6]

On the other hand, in *As You Like It*, for example, if either Rosalind or Celia had a mother at court, there would be less of a focus on their relationship. Rosalind and Celia seem more adventurous in travelling to the Forest of Arden because Rosalind's mother is not there. Lodge's *Rosalynde*, Shakespeare's source, already gets these effects from mother-absence.

It is arguable that the absent mother returns in many of Shakespeare's plays. Rosalind's language, for example, refers to motherhood more often than is necessary from the plot. In her disguise as Ganymede, she mocks naïve wives who can't defend themselves from criticism by saying 'that woman that cannot make her fault her husband's occasion, let her never nurse her child herself, for she will breed it like a fool' (4.1.165–8). This implies that smart mothers have a self-protective resourcefulness they can pass on to their children. The repression of motherhood, if that is what it is, breaks down in other comedies as well – for example, Beatrice imagines her mother crying in childbirth.[7]

More importantly, generalizations about the repression of mothers in Shakespeare's comedies need to be qualified by the recognition of larger exceptions. In *The Comedy of Errors*, Emilia, the mother of the main set of separated twins, reveals herself at a climactic moment, though in Shakespeare's source, Plautus's *Menaechmi*, she never makes an appearance. In Shakespeare's version, she is the Abbess whose convent has suddenly appeared as a refuge for two of the separated brothers. She has been giving marital advice, perhaps unfairly, to Adriana, who neither of them knows is her daughter-in-law. In spite of the presence of the Duke, Emilia stage-manages much of the last scene and has a fourteen-line summary speech at the end, full of maternal imagery:

> Thirty-three years have I but gone in travail
> Of you, my sons, and till this present hour
> My heavy burden ne'er delivered.
>
> (5.1.401–3)

Shakespeare borrowed the transformation of the mother lost at sea into an abbess from John Gower, whose *Apollonius of Tyre* he returned to as a source for *Pericles*. The location of a newly discovered mother in a convent could be seen as another indication of uneasiness about maternal sexuality, such as Mary Beth Rose (1991), Janet Adelman (1992) and Gail Paster (1993) have suggested. But an abbess would have the title of Mother, and it was one of the roles in which a woman could have some official power, whether we see it as supervising Catholic or Anglican nuns or vestal virgins in ancient Ephesus.

The Merry Wives of Windsor also adds a mother to the source plot. Margaret Page, one of the title characters, is the mother of Anne, for whom she and others are trying to find a match. But her major role in the play is as a friend of Alice Ford and a co-conspirator with her in a plot to humiliate Falstaff, who is wooing both of them, and cure Frank Ford of jealousy. The trick is her idea; she is witty and resourceful, good at mocking and flirting with Falstaff. In this plot, she seems clever. Yet, as a mother, she is not so admirable. She wants to marry Anne to a rich doctor who speaks with a comical French accent. Meanwhile, Anne and her poor, but higher-born wooer Fenton arrange to elope together. Mistress Page redeems herself for the comic audience by her good wishes to Fenton and final willingness to 'laugh this sport o'er by a country fire, / Sir John and all' (5.5.236–7).

Margaret Page could be taken as a good example of the humanist/equality feminist principle that mothers have many other sides than their motherhood. In the jealousy plot, she both vindicates herself and punishes Falstaff, showing that 'Wives may be merry and yet honest too' (4.2.100).[8] But she is not wise about motherhood. She plays a comic parallel to Lady Capulet's role, urging her daughter to an unwanted marriage. In this play, the comic vision is that at some time everyone is foolish.

A more sympathetic Shakespearean mother, the Countess of Rossillion, is an addition to the source of her play, *All's Well that Ends Well*. 'Giletta of Narbonne' tells us that Count Beltramo, as a boy, was brought up together with Giletta, whose father had been Beltramo's father's doctor, but never mentions either Beltramo's or Giletta's mother (Shakespeare 1993: 225). In *All's Well*, the Countess is both a mother to Bertram and an adoptive or foster mother to Helen. She observes Helen, deduces she probably loves Bertram, whose father has just died and who has just been called to the court by the King, his guardian. She tells her, 'I am your mother / And put you in the catalogue of those / That were enwombed mine' (1.3.139–41).

This affectionate speech is designed to lead Helen into confiding her love of Bertram and it works, as Helen insists she does not want to be his sister. With the Countess's encouragement, Helen cures the mysteriously sick King, and chooses marriage to Bertram as her reward. Bertram reluctantly marries her at the King's command – 'A poor physician's daughter my wife!' (2.3.116) – and then abandons her to go off to war. He writes her, *'when thou canst get the ring upon my finger, which never shall come off, and show me a child begotten of thy body that I am father to, then call me husband; but in such a "then" I write a "never"'* (3.2.55–8). The Countess' sympathy is much more with Helen, whom she sees as replacing Bertram in her family and affections.

The Countess is the only mother in Shakespeare whose relationship with a daughter is close enough for her to support her daughter's marriage choice. (Even the Nurse, who might also be considered a foster mother, eventually tells Juliet to marry Paris.) She is paralleled by a poorer and lower-ranking mother, referred to only as Widow, who is close enough to her daughter, Diana, that Diana discusses with her Bertram's pursuit. Diana, the Widow and Helen, who is following Bertram in disguise, plan a bed trick that enables Helen to get pregnant by Bertram. Bertram's first response to the revelation of her pregnancy is to apologize. But his last words are more conditional: 'If she, my liege, can make me know this clearly / I'll love her dearly, ever, ever dearly' (5.3.314–15).

There is no other Shakespearean play in which a mother plays such a strong role in promoting the marriage at the end. Indeed, the active roles of the two guardians, Countess and King, are unprecedented. Neely writes, 'The younger generation achieves its desires by remaining under the authority of and satisfying the needs of the older generation' (1985: 91). Though the Countess is remarkable and sympathetic, for centuries many readers have felt that Bertram is an unworthy goal of Helen's desires and that their marriage is not promising. Adelman, a feminist psychoanalytic critic, here focusing on fantasies about mothers, makes an explicit connection between the strong role of the Countess, Helen's association with her and Bertram's resistance to marriage with Helen: 'For Bertram, Helena has virtually no existence apart from his mother; ... she becomes the epitome of the maternal power that binds the child, especially the male child, who here discovers that she is always the woman in his bed' (1992: 80, 83). Bertram is apparently so obsessed with mothers that he even tries to seduce Diana by saying, 'Now you should be as your mother was / When your sweet self was got' (4.2.9–10).

Helen's last line is to the Countess, 'O my dear mother, do I see you living?' (5.3.318). If she is now Helen's mother-in-law, that gives Helen a reason to greet her as mother, especially as kinship names were used in the early modern period, but as Helen herself has earlier recognized, she is Helen's mother because of their own attachment as well. That is less ambiguous and less a doubtful good than the marriage.

There is no mother–daughter relationship in *The Comedy of Errors*, and the slightly later tragic picture of one in *Romeo and Juliet* presents Lady Capulet as both distant and controlling. However, *The Merry Wives of Windsor* and *All's Well that Ends Well*, with its addition of a strong and loving older woman, show an increasing interest in the mother–daughter relationship, which will culminate in *The Winter's Tale*. On the other hand, a man's flight from his mother's influence, important in *All's Well*, appears in both the history plays and the tragedies, as well as in a shocking soliloquy in the romance *Cymbeline*, in which a man quickly moves from doubting his wife to doubting his mother.

Mothers in the histories

King John and the first tetralogy of history plays include more mothers proportionately than the comedies, while the second tetralogy includes fewer. A few plays, *Richard III* in particular, also show the male hostility to mothers suggested in *All's Well that Ends Well*. Most mothers in the history plays are mainly defined by their care for their sons. Sometimes this is simply nurturing or mourning. However, their concern for their sons' rights or sorrow over their sons' loss may lead them to instigate or support violence. At the end of *Richard III*, bereaved mothers, including his own, pray for the defeat of Richard in battle, supporting what is presented as the side of justice. On the other hand, in *King John* neither mother's quest for her son's rights receives clear vindication.

Margaret of Anjou, queen of England as the wife of Henry VI, appears in the three plays named after him as well as *Richard III*, and in the later plays frequently speaks as a mother. Even before she marries Henry, Suffolk, who has wooed her ostensibly for his king but really for himself, sees her difference from stereotypical femininity as an advantage in her likelihood of producing royal children (Willis 1995: 183). In *3 Henry VI*, when she first speaks as a mother, she is protesting against Henry's disinheritance of him: her maternal and military roles blend. She calls Henry an unnatural father but also specifically credits her physical connection with Edward, saying that Henry would have kept him as heir, 'Hadst thou but lov'd him half so well as I, / Or felt that pain which I did for him once, / Or nourish'd him as I did with my blood' (1.1.227–9). She leads an army of 5,000 men against York, who pushed for her son's disinheritance. But when her son is killed she cradles his dead body in a way that could suggest the Pietà figure of Mary holding the dead Christ and the similar scene in the N-Town cycle of mystery plays.[9]

Her love of her son does not, however, lead to sympathy for other parents and thus the association with this religious figure of mercy is in part ironic. When York's son Rutland is killed, by her supporter Clifford and presumably under her direction, she mocks York and shows him a napkin stained with his son's blood to get him to weep. Yet after her own son is killed, she attacks his murderers thus: 'You have no children, butchers; if you had, / The thought of them would have stirr'd up remorse' (5.5.61–2).

While her role was drastically cut from the late seventeenth century on, Margaret was rediscovered in the mid-twentieth century, after performances by Rosalind Boxall (1952–3) and, especially, Peggy Ashcroft (1963–4). Randall Martin writes that Ashcroft conveyed 'maternal solicitude, problematizing the Amazon stereotype to which her male opponents always seek to reduce her' (2001: 88). Martin even compares her in her complexity to Lear (2001: 82).

The historical Margaret had died by the time in which *Richard III* was set, but the play keeps her alive (another mother added to the source) to curse Richard and to be cursed for her role in the death of Rutland by some of the other mourning mothers. None of the other mothers in the history plays is quite as bloody-minded, sexually transgressive or long-lived as Margaret, but they share what the play presents as her maternal qualities – they protect their sons' rights, influence them, mourn them and curse those who killed them.

If mothers' speeches in *Richard III* are largely laments and curses, in *King John* they are largely laments and insults. Juliet Dusinberre says this play has the 'biggest slanging match Shakespeare ever wrote for women' (1990: 49). Queen Eleanor's son John is the king, but Constance, whose dead husband was John's deceased elder brother, considers her young son Arthur the true heir to the throne. Both Constance and Eleanor, Duchess of Aquitaine in her own right and Queen of England by her marriage to Henry II, now deceased, want their sons to be recognized as the legitimate king by descent from Richard Plantagenet. Each defends her position and that of her son, partly by accusing the other woman of adultery. In England in Shakespeare's time, when women of all classes were insulted, this was the most common charge, but of course the stakes are higher when ancestry is supposed to decide who rules England (Gowing 1996). An ironic contrast to their charges appears with another mother/son relation – Lady Faulconbridge's son is recognized as part of the Plantagenet line only because he gives up his claim to legitimate birth.[10]

Both Eleanor and Constance defend their maternal claims eloquently. Which mother is actually in the right is not clear, and Shakespeare complicates the case in a number of ways, such as making Arthur younger than he historically was, and not interested in kingship. Each mother claims she regrets what she feels is the necessity of war. But as with Queen Margaret, motherhood does not make either Eleanor or Constance more peaceful.

Gynocentric feminism sometimes asserts that women's experiences of pregnancy, childbirth, nursing and child raising give them a greater appreciation of the value of human life and therefore make them more opposed to war and violence. Humanist feminism sometimes makes the same claim about child-rearing as an experience that has a similar effect on men who are active in caregiving.[11] But neither Constance nor Eleanor has broadened concern for her own son to an interest in helping other women's children. Eleanor does claim a connection with her newly discovered grandson, the offspring of Lady Faulconbridge and King Richard, but this is largely because she sees him as a strong fighter on her side. Her last attention to her younger grandson, Arthur, may even be in collusion with John's plans to have him killed, and she has no qualms about arranging for her granddaughter, Blanche, a marriage that has very little chance of bringing about the peace it is supposed to.

Thus the most salient repeated features of mothers in the histories are that they are concerned about their own children, they mourn them, they often curse and promote battle to redress their grievances, and, contrary to any belief in women's superior sympathies, they rarely care about the deaths of the children of their political opponents. One of the few places where a mother extends her sympathies more broadly could be said to be the exception that proves the rule, since it comes as part of an international settlement won in war: near the end of *Henry V*, when Queen Isabel of France gives her blessing to her daughter's marriage with Henry, promoting a union of the kingdoms, she concludes with a wish, 'That English may as French, French Englishmen / Receive each other. God speak this amen' (5.2.359–60).

Mothers in the tragedies

Several tragedies develop further the question of mothers' attitudes to killing. The three most vividly portrayed mothers in Shakespeare's tragedies are all involved with warfare; however, each of them is opposed to a sharply contrasting woman, in two cases another mother, who seems her polar opposite. In other tragedies, the play's language suggests that fantasies about mothers affect the relationship between the hero and the women closest to him, and this too may involve a polarized view of women, into good or bad mothers, whether in the hero's mind or in the actual characterization.

While no child of Lady Macbeth appears onstage, one of her most memorable speeches produces the image of her as a potential murderer of her own child.[12]

> I have given suck, and know
> How tender 'tis to love the babe that milks me:

> I would, while it was smiling in my face,
> Have pluck'd my nipple from his boneless gyms
> And dash'd the brains out, had I so sworn
> As you have done to this.
>
> (1.7.54–9)

In the early twentieth century A. C. Bradley asked, 'How many children had Lady Macbeth?' (1985 [1904]), and L. C. Knights wrote an essay with that title, using it as an example of what not to ask because characters are not real people (1946). Because of the high infant mortality rate of the time, the original audience might have assumed that she had had a child who had died, but the passage also suggests that if a child of hers had died, her violation of mothering might have been responsible.[13] Deborah Willis convincingly locates the reference to swearing in this passage in relation to the aristocratic 'honor culture, for whom keeping an oath "to do" assumes more importance than attachment to her child' (1995: 224).[14] Like Margaret, Lady Macbeth is imagined as both war-like and maternal, as when Macbeth exclaims, 'Bring forth men-children only! / For thy undaunted mettle should compose / Nothing but males' (1.7.73–5). Thus he 'imagines her as male and then reconstitutes himself as the invulnerable male child of such a mother' (Adelman 1992: 139). The play makes it easy to blame her for all Macbeth's subsequent murders, as if she has initiated him to an addiction. But she has no part in his plans for further murders. He takes on the pitilessness she has advised, 'giving up attachment to her for identification with her' (Willis 1995: 226). She suffers from this rejection, and we eventually hear her, talking in her sleep, guiltily remembering how much blood flowed from the murdered Banquo. Thus she is humanized, at least in part. She is somehow both the maternal helpmate invested in her husband's career, as well as the communer with the spirits of evil. She is also one of the courageous ancient Scotswomen described in Holinshed's *Chronicles* – though unlike Holinshed's description she imagines conflict between nursing and hardihood (Rackin 2005: 123–5).

The presentation of both Lady Macbeth and the Weird Sisters draws on the image of the witch as the bad mother. One unambiguously maternal figure in this play contrasts with them, Lady Macduff, another mother added to the play's source. When warned by a messenger of an attack coming, she knows that her innocence has no power to help her – 'Why then, alas! / Do I put up that womanly defence / To say, I have done no harm?' (4.2.76–8). Nevertheless, though she has been calling her husband a traitor for his absence, with her last words she stands up for him:

FIRST MURDERER Where is your husband?
LADY MACDUFF I hope, in no place so unsanctified,
Where such as thou may'st find him.
(79–81)

Lady Macbeth and Lady Macduff contrast on several key points – the first imagines murdering her child, the second wants to protect hers but faces others trying to kill him. The first criticizes her husband for being 'too full o' th' milk of human kindness' (1.5.16), the second criticizes hers for lacking 'the natural touch' (4.2.9) in not putting the instinct to protect his family first. But while the first begins with a sense of her power and loses it, the second feels powerless but speaks courageously in the last we see of her. Thus near the end they do not contrast as absolutely as they have earlier, and Lady Macbeth's sleepwalking question 'The Thane of Fife had a wife: where is she now?' (5.1.43–4) reinforces the sense of their shared complexity. Deborah Willis notes the 'unexpected hint of an identification with Lady Macduff ... the only instance in which Lady Macbeth shows any sign of feeling for another woman' (1995: 236).

Adelman has argued that *Macbeth* not only ends with a womanless world but also invokes a fantasy of male 'birth entirely exempt from women ... in effect an all-male family'

(1992: 139). When Macbeth keeps repeating the witches' promise, 'None of woman born / Shall harm Macbeth' (4.1.80–1), this suggests that he has come to see himself, by contrast to other men, as not born of woman and therefore invulnerable (Adelman 1992: 141). His invulnerability is a delusion, but the revelation that Macduff, his nemesis, was 'from his mother's womb / Untimely ripp'd' (5.8.15–16), while denying 'the fantasy of male self-generation', still sustains 'the sense that violent separation from the mother is the mark of the successful male' (Adelman 1992: 144). Furthermore, Malcolm, to whom his father's throne succeeds when Macbeth is defeated, describes himself as 'yet / Unknown to woman' (4.3.125–6).

Thus, though many women have found Lady Macbeth fascinating, both her trajectory and other fantasies about gender in this play make it more plausible to read this play as anti-feminist than feminist. Deborah Willis tries to refute this conclusion, arguing that the play does not finally associate all evil with women or wholeheartedly endorse the patriarchal order with which the play finishes. The witches have male masters, human males are too often negligent fathers, the 'honor-driven patronage system controlled by the king' and 'the vicissitudes of patrilineality' create tensions within Malcolm's order with no need for the weird sisters to spark them (Willis 1995: 236). These flaws in the final order are, however, subtle, and the image of the all-male community remains for those who want to see it as a victory of goodness. Or, alternatively, the final all-male community may be seen, as often in recent productions, as threatened by the persistent power of the witches. If we try to find inchoate feminism in the presence that Lady Macbeth still has in popular culture, that attempt is frustrated by the way that hostile comparisons to her continually poison the public conversation about women in politics.

By contrast to Lady Macbeth, Volumnia, the mother in *Coriolanus*, is relatively ordinary. Volumnia promotes the values of her culture rather than, like Lady Macbeth, transgressing them by consciously identifying with evil. She trains her son in Roman honour and military courage. Claiming credit for nursing him as well, she says, 'Thy valiantness was mine, thou suck'st it from me' (3.2.129).[15]

This emphasis on Volumnia's militaristic upbringing of Coriolanus is Shakespeare's invention. His source, Plutarch's 'Life of Coriolanus', rather than stressing Volumnia's educating him to love warfare, emphasizes his fatherlessness, sees his impatience as coming from a lack of education, and presents his interest in weapons and athletic competition as self-generated (1976: 314).[16]

Critics of the eighteenth and nineteenth century generally idealized Volumnia; Anna Jameson writes of her 'towering spirit' and the 'truth of female nature ... beautifully preserved, and the portrait, with all its vigour ... without harshness' (qtd in Bliss 2010: 48). It is hard to find a contemporary feminist critic with language at all similar.[17] This is as much because of changing attitudes towards war as changing attitudes towards women. After two world wars and many other conflicts, Coriolanus' constant readiness for battle has lost its appeal, and so has Volumnia's coaching.

As feminist critics sometimes note, Volumnia did not single-handedly establish Roman militarism, but she does embody and transmit it with particular intensity, and initially without respect for Roman citizens or even a pragmatic ability to pretend it.[18] However, when Coriolanus shows his scorn for the people as he begs for votes, she urges more diplomacy. Her values are more complex than his, but the play may encourage blaming her for his extreme warrior identity: her militaristic lines are more memorable than those of any male character except his, and she takes credit for his achievements. Not only does she use imagery of nursing him in valiantness, but, emphasizing her influence with language more often applied to fathers in the prevailing medical model, she says, 'Thou art my warrior: / I holp to frame thee' (5.3.62–3) (Kahn 1997: 148).

Virgilia, whom Coriolanus calls 'my gracious silence' (2.1.175), is a very different kind of mother than Volumnia.

Volumnia enjoys imagining him in battle with a bloody brow, and Virgilia responds, 'O Jupiter, no blood!' (1.3.39). Virgilia insists on staying inside their house to spin while Volumnia goes out with a similarly militaristic friend Valeria, as she ranges beyond home and family in her interests.

Virgilia's son with Coriolanus is a pugnacious little boy, introduced with a description of his angry attack on a butterfly. Volumnia's friend Valeria describes it enthusiastically and Volumnia herself indulgently compares his anger to 'one on's father's moods' (1.3.67). Her encouragement of militarism is an expression of a larger culture, against which Virgilia's gentleness has little chance.

Just as Lady Macbeth does not anticipate Macbeth's continued obsession with killing, Volumnia does not anticipate that Coriolanus will alienate Romans enough to be banished, and will then join Rome's enemies and return with them intent on burning down the city of his birth. In spite of their differences, the mothers are in agreement when Coriolanus returns. Volumnia pleads that assaulting his city is like treading 'on thy mother's womb / That brought thee to this world' (5.3.124–5) and Virgilia echoes her.

In spite of her silence after Coriolanus's submission to her and during the procession in her honour there is much opportunity for her facial expression and posture to convey feelings. She may appear proud of her power to protect Rome from her son's resentment, but in 1984 Irene Worth's silence showed 'mute devastation'. In 1992 Judi Dench's face suddenly became 'a mask of grief' and she entered Rome for the last time 'as a mourning statue of horror' (Bliss 2010: 59; Luckyj 2002: 113, see also 109–15). As Jeanne Roberts writes, 'there are few more heartbreakingly ironic moments in all of Shakespeare than her return to the city and the empty celebration of the people' (2002: 206).

Feminist psychoanalytic critics Kahn, Adelman and Willis have shown that motherhood in these plays figures not only as a role of key female characters but also as a fantasy that the tragic heroes are in many ways acting against. Adelman in particular has shown how in both imagery and actions, Macbeth and Coriolanus try to identify themselves as men by disidentifying with qualities they associate with women and mothers, and also by distancing themselves from Lady Macbeth and Volumnia. The plays are bleak companion pieces that 'enact the logic of a terrible either/or; 'either the excision of the female or the excision of the male, either the death of the mother or the death of her son' (Adelman 1992: 162).

Although no literal mothers appear in *King Lear* or *Othello*, fantasies about mothers are important in these plays. Kahn (1986) and Adelman (1992) read *Lear* as showing the return of the repressed mother. In Shakespeare's main source, a play where the name is spelled 'Leir', the division of his kingdoms and confrontation with the original of Cordelia take place just after his queen's funeral. Shakespeare omits that context. But Lear says he 'thought to set [his] rest / On [Cordelia's] kind nursery' (1.1.124–5); he hoped to find loving maternal care in her. The fool criticizes him for making his daughters his mothers: 'thou gav'st them the rod and putt'st down thine own breeches' (1.4.164–5). Facing the refusal of Goneril and Regan to nurture him as he wants, and sometimes imagining it to result from their possible origin in the adultery of their own mother, his wife, Lear speaks of his own emotional disturbance as 'this mother' (2.2.249). This term in the medicine of the time usually referred to a disease of women who showed the range of symptoms later associated with hysteria, a word which comes from the Greek word for 'womb'. The 'wandering womb' was thought to be the cause of 'the mother' but there are a few cases where medical records present it as a possible disease of males also. Kahn identifies it here with 'a searing sense of loss at the deprivation of the mother's presence' (1986: 40). Lear's inability to get the motherly love he wants from his daughters makes him feel like a weak woman. He tries not to weep since he considers tears 'women's weapons' (2.2.469), and attacks Goneril in terms of motherhood when he hopes that she will either be childless or have an ungrateful child.

The beneficent mother reappears after Lear has been thoroughly tested and stripped of everything. Cordelia is implicitly compared to the Virgin/Mother Mary – her tears are 'holy water' (4.2.31) – and to the Roman mother goddess Ceres, patron of natural fertility, who according to legend brought spring back to the earth by searching for her lost daughter (Adelman 1992: 120; Kahn 1986: 27). But her return is less as a psychically realistic character than as 'the creature of Lear's need' (Adelman 1992: 124). Adelman argues movingly that the audience responds to her return in part because of fantasies that 'spring from the ground of an infantile experience prior to gender' (1992: 125) – they are not just male fantasies.

> Daughters as well as sons require this sacrifice from those we make our mothers. Perhaps our task – if we read this play specifically as feminists – is simultaneously to acknowledge this place of common need and to measure its cost to the woman forced to bear its burden. (1992: 126)

In *Othello* also no literal mothers appear, but both Othello and Desdemona remember their deceased mothers, Othello in both his handkerchief stories and Desdemona in lines identifying with her mother quoted earlier. Both speak lines that suggest fantasies of maternal love in the background of their own relationship. Desdemona compares the advice she gives him about Cassio to urging him to 'feed on nourishing dishes, or keep you warm' (3.3.78). Othello refers to Desdemona as 'the fountain from the which my current runs / Or else dries up' (4.1.60–1), and when he adds, 'to be discarded thus' (61), this is 'the language of maternal abandonment' (Adelman 1992: 66). The impossible desire for a woman to be like a perfect mother emerges in the imagery of both of these tragedies, though in one case the woman is a daughter and in the other she is a new wife.

Both plays contrast with *Antony and Cleopatra*. Cleopatra is literally a mother, and there is a description of her enthroned together with Antony in Alexandria with her children (one by Caesar, several by Antony) at their feet. While the maternal aspects of the other women are frustrated in relation to the hero or he is frustrated by his search for an all-loving mother, Antony develops a masculinity that includes maternal generosity, so that the two have a more reciprocal relationship (Adelman 1992; Erickson 1985). Although Antony and Cleopatra have their fights, including some sparked by Antony's jealousy, they always forgive each other. Their relationship can be seen as one of the few examples in Shakespeare of the acceptance of a mother's sexuality.

The strangest visual image of a woman as mother in Shakespeare is probably Cleopatra's suicide, for which she clothes herself in royal garments and puts an asp to her bosom, saying 'Dost thou not see my baby at my breast / That sucks the nurse asleep?' (5.2.307–8). Neely argues that 'the asp is lover and child, phallic and gynocentric, death-bringing and immortality-conferring ... the love death is profoundly satisfying' (1985: 161).[19] Erickson, on the other hand, finds this maternal image 'poignant but nonetheless destructive' (1985: 145). Possibly audiences have always been split, with some finding 'Cleopatra's equation of baby with poisonous asp' (Erickson 1985: 146) too jarring, others drawn in by the power of her language and performance and perhaps by their knowledge that serpents could iconographically suggest wisdom and royalty (Lewis 1997: 140).

Mothers in the romances

Many critics have found *Antony and Cleopatra* a link with the romances, written soon after it, and Cleopatra's maternity can be seen as an anticipation of the maternal power in *The Winter's Tale*. Most of the romances, like many of the tragedies, use maternal doubling or mirroring – in *Pericles* and *Cymbeline*, the idealized Thaisa, Diana, Lychorida, Euriphile and Leonatus' dream-vision mother vs Dionyza and the Wicked Queen; in *Winter's Tale*, two good living mothers, Hermione and Paulina, and the Shepherd's dead wife. But while in the tragedies there are final rapprochements between more and less warlike women, in the romances the polarization of some of these female characters remains.

The two romances that are also jealousy plays, *Cymbeline* and *The Winter's Tale*, in different ways show the fantasies about an evil mother that are one side of polarization. The most wholesale connection of suspicions of adultery with mother-blaming is in Posthumus' soliloquy:

> Is there no way for men to be, but women
> Must be half-workers? We are all bastards,
> And that most venerable man, which I
> Did call my father, was I know not where
> When I was stamp'd.
>
> (2.4.153–7)

Told by a supposed friend, Iachimo, that his wife, Imogen, is unfaithful, he quickly makes the identification: 'yet my mother seemed / The Dian of that time: so doth my wife / The nonpareil of this' (158–9) and moves on to conclude that 'there's no motion / That tends to vice in man but I affirm / It is the woman's part' (172–4). And so on for fourteen more lines.

He orders a servant of his to kill his wife and assumes she is dead when the servant sends him a bloody cloth. But eventually he repents and, remarkably, sees her supposed adultery as 'wrying but a little' (5.1.5). He fights bravely on Imogen's side of a battle (British), is taken prisoner by the Romans, and has a dream-vision of his deceased family, including his now vindicated mother, who concludes, 'Since, Jupiter, our son is good, / Take off his miseries' (5.4.85–6). In the final scene he is set free, and discovers that Imogen is still alive, innocent and present – she has been serving him disguised as a boy.

Posthumus' mother-blaming and the resultant fantasy of male parthenogenesis are portrayed in such a blatant and extreme way, in a situation where Posthumus is clearly deceived, that the audience or reader is distanced from the suspicion. However, Imogen's fairy-tale-like wicked stepmother, the Queen, also plays an important role. She experiments with poisons on animals, with the hope to eventually use them against her husband, King Cymbeline, as well as Imogen. Another mother whose sympathy does not extend beyond her own blood family, she makes her plots on behalf of her son Cloten. Her death in despair at her son's disappearance (he is dead), unlike Lady Macbeth's end, has no suggestion of expanded humanity – rather we are told that she 'repented / The evils she hatch'd were not effected' (5.5.59–60). She is one of the closest to caricature of all Shakespeare's villains, though the original audience, and others since, might have been uplifted mid-play by her evocation of the ancient courage of Britain.

In *The Winter's Tale*, by contrast, the villainous mother exists only in the distorted version of Leontes' wife, Hermione, in his imagination. Hermione herself is the 'mother figure most fully and pointedly represented as traditionally maternal in Shakespeare's canon' (Rose 1991: 306). She is even visibly pregnant, thus literally embodying motherhood. Loving to her son, and soon to her newly born daughter, she also has characteristics not necessarily found in traditional mothers: 'wit, sexual frankness, and deflating banter' (Neely 1985: 196).

When she is accused of adultery by her husband, she defends herself stoutly, at greater length than Desdemona, and continues to maintain her innocence before Leontes and his court. But upon hearing of her ill son's death she faints, and her friend Paulina soon reports that she has died. In Shakespeare's source, Greene's *Pandosto or the Triumph of Time,* her original does die at this point, and this fate is what his first audience must have expected for her. Her daughter Perdita is taken at Leontes' command to the sea, abandoned on the shore of Sicily, and raised in a shepherd family.

Donna Woodford has pointed out that in Shakespeare Perdita's 'upbringing is a fantasy of an exclusively male nurture', by the old shepherd and his son, since unlike his prototype in *Pandosto* this shepherd does not anticipate his wife's response to his bringing home a baby (2007: 191). Sixteen years later, he remembers her as a warm and vivacious hostess, perhaps a better mother than the one in *Pandosto*, who is at first reluctant to keep the abandoned child. However, Perdita does not speak of any memories of her, even after the shepherd's recollection. Perhaps such memories are absent to stress the importance to Perdita of her reunion with Hermione.

Hermione returns after Leontes has done sixteen years' penance for his jealousy, under Paulina's supervision, and has welcomed back his daughter. Leontes and Perdita go to Paulina's house to see a statue of Hermione, and on the stage the statue is revealed as the real woman. She embraces Leontes, but her only speech is devoted to her daughter:

> Tell me, mine own,
> Where hast thou been preserv'd? where liv'd? how found
> Thy father's court? for thou shalt hear that I,
> Knowing by Paulina that the Oracle
> Gave hope thou wast in being, have preserved
> Myself to see the issue.
>
> (5.3.123–8)

As Adelman says, Hermione 'insist[s] on her own agency, her own version of the story', and through her turning away from Leontes, Shakespeare 'opens up a space for the female narrative – specifically the mother–daughter narrative – his work has thus far suppressed' (1992: 234).

The ending, with Leontes' delight at finding that 'she's warm' (109) and not a statue, emphasizes his acceptance of her physicality. Neely writes that she, Perdita, and Paulina are 'fully human figures "freed and enfranchis'd" [2.2.61] from the rigid conceptions and imprisoning roles projected onto them by foolish men' (1985: 209). However, not all feminist critics agree. Gail Paster argues that she is 'visibly altered and diminished by her experience of patriarchal discipline, as may be suggested by the silence in which she embraces Leontes'

(1993: 279). From an opposite anti-idealizing perspective, Peter Erickson writes, 'she remains an icon ... [their] respective roles as all-giving and all-worshiping are fixed' (1985: 163). But can she be an icon if, as observers within the play note, 'She embraces him! / She hangs about his neck!' (5.3.111–12)? These gestures can be read as more eloquent of forgiveness than any words, rather than as signs of her subordination.

Rather than continuing to stand worshipping Hermione, Leontes turns outside their relationship to the friend he accused of adultery with her, and to the rest of their family. He now revalues the earlier friendship of Hermione and Polixenes as 'holy' (148) rather than suspect. Adelman's conclusion seems appropriately qualified: *The Winter's Tale* recovers 'the sexual body' but 'reproductivity is split between Hermione and Perdita, deflected in one and deferred in the other' (1992: 236).

Influenced by feminism in the seriousness with which they treat Leontes' offence, some productions, since the late twentieth century, have shown Hermione as more reluctant to forgive Leontes. In the 1978 production in Stratford, Canada, she did not embrace him or hang about his neck and the lines describing those gestures were cut, though she did offer her hand, which he took. More drastically, in Edward Hall's 2005 production of the all-male Propeller Company, based at the Watermill Theatre, England, Hermione greets Leontes 'almost mechanically', then turns to a passionate embrace of Perdita, demolishing any chance of what Adrian Kiernander has called 'a heterosexual male fantasy of forgiveness' (1997). Paulina is too grief-stricken for the new husband he offers her, Perdita is too absorbed in her mother to be interested in Florizel – Leontes has alienated everyone and is left alone with the apparition of his dead son.[20]

Though critics often want to see a progress narrative, and my discussion of motherhood in *The Winter's Tale* may suggest progress, the staging of motherhood in Shakespeare's plays after *The Winter's Tale* does not support this idea. In *Henry VIII*, co-authored with Fletcher, Katherine of Aragon speaks only seven lines about her daughter, as a message to the king just before her own death, 'Beseeching him to give her virtuous breeding ... and a little to love her for her mother's sake that loved him' (4.2.134–7). (The daughter grew up to be Queen Mary, hardly remembered with fondness by most in the audience of the time.) There are no mothers in *The Tempest*, the last play Shakespeare wrote without a collaborator, though Prospero remembers his wife as virtuous and pledging that he is Miranda's father. Memories of Caliban's deceased mother, Sycorax, from whom he takes his claim to the island, persist more vividly: to Prospero she is a witch whose former servant, Ariel, he has saved from her torture. Ironically, critics have noted that Prospero's language describing his past achievements borrows from Ovid's mother-witch Medea, and also that his description of taking Miranda to the new island uses words suggesting pregnancy – but such appropriations of maternal language hardly mellow Prospero (Adelman 1992). Julie Taymor's conversion of Prospero to Prospera in her 2010 film challenges tradition by putting a mother in a role written for a patriarch.

Mothers are not absent from Shakespeare's plays, but neither are they central figures in the plays now most frequently performed. In the nineteenth century, *King John* with its two mourning and vengeful mothers was well known, and those roles were key, but that particular kind of sentiment no longer draws. *All's Well that Ends Well* and *Coriolanus* – two plays that focus most on a troubled relationship between a strong mother and her adult son, to both of which the mother is essentially Shakespeare's addition – are relatively obscure. In plays where the mother has a life of her own outside of motherhood, for example, *The Merry Wives of Windsor* and *Antony and Cleopatra*, she is less often thought of as a mother.

Much is indeed left out of Shakespeare's portrayal of motherhood, especially the development of the relationship between a mother and a daughter over time. When she returns at the end, Hermione has been absent for her daughter's whole life – and the same is true of the less vividly presented

Thaisa, in *Pericles*. But critique of the absence of mothers in his work might well be directed not just at him but at a larger literary and dramatic tradition, given the fact that in many plays he adds mothers to his sources and/or expands their roles. And several plays without mothers, especially *King Lear* and *Othello*, suggest profound insights into how men's – and sometimes women's – fantasies about mothers affect their other relationships.

For all their limitations, the mothers he portrays mostly vary in ways more complex than good vs evil, including fierce partisans as well as those relatively uninvolved with their children. Few give comfort to those looking for role models, but few experience a loss or a threat without some great lines of protest. Many of them are in tension with the sentimental image of the perfect mother – even the closest, Hermione, needs her maids' help with her young son, and both teases and tells off her husband.

Mary Beth Rose concludes that in Shakespeare's tragedies and comedies 'maternal desire and agency, conceived solely in terms of the private domain, can be represented visibly (corporeally) only as dangerous, subordinate or peripheral in relation to public, adult life … The best mother is an absent or a dead mother, and the ideal society is based upon the sacrifice of the mother's desire' (1991: 307). Certainly, Tamora and Lady Macbeth are dangerous, and Volumnia has herself contributed to the danger her son poses. But are Volumnia, the Countess, Hermione, Paulina, Margaret Page and Emilia (in *The Comedy of Errors*) 'subordinate or peripheral in relation to public, adult life'? How meaningful is the judgement that they are subordinate, if women are by definition subordinate in public life (except for reigning queens)? And how about Cleopatra, Queen Margaret, Queen Eleanor and Constance? Is it easy to demarcate the victories and defeats of all of these characters as only a matter of private life, since their family lives are public issues in their plays?

Many feminist critics have noted that cultural emphasis on Shakespeare's tragedies has resulted in popular ignorance of how important women are in his comedies. But the view that the only women to whom the plays give attention are young women on the verge of marriage also results from a partial look at his canon.[21] The history plays, the romances, and several lesser-known tragedies and comedies present an array of mothers Shakespeare has developed, many of them strong and complex, often with only a few hints from his sources. The persistent fascination of Lady Macbeth results in part from her aura of destructive motherhood, but more of his characters than often acknowledged have another kind of maternal power.

5

Language

The two topics most discussed in feminist analyses of language today are how women are spoken about and how women speak (Cameron 2014). While specific issues of both kinds in Shakespeare's plays are mostly different, these topics have a long history. The observation that women on the average have more difficulty speaking in public than men do and that women often feel silenced or attacked when they do speak is not a new one, nor is the sense that women are more often described in terms of their appearance than men are, in a way that trivializes their words and actions. Nevertheless, many of Shakespeare's female characters speak powerfully in spite of these and other circumstances.

Language traditions against women

Early modern English sermons and advice books repeatedly exhorted women to silence or to infrequent speech. Jestbooks and male characters in plays made fun of talkative women (Brown 2003; Woodbridge 1984: 207–10; Stallybrass 1986: 126–7). A woman's verbal facility could be considered a sign of sexual promiscuity, which was even more condemned. Linguistic customs going back at least to early Christian writers Jerome and Augustine, such as the categorization of virtuous women as maid, wife or widow, with the rest being whores, reduced women.¹ The double sexual standard also meant that many words attacked women for sexual activity that was rarely named critically when performed by men.² As Dympna Callaghan has pointed out, the word 'whore' has power partly because of its history of use to stigmatize and punish women, a history to which other women have also contributed (2000b: xii).

More apparently complimentary use of language can also be problematic. Nancy Vickers has influentially argued that a genre ostensibly praising women, the Petrarchan blazon, which enumerates a particular woman's various facial and bodily beauties with elaborate similes, is actually a verbal dismemberment of the woman described (1981). Other kinds of Petrarchan language have also been analysed as stereotyping women by idealizing them, putting them on a pedestal, fixing them as icons (Rose 1988: 21).

Shakespeare's women's language

How much do such traditions confine women in Shakespeare's plays? More than any other dramatist of his time, Shakespeare wrote roles of great expressiveness and variety for many of his female characters. As Inga-Stina Ewbank observes, Cleopatra is 'in command of all the resources of language: of a vast vocabulary, of images ranging from the cosmos to the milkmaid, and of a variety of styles and rhetorical approaches that she can adapt to the occasion and to her interlocutor' (1978: 224). Portia brings about a comic resolution largely by her speech, and Paulina's dialogue does much of the work of converting Leontes.

These female characters, and others, often convey a sense of agency by their language. In *All's Well that Ends Well*, Helena is confident that she can cure the King with her medical knowledge, though many physicians have given up on him; she goes off to court saying, 'Our remedies oft in ourselves do lie, / Which we ascribe to heaven' (1.1.216–17). Desdemona, 'in a setting whose formality and importance would silence many speakers', defends to the senate her wish to accompany Othello to Cyprus, saying 'That I did love the Moor to live with him / My downright violence and scorn of fortunes / May trumpet to the world' (1.3.250–2) (Magnusson 1999: 166).

As Gina Bloom writes, 'whether "voice" refers to the specificity of the female body, to feminine expression or to women's subjectivity, it functions as a shorthand metaphor for women's access to personal and political power' (2007: 13). Spectators and readers have often seen voice and power in many of Shakespeare's female characters, in spite of the social restrictions and biases in their worlds. His plays include many forceful and eloquent women who would laugh at the restraints advocated by prescriptive authors such as the Spanish Catholic Juan Luis Vives. Barbara Bellow Watson, like many other feminists, distinguishes between power as ability, competence and energy on the one hand, and power as dominance on the other (1975 [1927]: 113–14). In drama, language often links the two: a character's eloquence may be demonstrated by how she draws others to respond. Many of Shakespeare's women, for example Rosalind, Cleopatra and Paulina, manage other characters. Several are spoken of (by themselves or others) as teachers.

However, some, like Portia praising mercy and Isabella critiquing Angelo's abuse of power, may persuade the audience, or at least some of it, more successfully than they persuade the characters they are addressing. Sometimes speeches that move audiences and readers have little effect in the play. In analysing the role of language as in considering final marriages in the comedies, a major divide in feminist criticism is between those who emphasize women's power and those who emphasize structures that confine them. The relation of language to power has also been important in the history of how Shakespeare has been recreated by editors and directors. Editors and directors have sometimes removed speeches from female characters that did not fit with their idea of proper women's behaviour.

Scholars disagree about literacy rates in Shakespeare's society – it is not clear whether signing one's name with an X indicates inability to write, and it is even more dubious as a sign of inability to read (Hackel 2005: 56–8). Nevertheless, everyone agrees that fewer women could read than men could, and that no university admitted women, though a few had scholarly tutors and might occasionally become, for example, translators of literature from other languages. But the frequent circulation of letters, among other things, makes it clear that many of Shakespeare's female characters not only speak well but also read and write.[3] From the early play *The Two Gentlemen of Verona* to the late *Cymbeline*, women's ability to read is important.

The verbal power of Shakespeare's women is often related to class privilege. Lynne Magnusson points out that Desdemona at the beginning is 'an aristocratic speaker whose discourse is full of the assurance and self-confidence of her class habitus' and shows a 'history of access' and thus she is shocked when she learns she cannot rely on Othello's previous respect for her (1999: 169). But some female characters outside the aristocracy are also skilled in speech. Alice Ford and Margaret Page in *The Merry Wives of Windsor* and Maria in *Twelfth Night* can still have power to manage and punish presumptuous men through using language for trickery. They also have enough education to make jokes that depend on classical allusions: wooed by Falstaff, Margaret Page compares him to a mountain famous in Greek mythology when she says 'I had rather be a giantess, / and lie under Mount Pelion' (2.1.70–1).

On the other hand, Mistress Quickly in *The Merry Wives of Windsor* shows confident linguistic ignorance when she repeatedly interrupts Margaret Page's son's Latin lesson.[4] Quickly and Juliet's nurse frequently speak in what Katie Wales has called a 'familiar, chattering style, full of repetitions and digressions', reinforcing a 'stereotype of female empty-headedness' (2001: 196–7). Polonius is also full of repetitions and digressions – but these leave a different impression because they are the follies of a powerful man.

Still, even in a tragedy, a woman in a subordinate position may occasionally make a crucial and influential speech because of what she believes to be right, as when Emilia finally tells what she knows about Iago. Magnusson writes, 'The surprise of Emilia's voice power is not simply a matter of everyday verbal economics; the play positions her speech as extraordinary and grants her a measure of heroic agency, as she asserts the priority of her moral responsibility over her social role' (1999: 180). Perhaps the eloquent women in Shakespeare's plays always stand out against an underlying expectation that they will be seen and not much heard, as figure plays off ground. Instead 'all of Shakespeare's talkative women ... are, in a way, created out of an imaginative, and perhaps forward-looking, use of indecorum' (Magnusson 2001: 26).

Does the excitement of these plays need the persistence of conservative attitudes so that its progressive ones will create conflict rather than simply being accepted? Do they depend on an implicit bias? In the twenty-first century, women still hold fewer political offices and get less recognition for their writings, so we do not yet have a level playing-field world to test whether Shakespeare's plays still have appeal if there is no residual bias against women's speech. But perhaps it is in keeping with this assumption of most women's relative silence that so many of Shakespeare's plays contrast a forceful and eloquent woman, such as Beatrice or Cleopatra, with a quieter one, such as Hero or Octavia. Sometimes the contrast is within the same character. Ophelia, whose speeches show verbal and conceptual sophistication, can't get a listener until she goes mad. Then she changes speech style: disregarding social conventions, she raises taboo topics and interrupts (Herman 1995: 288–95).[5]

Women's ambiguous rhetoric

The relation of language to women's power can be ambiguous in several ways. In *The Taming of the Shrew*, Katherine's longest speech and the one for which she receives most public recognition is her defence of a hierarchical marriage contract. This can be described as an acknowledgement of conversion, as showing that she has learned to speak in a socially acceptable way or as the result of brainwashing. Other comic heroines make shorter speeches of marital self-commitment. Rosalind takes responsibility for her choice when she says to Orlando, 'To you I give myself, for I am yours' (5.4.115), but she has just said the same words to her father and, as Susanne Wofford has written, this could suggest that 'the only kind of performance that Rosalind as woman can utter is to give herself away to the men who already possess her' (1994: 164–5).[6] However, Sir Oliver Martext, a minister who has appeared briefly in the play, has already commented about another marriage, 'Truly she must be given, or the marriage is not lawful' (3.3.65–6), and thus the play stresses that Rosalind is unusual in seizing the power to give herself (Wofford 1994: 164–5).[7] Partway through *The Merchant of Venice*, Portia says to Bassanio, 'Myself, and what is mine, to you and yours / Is now converted' (3.2.166–7), but on the other hand she reserves the right to test his loyalty to his promise about keeping her ring, and upon returning to Belmont still speaks of 'my house' (5.1.227, 274) (Engle 1993: 97).

Feminists who study language, most influentially Robin Lakoff, have often characterized self-deprecation and super-politeness as among other features that characterize women's speech and reflect women's secondary position in male-dominated society (1975). Recent scholars have found that not all women speak with what Lakoff calls 'women's language', and that other subordinated groups are likely to use it as well (McConnell-Ginet 2011: 12–15, 24–9). In early modern Europe, even male politicians and intellectuals writing to each other were likely to try to show their graceful ability to sound modest. Magnusson argues that some aspects of language use result more from speakers' context and position than from their character: speakers, male and female, all use self-deprecatory language when in dialogue with Henry VIII in the play of that name. Queen Katherine several times uses 'negative politeness ... strategies conveying the speaker's effort to avoid assumptions about the hearer's condition or volition, to avoid coercion, to communicate the wish not to impinge, or to personalize the threat' (1999: 21). Near the beginning, Katherine tries to influence Henry by asking him to remove taxes imposed by Cardinal Wolsey. She introduces it by humbly calling him 'your majesty' (1.2.13), and, in what Magnusson calls 'transparent indirectness', saying that her position is for his own good, 'That you would love yourself' (14) and ends it by apologizing: 'I am much too venturous / In tempting of your patience, but am boldened / Under your promised pardon' (54–6). Looking in purely characterological terms, a reader may see her as lacking in confidence, but the argument that her language is strategic given her context is worth considering.

Power in mourning and cursing?

In spite of their low position versus male monarchs, can women have power in their use of language to mourn and curse? Such language is important in the history plays, especially *Richard III*. King Edward's Queen Elizabeth, Margaret, and Richard's own mother, the Duchess of York, also Edward's mother, all mourn the loss of children because of Richard. When King Edward dies, in 2.2, Elizabeth and the Duchess compete over who has suffered more. After Richard's henchman kills Elizabeth's children, in 4.4, Margaret joins the other mothers and at first it looks as if the competition in grief will continue, but finally the mood changes. After asking and receiving Margaret's help in cursing, Elizabeth and his mother confront Richard and prophesy his downfall in his battle with Richmond.[8]

Do women's curses here have power? Feminist critics differ. Deborah Willis argues that their words help to destroy Richard, and thus the play 'opens up a space for the mother as white witch, who heals with her destructive violence' (1995: 201–2). James Siemon finds political significance in their speaking in an alliance beyond self-interest, in Margaret's prophecies, and in their ability to mobilize public opinion and make Richard feel insecure (2009: 18–27). On the other hand, Jean Howard and Phyllis Rackin maintain that in these scenes the women are domesticated and 'lose their individuality and become an undifferentiated chorus of ritual lamentation, curse, and prophecy that enunciates the play's providential agenda' (1997: 116). Willis's approach is influenced by her work on the history of witch-hunting, and she is closer to gynocentric feminism, while Howard and Rackin affiliate with humanist and materialist feminism and are more interested in the play's relation to Tudor ideology as they set it among other histories. Siemon, also influenced by feminist scholarship, associates the public outcry of the women of *Richard III*, in its power, with female rioters, prophets and petitioners of sixteenth- and seventeenth-century England (2009: 24–5).[9]

The women of *Richard III* themselves discuss whether their words accomplish anything. Elizabeth says, 'Though what they will impart / Help nothing else, yet do they ease the heart' (4.4.130–1), but the Duchess responds to her, 'In the breath of bitter words let's smother / My damned son, that thy two sweet sons smother'd' (133–4). Gina Bloom argues that the Duchess's 'curse on Richard ... haunts him until his dying day', contributing to his loss of confidence and sense of guilt (2007: 91–3).

Scepticism about these women's power is both instantiated and heightened by the drastic cuts they have often received in productions from the eighteenth to the twentieth centuries (Lull 1999: 25, 28, 34).[10] Bill Alexander's 1984

RSC production is one of few that let the women keep enough of their lines to have some strength (Lull 1999: 36). Still, several late twentieth-century productions of *Richard III* have highlighted Margaret's importance, if not that of her companions. Barry Kyle, at Stratford in 1975, made her gesture like a stage manager; similarly, in the 1979 productions of the Rustaveli Company of Tbilisi, Georgia, Margaret, 'brandishing the text, prompted the actors', and in the 1992–3 production directed by Sam Mendes, near the end she 'appeared to reiterate the curses of 1.5 as the victims met execution', and actively contributed to Richmond's final victory (Siemon 2009: 115, 116, 118). While those productions may have presented her as achieving justice, her power may also be staged to seem ominous.

Questions about the power of women's language also arise in *King John*. Eleanor and Constance are splendidly theatrical roles, with many passionate speeches, and Victorian stars received much acclaim in them.[11] Juliet Dusinberre writes, 'up till the end of Act 3 the dramatic action is dominated by the women characters' (1990: 40). As in *Richard III*, there are references to the materiality of the breath they use in their speeches, which suggest the persistence of their influence (Bloom 2007: 87, 94).[12] But the play's final treatment of them is anticlimactic. Both appear for the last time in the third act. In 4.1, Arthur barely escapes murder and, in 4.2, the news arrives that both Eleanor and Constance are dead. Arthur dies in a fall, trying to escape, King John dies, perhaps from poison and his son, Henry, becomes King Henry III.

Both Eleanor and Constance have tried to act politically on behalf of their sons rather than simply suffer, and, as with women in the comedies, these histories may pose the question of which are more important – their speeches and actions during the play or their fate? But in the comedies, unlike these plays, the women are usually active and talkative until very close to the end, so the effect is neither as anticlimactic or as stunning in its surprise.

Women's resistance to language used about them

Shakespeare's plays show both uses of language restrictive of women and women's resistance to such uses. The impact of some male characters' descriptions of women has been compared to that of the objectifying male gaze in films. Patricia Parker notes how attention in *Othello*, for example, is directed towards 'the woman's secret place' (2004). Iago and under his influence Othello speak of Desdemona in a way that suggests they see her pornographically, suggest Parker (2004), Michael Neill (2004) and Lynda Boose (2004). However, the perspectives that multiple speakers provide in the theatre are less coercive than the perspective that a film may provide. The more spectators or readers identify with Desdemona, the more they would resist objectifying her; that identification might lead one to feel the pain of being so unintentionally targeted but also to look for places where Desdemona fights back.[13] For Desdemona does call Iago's clichés about women slander in 2.1, and articulately objects to Othello's suspicions, as does Emilia.

Shakespeare's female characters often also challenge and question poetic wooing language used by men or by male tradition. Olivia mocks Petrarchan blazons when she says, in response to Viola/Cesario's argument that she should not waste her beauty by failing to have children, that she will make an inventory of her attributes: 'item, two lips, indifferent red' (1.5.241). Juliet points out the irony of Romeo's poetic swearing constancy by the inconstant moon. Cleopatra calls Antony's first words of love to her in the play 'Excellent falsehood' (1.1.41). These critiques of ornamental language make female characters appear witty and realistic.

Descriptions and a divided audience

Sometimes no one onstage critiques the language used to describe a female character, and the audience may be divided over whether to admire the 'fine' language, judge it as the playwright's excess or see it as a revelation of the speaker's perspective. For example, several of the plays include oddly extended and jarring Petrarchan descriptions of women by men not clearly cast as villains. In *Titus Andronicus*, Marcus asks his niece Lavinia, whose tongue has been cut out after she has been raped, to name the man who violated her, describes the blood flowing from her mouth as 'a crimson river of warm blood, / Like to a bubbling fountain stirred with wind' (2.3.22–3) and wishes that the monster who cut her hands off had seen them 'tremble like aspen leaves upon a lute' (45). While Jonathan Bate analyses the length of this speech as showing Marcus' need to 'learn slowly and painfully to confront suffering' (2002 [1995]: 62), a feminist reading, such as William Carroll's, notes irony in the echoes of love poetry in this description: 'Marcus ... can only "see" Lavinia as an erotic object, with the only vocabulary available to him, that of male courtship' (2001: 96). A tribune of the people, Marcus appears to be a representative of order, yet this speech shows that he is inadequate to the violence of his world.

An analogous though less violently jarring moment is when Brabantio describes Desdemona as 'a maiden never bold, / Of spirit so still and quiet that her motion / Blushed at herself' (1.3.95–7), which is very far from describing the Desdemona who appears in descriptions of her elopement, Othello's immediately following narrative and shortly after onstage. Some spectators might accept Brabantio's description and wonder, with him, what magic Othello has used to transform her; others might credit love's transforming power or see Brabantio as having believed Desdemona a much more conventional woman than she was, perhaps because that was how he wished to see her, perhaps because that was what she pretended to be.

The audience might also be divided at the many points in which male characters criticize a woman for talking too much. This stereotype of women was often employed to urge women towards the conservative conduct-book ideal of submissive silence. As Woodbridge observes, women do not need to talk more than men to be considered talkative: 'Queen Margaret is derided [by King Edward] as a "wrangling woman" (2.2.176) after speaking only twenty-three of the 177 lines of [2.2] in *3 Henry VI*: her longest single speech in that scene is five lines long' (1984: 210).[14] Near the end of that play Richard, Duke of Gloucester, who will become Richard III in the play by that name, says of Margaret, 'Why should she live to fill the world with words?' (5.5.43), and King Edward kills her son while criticizing him for being like his mother: 'Take that, the likeness of this railer here' (38). Here, for many playgoers, the association of hostility to women's speech with murdering a woman and a child might work against taking Richard's and Edward's views as guides to women's proper behaviour. More conclusively, Leontes' attacks on Paulina's speech and Iago's attacks on Emilia's are undercut because they come when the men are insisting on false accusations against Hermione and Desdemona. Contrary to Leontes' view, Paulina's words really are 'medicinal' (2.2.37).

Editing women's language

Directors and editors, in all centuries, have ideas about how characters should speak and behave, and sometimes they remove women's words or transfer them to male characters, because of those ideas. From Rowe's 1709 edition, through most of the eighteenth and nineteenth centuries, for example, Rosalind was not allowed to say that her perturbation was not just for her father, but 'for my child's father' (1.3.11). This line, showing she was already anticipating sex with Orlando (presumably within marriage) was too forward and therefore 'unfeminine'. Instead, she was to claim to be upset 'for my father's child' (Brissenden 1993: 118n.). Others of her textual jokes about sex were often cut for stage performances during this time (Brissenden 1993: 190n., 193n.).

If a speech violated expectations of women, another option was to attribute it to a different character. Early in *The Tempest*, Miranda reproaches Caliban:

> Abhorred slave,
> Which any print of goodness wilt not take,
> Being capable of all ill; I pitied thee,
> Took pains to make thee speak, taught thee each hour
> One thing or other.
>
> (1.2.352–6)

In the late seventeenth century, already a time of great concern for literary decorum, Dryden suggested that Prospero must have said these lines, because the harshness and the reference to teaching would be out of character for a young woman, and many subsequent editors followed him. This contributed to an insistence on Miranda's passivity, which only a few recent critics, such as Jessica Slights (2001), have countered. The director-actor David Garrick adapted *The Taming of the Shrew* into *Catherine and Petruchio*, which dominated the stage from 1756 to 1886. This version gives most of the words of Katherine's last speech arguing for women's submission in marriage to Petruchio. Presumably this gives the speech more authority and also removes the complexity of showing Kate finding a voice in submission.

It is not always clear which text choice is the more feminist or gives women more power, let alone which one is more convincing. In modern editions of *As You Like It*, Hymen, the god of marriage, tells the Duke that he has brought Rosalind 'That thou mightst join her hand with his / Whose heart within his bosom is' (5.4.112–13). The First Folio, however, reads 'join his hand'. Perhaps this is because in manuscripts of the time 'her' is sometimes spelled 'hir', which is easy to confuse with 'his', and editors have long read 'her'. In 1709, the editor Nicholas Rowe added the stage direction, 'Rosalind in Woman's Cloths [sic]'. However, Maura Kuhn (1977) and more recently Jeff Masten (1997: 156) have argued in favour of keeping 'his' and imagining the original boy actor still in masculine clothes at this point – since there probably was not time to change costume during Touchstone's speech about the degrees of the lie.[15] This interpretation fits with the kind of feminism that favours deconstruction of gender roles, but does it make sense? The previous two lines have referred to Rosalind as 'her'. When Phebe sees Rosalind with Hymen, she says, 'If sight and shape be true, / Why then my love adieu' (188–9), alluding to her expectation of marrying Ganymede. This sounds like she now knows by sight (and did not before) that the person she thought was Ganymede is really female, and fits with the narrative in Shakespeare's source: 'In went Ganymede and dressed herself in woman's attire, having on a gown of green ... Thus attired came Rosalind in' (Lodge 1997 [1590]: 222). Perhaps the best defence of 'his' is as an error influenced by awareness that the actor is a boy.

Language, gesture and silence

Onstage there are other kinds of language in addition to words. Sometimes gestures and stage movements are implied by the text, but they also result from the creativity of the performers and the director, attempting to fill in what they think is a gap in the text. At the end of *The Taming of the Shrew*, Katherine directs wives to 'place your hands below your husband's foot. / In token of which duty, if he please, / My hand is ready, may it do him ease' (5.2.178–80). Does she then kneel? In some productions she does, in some she starts to and Petruchio stops her – in some productions after she kneels, he kneels to her.[16]

On the other hand, the director may ignore suggestions in the text. As Othello attacks Desdemona, for example, two of his lines suggest that she is actively struggling with him: 'Down, strumpet!' (5.2.78) and 'Nay, if you strive – ' (80).[17] However, for over a century directors and audiences preferred a motionless Desdemona, one who did not 'strive' (Siemon 2004). But as early as 1610, in one of the first examples we have of a spectator's response to Shakespeare, Henry Jackson remembers an active Desdemona whose facial expression was also a kind of language: she 'pleaded her case very effectively throughout, yet moved (us) more after she was dead, when, lying on her bed, she entreated the pity of the actors by her very countenance' (Yachnin 2001: 127).

As Deborah Cameron writes, 'silence, too, communicates, and in that sense is part of language' (2014: 246). But silence can mean many different things. Philip McGuire describes three different performances' approaches to Isabella's silence at the Duke's proposal to her in the final lines of *Measure for Measure*. Like the ending of *The Taming of the Shrew*, this is one of the more problematic moments in the comedies because of the questions it raises about marriage in relation to a woman's power. In Barry Kyle's 1978 RSC production, Isabella and the Duke 'exited side by side ... Her silence arose from and expressed the power she came to have and to exercise during the final scene' (McGuire 1985: 90–2).[18] Robin Phillips at Stratford in 1975 gave Isabella a long silence, as the Duke stood with arms outstretched towards her; he became embarrassed and angry (92). Keith Hack, with the RSC in 1974, had the Duke enfold 'her stiff, resisting body within the vast golden robes of his office'. Isabella's silence here 'conveyed her horrified, even hysterical helplessness' (86, 88). Silences and gestures in these productions, along with cutting, line interpretations, and many other details of staging, contributed to very different overall impressions (86–92). Isabella's silence suggested power in Kyle's and Phillips' versions and powerlessness in Hack's.

The variety of stagings of silences McGuire describes fit with the multiple meanings of silence that Christina Luckyj finds even in early modern ethical discourse. In spite of the tradition that associates silence with female submission, advice books may praise silence in gender-neutral terms as 'prudent self-containment', 'judicious sagacity' or 'necessary protection' or criticize it as stubbornness (2002: 51, 53, 55, 60). On the other hand, as is still true today, it can be seen as resistance to tyranny. And just as many scholars are now admitting that there may be no one best text, many are also now open to the possible validity of many different performance decisions, with regard to interpreting silence as well as to choosing gestures and emotions.

Language and women today

The meanings of any kind of language, and its implications for women's position, this chapter suggests, may not be easily pinned down. And the situation is complicated further by linguistic and social change since Shakespeare's time. Desdemona's penultimate sentence, 'Commend me to my kind lord' (5.2.125), must sound even more jarring to a modern audience than it did in its early performances, since it is no longer common for a woman to refer to her husband as her lord.

Nevertheless, student evaluations, popular views of women in politics and much other evidence show that women, on the average, still have a more restricted range of acceptable language and gestures than men do. And women whose opinion pieces appear online are more likely to be the target of sexualized hostile comments. Many things have changed, but women's negotiations with language may still be more complicated than those of, at least, men from comparably privileged groups.

The language of Shakespeare's female characters is not always clear. Sometimes words for the transition between one feeling and another seem to be missing; sometimes their words can be interpreted in opposite ways. But they can still speak to us, as we read and as performers interpret them, with their words, their eyes and their gestures. Feminist critics may analyse the gaps or fill them in, test what other characters say about those female characters against what they themselves say and do, and probe the cultural significance of how directors and editors have re-imagined them in different times and places. And women writers have sometimes re-imagined them today, creating plays, novels and poems in which they can tell more of their story. Recently, Toni Morrison, in her libretto for an opera, imagines Desdemona in the afterlife talking with Emilia, with her mother's black maid (whose real name, in this version, she didn't even know) and, finally, with Othello (Morrison and Traore 2012).

6

Between women

'Sisterhood is powerful' was a slogan of feminism of the late 1960s, and feminists have often struggled against the assumption that women are always in competition with each other, and emphasized the importance of friendship and female bonding and alliances. Feminist theory in the difference mode, developed influentially by Nancy Chodorow (1978), Carol Gilligan (1982) and others, says that women have a great capacity for empathy and therefore are drawn to cooperative rather than competitive behaviour. These theorists argue that such behaviour should be more culturally valued and can be developed by men as well.[1] At the same time, other feminists such as Katha Pollitt and Ellen Willis have argued that an emphasis on women's empathy and cooperation is too close to Victorian stereotypes, and many others assume that that competition is good and/or inevitable and that women need more opportunity to compete, with each other as well as with men (Pollitt 2015 [1992]: 164).[2]

Since the 1980s, even more feminist theorists and activists have stressed the idea that women's experiences are affected by other aspects of their identities such as race and class, and will differ depending on, for example, class privilege. More privileged women may oppress the less privileged by assuming they are allies. Audre Lorde writes of 'a pretense to a homogeneity of experience covered by the word *sisterhood* that does not in fact exist' (1984: 116). 'Intersectionality' is the word that feminist theory has often used to emphasize the idea that an upper-class woman's situation is different from a lower-class one, a white woman's is different from a black woman, with many other corollaries (Crenshaw 1991).

To summarize, we can divide views on relations between women into three categories:

1 Women compete with each other, whether because it is women's nature, women's socialization or human nature.
2 Women cooperate with each other much more than men do.
3 Women may either compete or cooperate, and cooperation is often more difficult between women positioned differently with regard to rank, class, race, religion or some other category or set in competition with each other by another social structure.

The relations portrayed among women in Shakespeare's plays could affirm each of these views. Part of the appeal of Shakespeare's plays to feminists has been that the plays take women's friendships and other bonds seriously. He presents female friendship in depth in *As You Like It*, *The Merry Wives of Windsor*, and *The Winter's Tale*, shows characters mourning its loss in *A Midsummer Night's Dream* and *The Two Noble Kinsmen* and portrays women confiding in, defending and helping each other in *The Merchant of Venice, Much Ado about Nothing, All's Well that Ends Well, Measure for Measure, Othello* and *Antony and Cleopatra* (Neely 1985; McKewin 1980).

However, the plays give more than a rosy picture of relations between women. Some are at odds because they are similarly positioned and compete for favour – most obviously, Goneril and Regan in *King Lear* and, to a lesser extent, Katherine and Bianca in *The Taming of the Shrew*. Cleopatra and Octavia are in conflict (though they never meet in Shakespeare's play) because Cleopatra is Egyptian and Octavia is Roman but even more because they are in competition for Antony. And the plays also show some of the intersectionality-related tensions discussed by recent feminists: class conflicts, colour differences.

Women's friendships

Nevertheless, in spite of various tensions, friendship between women is a notable feature of most of Shakespeare's comedies, including the problem comedies, and of *Othello* and the later play that rewrites its jealousy plot, *The Winter's Tale*. Furthermore, other plays as different as *Richard III*, *Macbeth*, *Hamlet* and *Coriolanus* move towards some form of rapprochement between women who have been separated from or hostile to each other earlier. This is especially notable because in Shakespeare's time most authors who wrote about friendship were men who didn't consider women capable of friendship. When friendship and marriage were opposed to each other in an argument about which to choose, it was assumed that a man was the chooser and the friendship would be with another man.[3]

At least one of Shakespeare's recent predecessors did write a story in which women's friendship is important – Thomas Lodge, the author of *Rosalynde*, in which Rosalind's cousin Celia's original, Alinda, says, 'So shall the world canonize our friendship, and speak of Rosalind and Alinda, as they do of Pylades and Orestes' (1997 [1590]: 122).[4] Speeches such as Celia's defence of Rosalind to her father and Rosalind's proposal to protect Celia by disguising herself as a man have their origin in Lodge. In Lodge, also, the two women set up a household together in Arden.

As You Like It, however, adds more tension to the relationship: it is Shakespeare's change that Celia seems more cautious about men than Rosalind, saying 'Love no man in good earnest' (1.2.26), when Rosalind proposes falling in love as a sport. Alinda, as Aliena, has the idea of playing the priest and saying the words to marry Rosalind in her disguise to Orlando's original, Rosader; Celia, in Shakespeare's version, says 'I cannot say the words' (4.1.121) when Rosalind proposes this play-acting. Celia, several critics have suggested, is more invested in Rosalind than Rosalind is in her, and she is threatened by the idea of losing Rosalind to a man. Developing this line further, Valerie Traub proposes that Celia's attachment to Rosalind is one of the places where homoerotic feeling circulates in the play (2002: 171).[5]

Does Rosalind's marriage to Orlando means a separation from Celia? Some critics say it does (Traub 2002: 174). However, Julie Crawford has argued that this marriage, and Portia's to Bassanio in *The Merchant of Venice*, maintain rather than threaten the bonds between women. Rosalind and Celia marry brothers and thus their relationship is cemented by the glue of extended family, as would have historically been the case in early modern England (2003: 152).

In *The Merry Wives of Windsor*, Alice Ford and Margaret Page are close enough to show that Shakespeare does not necessarily imagine marriage as precluding female friendship. The wives spend so much time together that Ford jokes, 'I think if your husbands would die, you two would marry' (3.2.13–14). Margaret Page's reply is 'Be sure of that – two other husbands' (15), but no one can doubt their strong companionship. Margaret supports Alice through her husband's jealousy and urges her into a shared joke on their joint money-seeking egocentric suitor Sir John Falstaff by leading him on and then subjecting him to humiliation while trying to escape. Crawford even argues that 'the substantive, and substantively vindicated, economy of *The Merry Wives of Windsor* is not ... marital; it is female homosocial' (2003: 152).

Another generally supportive relationship, though not as close, is the one between another pair of cousins, Beatrice and Hero, in *Much Ado about Nothing*. Though they are temperamentally more different than Rosalind and Celia – Beatrice is talkative and assertive, Hero is quiet and submissive – they frequently speak up for each other. Hero explains Beatrice's meaning when others find her jokes confusing, and Beatrice urges Hero to use her veto power if her father offers her a husband she finds unattractive. Most importantly, Beatrice is Hero's staunchest defender when her fiancé Claudio accuses her of sex with another man. Even in Beatrice's big love scene, Hero's wrongs are so close to her mind that she demands of Benedick, 'Kill Claudio!' (4.1.287).

As with Rosalind and Celia, there is some strain in this relationship: Hero's longest speech in the play comes when she is pretending to believe that Benedick is in love with Beatrice, and she criticizes her pride and mockery of men. Each of the cousins urges her own attitude, resistant or accepting, on the other, but their relationship continues.

In *The Winter's Tale*, as in *Much Ado* and *The Merry Wives of Windsor*, a staunch female friend strongly defends a woman against a jealous man. Paulina needs even more courage than Beatrice or Mistress Page since the man is not only Hermione's husband but the king. But she has that courage, and is even willing to call Leontes 'tyrant' (3.2.173) after Hermione has fainted upon hearing both that Leontes rejects the oracle exonerating her and that their young son has died. She reports Hermione's death, leads Leontes through sixteen years of penance, warns him against remarrying, and orchestrates Hermione's return, apparently in the form of a statue but still (or magically again) alive (Neely 1985: 199–200, 206).

Several Shakespearean plays also show bonds between women developing in situations of potential romantic competition or at least envy. In *Twelfth Night,* Viola, in her disguise as Cesario, is willing to follow her master's orders to woo Olivia for him, although she is secretly in love with him. When she sees Viola is more interested in the messenger than the sender, she feels sympathy, seeing the unrequited love that both of them experience: 'My state is desperate for my master's love: / As I am woman (now, alas the day!) / What thriftless sighs shall poor Olivia breathe' (2.2.37–9).[6]

In the problem plays, alliances extricate women out of other unhappy situations. In *All's Well that Ends Well*, forced to marry Helena by the King, Bertram leaves her, goes to war, and woos Diana; Helena follows him and finds that Diana is willing to help her by making a night-time assignation where she can substitute herself for Diana, giving their marriage legal force and Bertram the pregnancy he has set as the apparently impossible condition for returning to her. Dubious husband as Bertram is, this counts as a victory for Helena that only Diana's cooperation makes possible. Isabella and Mariana make a similar pact in *Measure for Measure* (Neely 1985: 73–5, 93).

In some comedies and romances, women long for a friendship that is or seems past. Sometimes it is past because the friend is dead, as in in *Two Noble Kinsmen* when Emilia looks back to when she was eleven, or in *A Midsummer Night's Dream*, when Titania, the queen of the fairies, remembers the mortal woman she spent time with when they were both pregnant. Sometimes it appears to be broken – but a production could emphasize reconciliation at the end.[7] In Shakespeare's tragedies, death or its possibility may bring women together who have been in conflict earlier or, at any rate, of contrasting temperament and different values. After Ophelia's death, Gertrude, who had refused to speak with her in her madness, says, 'I hop'd thou shouldst been my Hamlet's wife' (5.1.242). Coriolanus' warlike mother Volumnia and his peaceful wife Virgilia are united near the end in begging him for mercy on Rome.

One female alliance in Shakespeare in which characters call each other sisters is unique, that of the witches in *Macbeth*. In some ways these characters exist on a level of reality similar to that of the fairies in *A Midsummer Night's Dream*, in that they have powers over humans, though in a more nightmarish way. However, in Shakespeare's society humans could be identified as witches, and some of his contemporaries wrote plays in which characters on the same level of existence as the others were so labelled – and, in Middleton's *The Witch of Edmonton*, the process of how being repeatedly called a witch can make a woman call herself a witch is theatrically presented.

In the twentieth century, some feminists not only cited the persecution of witches as one of the worst historical crimes against women (since many fewer men than women were so called), but also identified witchcraft with hidden female powers demonized by a repressive social order.[8] Terry Eagleton uses Julia Kristeva's deconstructive feminism to interpret the witches in *Macbeth*: 'They are poets, prophetesses, and devotees of female cult, radical separatists who scorn male power and lay bare the hollow sounds and fury at its heart' (1986: 2).[9]

Psychoanalytic critics have often seen both the historic persecution of witches and their portrayal in Macbeth as based in unconscious hostility to mothers; they may link the witches with Lady Macbeth in this respect (Adelman 1992: 134–40; Willis 1995).[10] In Holinshed's *Chronicles*, Shakespeare's source, they are described as possibly the 'Weird Sisters, that is (as ye would say) the goddesses of destiny'. 'Weird' derived from the Anglo-Saxon word for fate, 'Wyrd' (Holinshed 1999 [1587]: 142). As Deborah Willis writes, they also seem to come from the world of poor old village women beggars who might become the target of witchcraft accusations when misfortune struck a family that had refused them food. However, the three witches are different from any other sisterhood in Shakespeare not only in that they seem to have more than human power but also in that they are never shown as being in conflict.

Women in competition

Although female friends in Shakespeare are often compared to sisters, two of the three pairs of literal human sisters in his plays are hardly good models. The relation of the lesser-known third pair, Adriana and Luciana in *The Comedy of Errors*, might be a sketch for that of Beatrice and Hero, except for their difference in marital status: Adriana, the married one, is more rebellious, while Luciana, who is single, urges her to be patient. But when Adriana is reproached (by the Abbess, who turns out to be her mother-in-law) for her complaints to her husband, Luciana defends her: 'She never reprehended him but mildly / When he demean'd himself rough, rude, and wildly' (5.1.87–8).[11] By contrast, the sisters in *The Taming of the Shrew*, Katherine and Bianca, have ill will that outlasts changes in their behaviour; they begin the play resenting each other and end the same way (Bianca and her husband have lost a lot of money because she didn't obey him and Katherine is lecturing her about obedience). Early in the play it is clear that Bianca can pretend submission in order to get what she wants. Katherine may be doing so at the end, but the two women never use the same strategy at the same time.

Goneril and Regan begin *King Lear* with competing declarations of love to win land from their father. They join forces for a while, but then both fall for Edmund, the leader of their forces in battle opposing Lear and, at the end, Goneril kills Regan and then herself. The play does not show the conflict between the sisters as inevitable, rather it suggests Lear's role in creating conflict, as *Taming* hints at Baptista's responsibility for creating conflict between Kate and Bianca. In both *Lear* and *Taming*, sisters who successfully pretend to be dutiful daughters are shown as self-serving by the end, though in Bianca's case this is not such a terrible thing.

Apart from *Lear*, surprisingly few Shakespearean plays dramatize conflict between women over their erotic relationships with a man, the situation in which such conflict would be most expected from the stereotype. Such conflict occurs in a farcical mode in the forest of *A Midsummer Night's Dream*, when under the influence of the magic potion both Lysander and Demetrius woo Helena and she attacks Hermia because she believes Hermia is in collusion with them to mock her. But this is resolved in the conclusion.

Titus Andronicus is the play before *Lear* in which resentment between women, Lavinia and Tamora, is most fully dramatized. In this case, as in *Antony and Cleopatra*, the resentment could be related to national/ethnic issues – here between Roman and Goth, as well as between Roman and Moor, with the Roman woman again presented as the one with more traditional virtues – but it also develops out of erotic competition, as well as maternal desire to avenge a son. The Roman general Titus has the Goth queen Tamora's son, Alarbus, executed in compensation for the twenty-five sons he has lost in battle with them; he refuses the position of emperor and gives it to Saturninus, promising him his daughter, Lavinia. But when Saturninus sees Tamora, his immediate response is to praise her beauty: 'A goodly lady, trust me, of the hue / That I would choose were I to choose anew' (1.1.265–6). He sets her and the other prisoners free – and immediately Bassianus, Saturninus' brother, claims Lavinia as his and Titus' other sons support him. Lavinia says nothing in this scene, except denying that she is displeased by Saturninus' generosity to Tamora.

Though a production would be likely to show her happy to be taken by Bassianus, Lavinia, like Hero and Cressida, is passed around like a football and then attacked for fickleness. Saturninus renounces the 'changing piece' (314) for Tamora, who pretends to counsel him to be reconciled with Titus and his family, but in an aside tells him, 'I'll find a day to massacre them all' (455). Soon afterwards, she encourages her sons to take vengeance on Lavinia, and they rape her and cut off her hands and tongue. Lavinia is, nevertheless, able to assist her father in killing Demetrius and Chiron and baking them into a pie for Tamora to eat, before Titus kills her too out of shame.

Tamora and Lavinia are initially contrasted in terms of their nation and their morality, and Tamora is shown as more forceful than Lavinia throughout, but they are both willing to participate in a revenge killing. Lavinia is also made more complicated than an innocent victim because of the sexual knowingness she shows in a verbal attack on Tamora (Berry

1999: 53). The forms of their deaths are both terrible. Lavinia dies because her father believes that she should not survive her shame – thus she dies from toxic beliefs about family honour. Tamora, in almost the last lines of the play, is doomed to be torn apart by wild beasts and vultures. This may well seem justice for urging her sons to rape Lavinia. Tamora seems outside the human community. On the other hand, she, too, might be seen as defending her family in a perverse way, since the rape, in the patriarchal view of the time, punishes Titus for killing her son.

The plot and characters of this play are echoes and multiplications of many details from Roman history and mythology, combined in an over-the-top stew of violence that Shakespeare never attempted again. Oppositions between transgressive and relatively dutiful female characters are also portrayed in *Hamlet*, *Macbeth*, *Coriolanus* and *Antony and Cleopatra*, but in the first three of these with the concluding gestures of reconciliation already noted and in no other tragedy with enmity such as in this play. Even the hatred in *Lear* of Goneril and Regan for each other, as well as for Cordelia, takes up a smaller portion of attention.

Class: Ladies, companions, maids, prostitutes

Many of Shakespeare's maidservants, such as Maria and Emilia, are ladies-in-waiting, also referred to as companions, a relationship in which the degree of subordination is often ambiguous, but the sharing of confidences is often dramatically marked.[12] The class contrast between Juliet and her nurse is more obvious, but it does not keep Juliet from discussing Romeo with her. In *Henry V*, Katherine of France, preparing for a possible political marriage, learns English from an elderly servant, Alice, and wrestles, in their conversation, with the French obscenities she hears in the English words.

Nerissa, in *The Merchant of Venice*, laughs with Portia at most of Portia's suitors and ends up marrying the companion of the most successful one. These scenes reveal the heroines' feelings to the audience while often presenting them as witty and sociable, but the servants' acuity may also be on display.

Nerissa accompanies Portia in a boy's costume to the courtroom and later repeats Portia's trick of asking her husband for a gift in her disguise. However, in two other comedies a female companion or maid goes too far in imitation of her mistress and in one of them also takes on the role of her mistress's cousin, though neither one is punished at the end of the play. The plot of imitation that can go too far suggests something of the mixed feelings that a companion or maidservant may have, a hint also developed in *Othello*.

In *Much Ado*, the maidservant Margaret tries out imitation at two marked points. The less consequential instance occurs when she plays Beatrice by making jokes in an all-female pre-wedding scene during which Beatrice is unusually quiet. Many of the jokes have sexual meanings; for example, 'A maid, and stuffed! There's goodly catching of cold' (3.4.60–1). Margaret's new role is explicit here:

BEATRICE   How long have you professed apprehension?
MARGARET   Ever since you left it.

(62–4)

The more significant moment is implied between the scenes, when Claudio doubts the faithfulness of his fiancée Hero because he sees a woman at Hero's window with another man. This woman is really Margaret with Borachio, the servant of the plotting, resentful Don John. A textual issue that critics have sometimes wondered about – Borachio says that if Claudio comes to the window he will 'hear me call Margaret Hero, hear Margaret term me Claudio' (2.2.40–1) – can easily mean that Borachio will ask Margaret to 'play Hero and Claudio' with him; on the evening of their wedding this has an obvious sexual suggestion.

During the wedding scene where Claudio denounces Hero and Beatrice defends her, Margaret is not present. In a realistic novel, a character in Margaret's position might learn about what happened to Hero and face her role in it. Perhaps the omission of this possibility shows the play's lack of interest in a mere lady's maid (Huston 1981: 124). Nevertheless, her involvement is discussed after Hero's name has been cleared. Leonato says that she 'was pack'd in all this wrong' (5.1.291) and Borachio defends her: 'No, by my soul she was not, / Nor knew not what she did when she spoke to me' (292–3). Of course talking with a man at a bedroom window was transgressive according to official early modern mores, but the many spectators who accept it in *Romeo and Juliet* would not be far from accepting it in Margaret. Mihoko Suzuki (2000: 134) says that she is for a while 'a demonized double' for Hero, but 'finally exonerated'; Leonato concedes that her 'fault' was 'against her will' (5.4.4–5). In Kenneth Branagh's film, which downplays some possible tensions in the play, Leonato dances with Margaret at the end.

Twelfth Night, unlike *The Merchant of Venice* or *Much Ado about Nothing*, includes only a few lines between the mistress, Olivia, and her companion, Maria. However, Maria does frequently speak on behalf of Olivia, who has declared that she will not admit any suitors for seven years since she is mourning her dead brother. She frequently presents herself as telling others what Olivia feels. In their first scene together, Maria tells Olivia of the young gentleman at the gate, and follows Olivia's lead, after Cesario (Viola in disguise) is admitted, in inviting him to leave – though at this point Olivia changes her mind. The relationship between Olivia and Maria seems to be largely one of business, which contributes to a sense of Olivia's isolation except when with Feste or, later, Cesario.

Maria can be seen as a double of Olivia – she too is divided between a belief in order and a wish for fun. At the beginning of the play, we hear she has sent away Orsino's messenger Valentine, and she criticizes Toby for his drinking and Feste for his absence, in both cases by saying that Olivia is unhappy with them. But she also flirts with Olivia's foolish would-be suitor Sir Andrew, and is drawn into joking with Feste as Olivia will be. Just as Olivia soon abandons herself to the love of Cesario, Maria definitively moves to the revelry side when she mocks Malvolio after he appears to reprimand the merrymakers. She writes a letter, forging Olivia's handwriting and inviting him to pursue Olivia, and then, pretending concern and conscientiousness, tells Olivia that he is mad and dangerous.

At the end of the play all three female characters are promised marriage – Maria to Sir Toby, an outcome that Feste may hint she wants when he says, 'If Sir Toby would leave drinking, thou wert as witty a piece of Eve's flesh as any in Illyria' (1.5.26–8). She and Toby have a companionable relationship, in which she can good-naturedly give him advice; she does not reveal romantic illusions about him, but marrying Olivia's uncle secures and improves her place in the household. Yet she is absent from the announcement of her marriage (as is he). And when Olivia's servant Fabian explains the plot against Malvolio, he leaves out her role in planning (not just writing) the forged letter, thus blaming himself and Sir Toby, probably an attempt to protect her from more of Olivia's displeasure. Thus tensions from Maria's imitation of Olivia remain in spite of the marriage that solidifies their relationship.

Shakespearean plays that include women of markedly different classes who are not mistress and maid to each other often keep them apart. There is no meeting in *2 Henry IV* between Lady Northumberland or Lady Percy, on one hand, and Doll Tearsheet and Mistress Quickly, on the other. Nor does Isabella or Mariana meet Mistress Overdone in *Measure for Measure*. Several other plays, however, do dramatize the interactions of women of different classes, from different households, in contrasting ways.

Some plays treat hostility between women related to resentment about their difference in rank and the higher-ranked one's feeling that the other is too presumptuous for her position. In *2 Henry VI*, Queen Margaret, herself an ambitious woman, speaks with hostility of the ambition and pride of the lower-ranked but still aristocratic Duchess Eleanor, who, she says, 'sweeps it through the court with troops of ladies / More like an empress than Duke Humphrey's wife' (1.3.78–9), and even gives her a box on the ear for not picking up for her a fan that she has dropped.

In her disguise as Ganymede, Rosalind frequently makes fun of Phebe, with comments on her rough hand (a class indicator of her lower rank as a shepherdess, though perhaps also a joke about the boy actor playing the role), as well as on her presumptuousness in refusing to accept Silvius's love – 'Sell when you can, you are not for all markets' (3.5.60).[13] Thus Rosalind, who could be seen as similar to Phebe in the fact that her disguise is maintaining her independence from her wooer Orlando, is asserting her contrast to Phebe. But her attack on Phebe also emphasizes Phebe's dark hair and eyes, a link to the common Elizabethan attack on dark skin as suggesting the suntan resulting from the outside work of the lower orders as well as different ethnicity, and a preference for the blond woman with blue eyes – in a frequent pun, the 'fair' woman – a source of conflict that will be discussed later.

In *The Merry Wives of Windsor*, the class lines do not keep women strictly apart or lead to hostility. Mistress Quickly is Dr Caius' maid and perhaps his sexual convenience, hinted at when Simple says of their relationship after she has enumerated the housework she does, "Tis a great charge to come under one body's hand' (1.4.92–3). But Mistresses Page and Ford and Ann Page have no problems with using her as a go-between, both for Ann's wooing and for their deception of Falstaff, and she even plays the role of the Fairy Queen in the final pageant, miraculously speaking in poetical and grammatical English (or perhaps the character heading is misleading and just indicates that the performer who plays her also plays the Queen). The only sign of tension appears when Mistress Page eventually complains about Quickly's constant interruption of her young son William's Latin lesson. The relaxation of class lines between women here may be a reflection of the setting of the play in a more middling rather than aristocratic circle.

In *Pericles*, Marina is kidnapped by a pander and a bawd; they attempt to set her up in their brothel, but she saves herself by her miraculously persuasive power of speech against prostitution, combined with her skills at singing, dancing, weaving and other arts which enable her to earn money. Her interaction with the bawd has a fairy-tale quality, featuring sudden escape from a figure presented as monstrous. Although their classes contrast, the main effect is a confrontation between good and evil.

Othello develops the tension between mistress and companion further than the tension in *Much Ado about Nothing*, in that, at Iago's request, Emilia is willing to steal Desdemona's handkerchief. But eventually Emilia defends Desdemona as strongly as Beatrice and Paulina stand up for their friends accused of infidelity. And *Othello* also includes a more dramatic confrontation between Emilia and Bianca, who, even if she is not the prostitute that she is called, acts outside the 'respectable' customs of the time in entertaining a man at her home alone.

Like Margaret, Emilia is complicit in the chain of events that lead her mistress to be falsely accused, because she goes along with the plot her husband, in this case, has devised. (Shakespeare adds this detail to his source, in which Iago himself steals the handkerchief.) Unlike Margaret, she is present during scenes in which her mistress is cruelly denounced for a sin when she knows her mistress is innocent. Critics have sometimes wondered why she doesn't defend Desdemona earlier. Perhaps it can be explained by the subordination to Iago that she expresses in stealing the handkerchief when she says, 'I nothing, but to please his fantasy' (3.3.303). The absence of any verb of which 'I' is the subject here reinforces the impression that she lacks a sense of agency (Pechter 2004: 371). Also, she may fear both the rage she can see building in Othello, and possible anger at her from Desdemona.

In several scenes, Emilia accompanies Desdemona and says nothing – usually while Othello is berating Desdemona. In spite of her possible fear, these scenes may eventually motivate Emilia to support Desdemona, as she can see that, somewhat like her, Desdemona now also is mistreated by her husband.[14] These scenes lead up to Emilia's great speech about the unfairness of the double standard in marriage, in which she is clearly thinking of the similarity of her situation to Desdemona's.[15]

However, class contrast between women appears again in Emilia's attitude towards Bianca. Though Bianca comes to the aid of Cassio when he is wounded by Iago, showing she loves him, Emilia, like Iago (and like, in Bianca's absence, Cassio as well), scorns her as a strumpet. Her speech against the double standard and her previous jokes about the price for which she would make her husband a cuckold would suggest that she should have a different view. As Michael Neill points out, there is no clear evidence that Bianca is actually a prostitute or a courtesan, a Venetian position of relatively higher status, the label the First Folio, but not necessarily Shakespeare's intention, gives her (2006: 194). Rather, she maintains, 'I am no strumpet / But of life as honest as you, that thus / Abuse me' (5.1.121–3), which 'calls into question the value of the purely technical chastity by which the male world sets such frantic store' (Neill 2006: 177). Bianca speaks here against attitudes towards sexuality which disadvantage all women, including Emilia, who can critique them one moment and use them against other women the next.

Overall the plays show a range of relations between women of different classes, ranging from simple close alliance through the occasionally ambivalent relations of mistress and maid to morally polar opposition. One of the fascinating aspects of *Othello* is the way it joins elements of most of these in the combination of how Desdemona and Emilia treat each other and how Emilia treats Bianca, and also adds Bianca's defence of her own honesty. Here the feminist critique of the double standard is developed even past Emilia's speech about it.

Race, colour, ethnicity, religion

In a play in which references to white and black, fair and foul, are so frequent – Desdemona is frequently described by Othello as fair – Bianca's name means white.[16] Several recent productions, however, have cast a woman of colour in her role, suggesting the coalescence of race-based and class-based prejudice frequent in the US and many other countries today and the way both kinds of prejudice also are inflected by gender (Neill 2006: 108–9). These productions underline Emilia's (and Cassio's) scorn of Bianca by making it seem at least partly racist.

Shakespeare's texts do not explicitly give any female characters a clearly different race than white, apart from, somewhat ambiguously as we shall see, Cleopatra. Yet the contrast between dark and fair women, perhaps related to the praise of golden hair and white skin often found in Petrarchan poetry, appears explicitly in several of his plays and implicitly in others. Many men in the plays speak disparagingly of women with dark skin and eyes, while women are never criticized for being white; the sonnets and many of the plays represent a world in which darker women are differently positioned than lighter women (Hall 1995: 27–32).[17] In the sonnets, the contrast is temporarily given a paradoxical turn and then resumes the usual moral valence with the difference that the fair love object contrasted with the dark sex object is a young man rather than a woman.

In British and American literature, as Kim Hall has noted, there is a tradition of the 'dark/light pair of women' (1995: 179–80). However, Shakespeare's use of this contrast is ambiguous. When his characters attribute 'fairness' to women, the word's descriptive quality is sometimes undercut because of the speaker's unreliability, combined with the double meaning of fair as 'white' and 'beautiful'. For example, in *A Midsummer Night's Dream*, after a magic potion has been put on his eyes, Lysander argues that it is just rational for him to transfer his love from Hermia to Helena because 'Who will not change a raven for a dove?' (2.2.113). We know it is the potion and not reason. He calls Hermia 'Ethiop' (3.2.257) and 'tawny Tartar' (263).[18] But earlier Helena has refused to accept Hermia's description of her as fair, saying 'Demetrius loves your fair' (1.1.182).

In *Love's Labour's Lost*, Berowne complains that he has fallen in love with a woman 'with two pitch-balls stuck in her face for eyes' (3.1.196) and with no evidence but a few words' interchange, assumes that she is sexually free: 'one that will do the deed / Though Argus were her eunuch and her guard' (197–8). Like the speaker of the sonnets, he sometimes defends her 'blackness' with paradoxes: 'O, if in black my lady's brows [*sic*] be decked, / It mourns that painting and usurping hair / Should ravish doters with a false aspect; / And therefore is she born to make black fair' (4.3.254–7). His reference to her 'white hand' (3.1.167) may indicate that the blackness does not extend to her skin – however, there may be some suggestion of at least a tan later when his oath is 'By this white glove – how white the hand, God knows!' (5.2.411).

In other plays, no woman is identified as black, but a lover's praise involves an implicit comparison with other women, not necessarily those in the play. However, this may also be ambiguous. For example, Troilus praises Cressida by saying that in comparison to her hand, 'All whites are ink / Writing their own reproach' (1.1.55), so her hand is whiter than all other hands. He has just called her 'fair Cressid' (30), but her uncle Pandarus says that her hair is 'somewhat darker than Helen's' (41–2).[19] And the use of 'fair' becomes even more paradoxical when he attributes Helen's fairness to painting with the blood of the wounded and dead on both sides of the Trojan War (89–90).

In spite of such ambiguities, there is still a background association of blackness with ugliness (Hall 1995). In several of the early plays, women who feel rejected speak of their dark skin, making explicit the source in suntan, which was then not glamorous because it was associated with having to work outside. In *The Two Gentlemen of Verona*, for example, when Julia, in disguise as a page, is telling the story of her former lover Proteus' fickleness, she says that Julia, 'when she did think my master lov'd her well' (4.4.147), was fair, but,

> since she did neglect her looking-glass
> And threw her sun-expelling mask away
> The air hath starv'd the roses in her cheeks
> And pinch'd the lily-tincture of her face,
> That now she is become as black as I.
>
> (4.4.149–53)

Claudio says he is repentant enough to marry Hero 'were she an Ethiope' (5.4.38). Pandarus, when claiming to be giving up on matching Cressida with Troilus, says, 'I care not an she were a blackamoor' (1.1.76). This association of dark skin with ugliness is found in descriptions of men as well, for example Portia's rejection not only of Morocco but also of 'all of his complexion' (2.7.99).[20]

Still, although *The Merchant of Venice* is the comedy that deals most explicitly with ethnic and religious otherness, it does not present a clear dark/fair contrast between women. Much later, in *Ivanhoe*, Sir Walter Scott would juxtapose the dark and Jewish Rebecca with the fair and Christian Rowena. But we hear nothing of Jessica's darkness in *The Merchant of Venice*. Lorenzo, her love, calls her 'fair ..., if that mine eyes be true' (2.6.54). Mocking Shylock, Salerio says to him, 'There is more difference between thy flesh and hers, than between jet and ivory, more between your bloods, than there is between red wine and Rhenish' (3.1.35–8). As a matter of ideology and custom, it was thought easier to assimilate a Jewish woman to Christianity than a Jewish man.[21]

However, dark or fair, Jessica is not clearly assimilated at the end of *The Merchant of Venice*. Portia and most of the other characters speak directly to Lorenzo but hardly at all to her (Adelman 2003).[22] After Lorenzo's speech about the music of the spheres, all she can say is 'I am never merry when I hear sweet music' (5.1.69), her last words in the play. Recent productions, however, have very often focused on her at the very end, whether to show her singing a Hebrew song, cherishing the ring that she was said to have gambled away or crumpling up and throwing away the deed of gift from her father.[23]

Shakespeare's Sonnets 127, 130, 131, 132, 137, 144, 147 and 152 are his works in which a woman's darkness is most stressed. These are among the 'Dark Lady Sonnets', a euphemistic term since the woman is never addressed as a lady and apparently is not a lady by either rank or decorum. The woman's blackness, or more specifically the blackness of her eyes and hair, is praised in some of them, but it is always through paradox – blackness is appropriate either because it is mourning for true beauty in a time where most women simulate beauty with cosmetics ('such who not born fair, no beauty lack' [127]) or because it is in sympathy with the speaker, who feels his love is disdained (132). However, the most specific contrast is not with pseudo-fair women but with 'a man right fair' (144). Most of the poems that refer to women's blackness associate it with moral evil, sometimes specifically sexual infidelity. And though the fair man is also sometimes presented as deceitful (in 144), which most explicitly sums up the triangle, his sin is presented as the result of the woman's temptation.[24] The picture of female blackness here may have developed out of the association of sun-tanned skin with a lower social position, but it is parallel to the stereotype that developed in the US largely as a result of slavery. And in both early modern England and the US after the racialized slave trade developed, as with the casting of Bianca, the association with sexual transgression was probably heightened by the association of blackness with racial otherness.

Antony and Cleopatra: Race, class, competition and friendship

In *Antony and Cleopatra*, there are suggestions of the link between a dark woman and sexual freedom made in the sonnets and in *Love's Labour's Lost*, but the treatment of Cleopatra is still different. When Antony calls Cleopatra 'the foul Egyptian' (4.12.10) and 'triple-turned whore' (13), it is because of his suspicion of political betrayal after her ships failed to join his in battle against Rome's. Cleopatra is the one sexually active woman in Shakespeare whose lover or husband forgives her for her past affairs.[25] She is also the one woman who turns her dark skin into a sign of having enjoyed her life – referring to herself as 'with Phoebus' amorous pinches black' (1.5.29).[26]

As Ania Loomba (2002: 112–19) notes, there is not a clear physical description of Cleopatra in this play, although Philo calls her 'tawny' (1.1.6). The historical Cleopatra was of Greek ancestry but identified with the Egyptians she ruled. The character also so identifies. Although even in recent years, only a few women of colour have played Cleopatra on the US, British and Canadian stages, the text of the play suggests that the typical Roman attitude towards her was influenced by the Roman construction of Egyptian women as likely to be both wanton and powerful (Dusinberre 2011; Rutter 2001: 57–103). Related images of women's wantonness are evoked by the references to her as a gypsy.

Shakespeare shows Cleopatra's resentment of Antony's wife Octavia in her violence towards the messenger who tells her of their marriage, and in her hostile words about Octavia at other times, but, unlike his adapter Dryden, he never shows the two women together. Their opposition can be related to national difference, Roman vs Egyptian, which in modern productions might well be shown as racial, but it is most emphasized as a conflict over Antony. The play also emphasizes a temperamental difference between the two women, related to contrasting associations of Rome and Egypt. Cleopatra is presented as, like the Nile, overflowing boundaries that Octavia stays within. Octavia is torn by the conflict between her husband and her brother that her marriage was supposed to have resolved; Cleopatra is much more in a position of power.

The relationship between women given the most space in this play is not the competition between Cleopatra and Octavia, but the relationship between Cleopatra and her maidservants, Iras and Charmian. At least one of these characters, beginning in 1953, has, unlike Cleopatra, usually been played by a woman of colour or at least in blackface (Rutter 2001: 57–67). Their names and deaths with Cleopatra are found in Plutarch's biography of Antony, but Shakespeare expands their roles considerably.[27] They appear in the second scene of the play, imitating their mistress in their talkativeness, playfulness, and zest for life – especially Charmian, who says to the soothsayer, 'Let me be married to three kings in a forenoon and widow them all. Let me have a child at fifty to whom Herod of Jewry may do homage. Find me to marry me with Octavius Caesar' (1.2.27–31). The two are playfully competitive: Iras says of Charmian's fortune, 'Am I not an inch of fortune better than she?' (58).

But although Charmian's language and wishes sound like an attempt to imitate Cleopatra, later passages show her playing a role of the confidante who gives more conventional advice, something like what Celia does for Rosalind. Iras says much less. Charmian advises, after Cleopatra has told another servant to report her as in the opposite of Antony's mood, 'In each thing give him way' (1.3.10). She is an audience for Cleopatra's words about her love for Antony, but one who speaks out with no fear of offending her mistress. She even protests against Cleopatra's threats to the messenger who tells her of Antony's marriage to Octavia.[28]

The scenes with Charmian and Iras help to flesh out the sense of Cleopatra's court as representing the culture of Egypt, making Cleopatra less isolated. Their obvious affection for her adds to the sense of her charm, and in the genre of tragedy their death with her is another tribute to her, parallel to the suicide of Antony's attendant Eros, who refuses to kill him.[29] Along with Emilia, they are the only ladies in waiting in Shakespeare who die a tragic death. Charmian gives Cleopatra eloquent words of farewell, calling her both 'a lass unparalleled' (5.2.314) and 'a princess / Descended of so many royal kings' (324–5). A class-conscious reader might think of the custom of burying servants in Egyptian pyramids when their master died, but these women, like Cleopatra, are also saving their dignity from the conquering Romans. Trying to save their lives instead would be an action more like Enobarbus' departure when he sees Antony is losing, which he repents bitterly. This play thus is an effective translation into tragic terms of the theme of women's friendship across class lines, as well as a unique presentation of women for whom a dark/light contrast does not seem to be an issue.

Friendship and difference

A look at Charmian and Iras adds to the evidence that friendships between women occur in many of Shakespeare's plays, in all genres, and the plots do not necessarily move towards dissolving them. Still, the plays also show tensions and even hatred of various sorts between women, variously related to competition, class difference, difference of appearance suggestive of racial/ethnic difference and moral contrast.

Tensions related to competition have their counterparts in relations between male characters.[30] However, between men, tensions from moral contrast are less about sexuality, because of the double standard. Apart from Othello's, men's contrasts in appearance are less discussed than women's. In a contrast that could be related to theories of women's greater empathy, men are rarely shown confiding in servant/companions as Portia, Desdemona, Juliet and others do (some do confide in servants who are not adult males, or at least not normative adult males in the play's terms, as with Orsino's closeness to Viola/Cesario, Lear's to the Fool, and Prospero's to Ariel).[31] Male friendships in the two plays that give them the most titular emphasis, *The Two Gentlemen of Verona* and *Two Noble Kinsmen*, are, arguably, violated more drastically than happens to any female friendships in Shakespeare.

Still, the range of relationships between women in Shakespeare's plays shows not only occasional improbable generosity, as with Isabella's final assistance to Mariana, but also polarity between good and evil, as with Marina and the bawd, and full-throated hatred in which both parties may be at fault. The most simply cooperative sisterhood is, ironically, among the witches of *Macbeth*. Most of the relationships are in the zone of ordinary human complexity, including friends with tensions and servants with aspirations. How relationships between women are affected by their racial, ethnic or religious differences is usually left ambiguous, but the plays make clear the general negative valence of words like 'black' and 'Jew' in Shakespeare's culture. Criticism and productions that have been sensitive to the relationship between Jessica and Portia, for example, have often highlighted these issues. But while many recent productions have visually suggested that while parallel in being disillusioned with their marriages at the end, they are isolated from each other, the 2010 Al Pacino version ends with Portia intently looking out from her tower at Jessica.

7

Work

Feminist activists, arguing from both likeness and difference approaches in feminist theory, have had several goals with regard to work: opening non-traditional fields to women, valuing work that women have traditionally done, and making women's pay and working conditions equitable. Trying to explain the difficulty of accomplishing these goals, feminists have sometimes presented the contrast between a female domestic sphere and a male public sphere as a transhistorical constant. Clearly, it can be found in ancient Greece and Rome. However, Alice Clark, in *Working Life of Women in the Seventeenth Century* (1919), using materialist analysis, saw a middle and late seventeenth century development of capitalism in England as a crucial point of transition after which women were more restricted to domesticity.[1] Considering household activities in detail, some more recent feminist historians and critics also argue that the spheres were not as divided or as unequal in prestige in Shakespeare's day, when women might make and sell goods from their home, as they became later.[2] Wendy Wall, for example, writes, 'How could women be "relegated" to the household at a time in which it had not yet even superficially withdrawn from economic life or from some yet unborn public sphere?' (2002: 9). However, the controversy continues. Natasha Korda argues that Shakespeare's plays show that the housewife's role as household manager, for example in *The Merry Wives of*

Windsor and *Othello*, requires self-supervision which 'works to reinforce the emergent privatization of the household and its differentiation as a specifically feminine sphere' (2002: 92). In a careful review of the question, Ann Christensen concludes that during this time, 'Though not yet "separate spheres," housewifery and business became constructed as women's work and men's work respectively, and contemporary discourses document ambivalent representations of the value of housewifery' (2014).[3] And when women worked outside their household, as they did, their work was generally devalued and considered part of an informal economy (Korda 2011: 20–53).

This chapter deals with four questions related to feminist theories of work. How, if at all, do Shakespeare's plays support the expansion of women's possible kinds of work? How, if at all, do the plays underscore the importance of women's traditional work? Which of two contrasting feminist approaches to sex work do the plays support, if either?[4] And last, what kinds of women's work in Shakespeare's time had or might have had an impact on his theatre, and what new perspective does knowledge of this give to the exclusion of women from work as performers in the English public theatre of his time?

Non-normative work

As Christensen implies, certain kinds of work excluded most women in Shakespeare's day. Several of these are occupations that until the late twentieth century only exceptional women could enter: law, medicine, government, the military. Early Shakespeare critics such as Juliet Dusinberre (2003 [1975]) and Irene Dash (1981), and later Theodora Jankowski (1992), have discussed examples of women doing such work in Shakespeare's plays. Portia has obvious success in a male-dominated venue, as she defeats Shylock in the Venetian courtroom, though the religious and anti-alien bias in her victory is open to criticism. Helena cures the King of France when all his professional physicians have failed. She might be seen as a precedent for women in medicine since she learned her skills form her physician father. There already was a tradition of women healers – struggling with male physicians over their turf – and some viewers might have aligned her with them.[5] She does not show any signs of wanting to continue her healing work, though it might be imagined as more likely than Portia arguing in a later courtroom.

The pictures of women's governmental and military work in Shakespeare are more problematic. Joan of Arc's military success is attributed to demons. Cleopatra leads her ships out of a sea battle because of her fear. Queen Margaret is a strong leader in battle, but even feminists Howard and Rackin call her 'monstrous' for her cruelty (1997: 94).

How about women as rulers? Scholars have demonstrated that Shakespeare de-emphasizes the historical Cleopatra's governmental achievements to stress her relationship with Anthony, but on the other hand Jankowski argues that she has political power because of her ability as a dramatist, director and performer (Jankowski 1992: 158–62). Many of his other plays were written during the reign of Queen Elizabeth, phenomenally successful as a ruler by most measures. It would have been very difficult to portray a female ruler on stage during her reign without it being taken as a comment on her. In *Henry VIII*, however, Cranmer's prediction of England's prosperity during her future reign at her baptism pays her tribute. Many of Shakespeare's plays portray exceptional women, and a few of them are successful in work unusual for women, but this is not his consistent concern.

Another kind of work for women outside the normative household, prostitution, appears in at least five plays. The location of the Globe Theatre, in Southwark, was near the brothels, and prostitutes often solicited near the theatres and in the audience. The plays do not literally show them at work, but we see several of them interacting with previous and potential customers. The Bawd in *Pericles* (written when

Shakespeare's players were less often performing at the Globe) gives most support to the feminist anti-prostitution argument that it is exploitation. She overworks her employees, speaks callously about them – 'we have but poor three, and they can do no more than they can do; and they with continual action are even as good as rotten' (4.2.6–9) – and does her best to force Marina into prostitution, though Marina escapes, apparently through skill at persuasion of her first customer. The two prostitutes who appear briefly in *Timon of Athens* are, like the Bawd, caricatures of greed.

The other sex workers are quite different. The plays do not make an argument that prostitution can be a rational choice, but they do not provide clear counter-examples to that view. In *The Comedy of Errors*, the Courtesan is described by Antipholus of Ephesus as 'A wench of excellent discourse, / Pretty and witty; wild, and yet, too, gentle' (3.1.109–10). Although the play is set in Ephesus, the term and description links her with the 'famous courtesans of Venice – learned, beautiful, wealthy women who were compensated sometimes just for their verbal conversation' (Wayne 1998: 194). Further down the economic and social scale is the madam Mistress Overdone of *Measure for Measure*. She is matter-of-fact about the threat to her and other brothels from Angelo's enforcing the law against sex outside of marriage, but she can see the superiority of Claudio to her customers. When she is taken off to prison many in the audience probably sympathize with her. She has kept the child of her employee Kate Keepdown, though this might be as another eventual worker. In *2 Henry IV*, Doll Tearsheet, though drunk, provides both affection and moral advice for Falstaff. After calling him 'as valorous as Hector of Troy, worth five of Agamemnon' (2.4.218–19), she asks when he will 'begin to patch up [his] old body for heaven' (232–3). These three plays, and *Othello* if we consider Bianca as a prostitute, do not idealize or defend sex workers, but they are not simply evil temptresses or exploited victims (Stanton 2000).

Mistresses and servants

Several other kinds of more normative ordinary women's work are presented or referred to in Shakespeare's plays: governing a household, working as a maidservant, textile work, laundry and food preparation. Does the presentation of these kinds of work emphasize their value, make them seem limited or degrading or emphasize their gendering? A few lines clearly gender them. When Othello imagines as an example of an unlikely humiliation, 'Let housewives make a skillet of my helm' (1.3.274), the opposition of male and female kinds of work, and their value difference, is emphasized. In spite of the argument that the spheres were not yet separate, when Adriana protests against men, 'Why should their liberty than ours be more?' (2.1.10), her sister, Luciana, answers, 'Because their business lies still out o'door' (11). Adriana sees the household role as confinement, part of the subordination of women.

However, women did have some mobility outside the home, as we can see not only in the portrayal of the extraordinary Cleopatra but also in the multiple locations of, for example, Alice Ford, Margaret Page, Helena, Isabella, Volumnia, Juliet's nurse and Paulina, as well as female characters who are exiled or shipwrecked. A number of plays, on the other hand, show women skilfully governing their household, servants and property. Showing that such ability does not depend on marriage, one of the characters most explicitly praised for household management is Olivia in *Twelfth Night*.[6] Sebastian admires her ability to 'sway her house, command her followers, / Take and give back affairs and their dispatch' smoothly and discreetly (4.3.17–18). And clearly the mobility of Alice Ford and Margaret Page does not keep them from domestic skills.

The position of maidservant, discussed in the previous chapter mostly in terms of relation to a woman of higher status, was sometimes a stage of life rather than a class position. Viola is one of the most romanticized of servants, not only in that she is disguised as a boy: her economic condition (she has gold to give the captain who saves her) is closer to that of the aristocratic women for whom service was merely temporary, than to the financial hardship of most women in service.[7] Though her situation, shipwrecked in a foreign country, suggests desperation, her entry into service seems adventurous, a 'choice rather than need', and her quick intimacy with Orsino has the acceleration of dramatic fantasy (Dowd 2009: 25). As Michele Dowd writes, her marriage could be reassuring to 'those who might be concerned about women's ambiguous position within a volatile service economy – one that was newly based on yearly contracts and variable wages' (2009: 2).

Maria's position is not as idealized as Viola's. There is no hint that she has chosen to be a servant and, unlike Viola, she never expresses love or the wish to marry the man with whom she is eventually paired off (Dowd 2009: 39, 46). However, she clearly has an unusually outspoken relationship with Sir Toby, as a servant giving advice to and sharing revelry with her aristocratic mistress' kin. Toby is not an ideal catch, but marrying him gives her a more secure position in Olivia's household. Toby presents his marriage to Maria as a recompense for her deception of Malvolio. Her ability to copy Olivia's handwriting is crucial in this, and this outcome dramatizes the fact that literacy was indeed becoming 'an increasingly valuable skill for servants'. Toby even says he would 'ask no other dowry with her but such another jest' (2.5.178–9), thus providing an appealing fantasy to contrast with the usual economic requirements of marriage at the time (Dowd 2009: 42, 38).

No female servants in Shakespeare are beaten by their masters, as are male servants in *The Comedy of Errors* and *The Taming of the Shrew*. The one whose domestic occupations are most stressed is Mistress Quickly, who works for Doctor Caius. She says, 'I keep his house; and I wash, wring, brew, bake, scour, dress meat and drink, make the beds and do all myself' (*MW* 1.4.89–91). She talks about how much work she does for him – and yet she seems to enjoy taking on other tasks, such as carrying messages. The play does not emphasize her exploitation any more that it emphasizes exploitation in the household work of Alice Ford and Margaret Page.

Textile work

Orsino refers to and romanticizes still another kind of woman worker when he asks Feste to sing a song that comes from 'The spinsters and the knitters in the sun, / And the free maids that weave their thread with bones' (2.4.44–5). The allusion at the end is to makers of bonelace, which required counting (McNeill 2007: 48–50).[8] He is framing it poetically, but something sung while weaving would have been an occupational song that helped to make weaving accurate. According to McNeill, these maids are 'impoverished workers losing their health to the mechanized labor and pauper wages of lacemaking'. They 'used the line-length of the song to remind them when to start a new line of weaving'. Paradoxically, women who were 'free' and working at such a job actually had less freedom than a single woman in service to a household, like Viola and Maria – since a masterless woman could be subject to correction by the court (McNeill 2007: 55, 151–2).[9]

Textile work of many kinds, done by women, was the basis of the English economy at the time, and 'cloth was England's largest export commodity' (McNeill 2007: 29). Women of all classes up to royalty were advised to spin, but 'it was poor women who did most of the spinning' (McNeill 2007: 28). McNeill discusses at length the association of spinning, which paid less than a subsistence wage, with poverty (2007: 29–34). It was a frequent occupation of women who could not be clearly classified as 'maid, wife, or widow', the official taxonomy of identity. The word 'spinster' might be used to refer to their occupation, but it was an occupation for which, unlike many others, there was no official apprentice or guild system (McNeill 2007: 32). Such women generally appear in Shakespeare's plays only at the margins, as in Orsino's speech.

Needlework was so frequent and so acceptable an occupation for women that it was frequently the meaning when the single word 'work' was used in early modern England. Sewing scenes among more aristocratic women are frequent in early modern English drama (Orlin 1999). Shakespeare has two: Coriolanus' wife, Virgilia, and mother, Volumnia, are sewing while he is away fighting. A visitor, Valeria, persuades Volumnia to leave, but Virgilia continues to sew, emphasizing her persistence in following a domestic ideal. In *Henry VIII*, Katherine of Aragon is sewing with her maid as two Cardinals visit her to persuade her to follow her husband's plans for her rather than to resist. Again, the scene emphasizes her virtue, innocence, and devotion to the domestic sphere. Desdemona, another wrongly suspected female character, is also talented in needlework, as are Bianca (in *Othello*) and Marina, and needle images come readily to Imogen (*Cym.* 1.2.99, 1.4.19), but this does not imply as much a restriction to the domestic sphere.

Othello is not only the play with the most thorough consideration of women's position, but also the play with the most attention to various aspects of one piece of cloth, Desdemona's handkerchief. As a gift that Othello gives her but charges her to keep safe, it embodies the ambiguity about married women's possession of property (Korda 2002: 40–5, 150–8). According to the law of coverture, a wife's property belonged to her husband, and it was part of her work as a wife to guard it. Cassio asks Bianca to copy it, and for those who see her as a prostitute, this resonates with the fact that sewing paid so little that women in the needle trades often did resort to prostitution.

The most extraordinary aspect of the handkerchief is the first description that Othello gives of its origin:

A sibyl that had numbered in the world
The sun to course two hundred compasses,
In her prophetic fury sewed the work;

> The worms were hallowed that did breed the silk,
> And it was dyed in mummy, which the skilful
> Conserved of maidens' hearts.
>
> (3.4.72–7)

The mythically prophetic and long-lived sibyls were mostly linked with Greece and Italy, but some were supposed to have come from the Middle East, Persia and Egypt. Mummy, in this case, was a liquid derived for medicinal purposes in various ways from human bodies, very frequently dead ones. Like another kind of mummy, it was often associated with Egypt, but it was in use in parts of Europe, including London, in Shakespeare's time.[10] This passage has been described as 'probably the most beautiful account ever written of women's ubiquitous labor in the field of textiles', but the source of the blood is dead maiden's hearts and so it is also an unsettling picture of human sacrifice, closely related, as Desdemona's death will be, to the victimizing glorification of female chastity (Callaghan 2001: 77). Dympna Callaghan makes the description evidence that 'the invisibility of women's work as well as the creation of an absolute distinction between aesthetic and productive labor is a relatively new phenomenon, and one which certainly postdates the Renaissance', but the role of virgin sacrifice as well as the context in an attempt to frighten Desdemona should not be forgotten in analysing this as a picture of women's work (2001: 78).

Women were not only the weavers of textiles and in charge of their household use; like Mistress Quickly, they were also usually in charge of cleaning them. But the chief importance of laundry in Shakespeare, apart from Desdemona's sheets, is in the humiliation that Falstaff receives when he escapes being caught as an illicit visitor to Alice Ford by hiding in a laundry basket that is carried away by servants. Over and over again Falstaff repeats his disgust at being surrounded by smelly and dirty linen. Though not themselves carried in baskets, dealing with laundry was of course an ordinary experience for many women in service. But the other characters also act shocked when Ford searches through the basket the next time he suspects Falstaff – a man is expected to be 'ashamed' (4.2.130) to handle dirty laundry, thus reinforcing the idea of a gendered division of labour, with women's share associated with dirt, even though the result of doing laundry is the removal of dirt.

Food preparation

While there were men who specialized in cookery and wrote cookbooks in Shakespeare's time, the ordinary home kitchen, like the laundry, was more female territory than male and even in a house as great as the Capulets, the master is mocked by the Nurse as a 'cot-quean' (4.4.6) as he tries to supervise preparations for Juliet's wedding to Paris. However, many of the meal scenes exclude women: consider the Duke's picnic in *As You Like It* and the banquet in *2 Henry IV* (Erickson 1985: 28–9). The servants in *The Taming of the Shrew* and the fairies who bring Bottom food in *A Midsummer Night's Dream* all have male names. Eating scenes in *1 Henry IV* and *Henry V* are apparently set in womanless taverns. On the other hand, there are Mistress Quickly in *2 Henry IV*, Marian Hacket, the alewife in the induction to *The Taming of the Shrew*, the kitchen-maid described, heard once, but never seen, in *The Comedy of Errors*, and, oddly in this company, Imogen in her disguise as Fidele. S/he is the character most praised for cooking skills: one of her unknown brothers, who she has met by chance in the caves of Wales, says that she 'sauced our broths as Juno had been sick, / And he her dieter' (*Cym.* 4.2.50–1). This praise could be taken as related to her hidden female gender, but it could also suggest skills developed by experience at court.[11]

Why do the plays show many more males serving food than females? Is the case of the good cook in boy's clothes the exception that proves the rule? Many social historians conclude that 'at least within the noble household, there was little place for women beyond the meanest menial tasks and the more elevated but confined role of waiting upon and providing companionship to its lady' (Schalkwyk 2008: 36).[12] Shakespeare occasionally makes reference to women in menial kitchen roles – in addition to those previously mentioned, the 'kitchen malkin ... / Clamb'ring the walls to eye him' (2.1.208–10), becomes a measure of Coriolanus' celebrity, and the song at the end of *Love's Labour's Lost* concludes with 'greasy Joan doth keel the pot' (5.2.911, 920). Not much more.

There were a limited number of boy actors that could play women in the company, and they were more needed in roles that had dialogue than in simply bringing in the food. Theoretically, of course, kitchen-maids could have had speaking parts in other plays than *The Comedy of Errors*. This would change the effect of their scenes somewhat: if Petruchio had female servants in *The Taming of the Shrew*, Katherine might appear less isolated. By contrast to the all-male banquets and several others in which guests are all or almost all male, one all-female dinner is implied, in *All's Well that Ends Well*, when Helena hosts Diana and her friend Mariana at Diana's mother's inn. This corresponds to the unusual power of women in this play.[13]

Theatrical work

The absence of parts for women who serve food is one of the less obvious likely consequences of the absence of women performers from the stage at Shakespeare's Globe. This larger absence was not paralleled on all kinds of stages at the time. Women had participated in guild pageants earlier, and in many kinds of parish entertainment. There were female performers in the *commedia dell'arte* players from Italy who visited London during Shakespeare's career. Englishwomen acted in plays and masques at court and in households (Korda 2011; Brown and Parolin 2005; Rackin 2005: 41).

Although women were not performers on the public stage, Natasha Korda has recently shown that they helped London theatres in many other ways. They mended and sewed spangles on costumes. They worked as tire women; that is, they made elaborate headgear, wigs and other accessories such as fans, and dressed the performers. They starched and laundered clothes and ruffs. They collected entrance fees and during performances they sold food (though this was sometimes more competition for attention than help). Elite women hosted entertainments at court and women owned three of the four London inns that served as playhouses. And, of course, as has long been known, they were paying customers (Korda 2011).[14] So the theatres where women couldn't perform not only appealed to women as spectators, they had many kinds of women in their system of production.

Gender-related apparent inequities in culture industries are still with us in the twenty-first century. In the US, more women read books than men, but more men than women have books published, reviewed and rewarded.[15] But the fact that women acted on the public stage in some other European countries when they didn't in England suggests that there was a more specific cause. The English theatre was under attack by Protestant preachers (whose Christianity, more than Catholic tradition, emphasized the importance of an earthly vocation for all) as encouraging idleness, both on the part of the spectators and on the part of the actors, who were not doing what was considered honest work.[16] Stephen Gosson, for example, wrote that acting was 'a softe, a silken, a Courting kind of life, fitter for women than for men', and Thomas Beard said that it made people 'idle, effeminate, and voluptuous'. Keeping women off the stage thus was a way the theatre attempted to legitimate itself as 'honest' and 'manly' work – nevertheless, it did open up some work opportunities for women, even if not as actors (Korda 2011: 51–3).

Korda also argues that the activities of women behind the scenes influenced some early modern English plays. For example, women lent money to the theatres. Indeed, there were many female money-lenders, usually widowed or never married women, in early modern England, and some polemicists defended women's moneylending as an 'expression of God's mercy' (2011: 68).[17] This provides an interesting context for Portia in *The Merchant of Venice*. She sees other connections between women's work offstage and plots onstage: for example, the practice of sending dirty clothes out to immigrant Dutch laundry women might have suggested the carrying out of Falstaff in a laundry basket (2011: 115).

In another influence from offstage women, the actresses of the *commedia dell'arte* may have provided hints for Shakespeare's Viola, Portia and Rosalind. As Pamela Brown shows, the Italian women of those troupes first performed lengthy and passionate roles in England in the 1570, the same decade in which English playwrights, first John Lyly, then Thomas Kyd, then Shakespeare, wrote female roles with 'generic versatility, self-awareness and emotional volatility' (Brown 2012: 150). Rosalind as a character is herself an actress in everyday life, with 'pleasure in performance itself', suggesting the French court as well as the Italian *commedia dell'arte* (Brown 2012: 153).[18] In her disguise as Ganymede, Rosalind claims to have the great variety of changeable emotions attributed to women by antifeminists, because 'boys and women are for the most part cattle of this colour' (3.2.403–4), a boast about the metamorphic virtuosity that Rosalind the character, Ganymede her creation, and the boy actor behind them all possess. So did the Italian actresses, some of which had much more professional autonomy, fame and lengthy careers than did the boy actors even at their most successful. Rosalind's traits 'defy early modern notions of gender decorum but conform to the new actress-driven trend in comedy' (Brown 2012: 158). Thus they prepare for the character's success as, beginning in the late seventeenth century, she, along with other women written by Shakespeare, would be portrayed by many women over the centuries.

Feminist criticism and feminist theory are both diverse communities with many different methodologies, so much so that many recent books use the plural form and title themselves with reference to 'feminisms'. Accordingly, it is not surprising that this book shows disagreements among feminist critics of Shakespeare. With regard to work, also, Shakespeare's plays give a picture from which critics can draw many different conclusions. Some plays show women successful in extraordinary positions, and thus seem to favour the expansion of women's possibilities, but a critic can also find suggestions that they may fail in a crisis and/or that masculine disguise is necessary. Some of them show women governing their household well; this would be welcomed by difference feminists but might be critiqued by some equality feminists. One materialist feminist might note absence of the voices of women who do menial work, but another might note the protest against prostitutes' working conditions in *Pericles* and Mistress Overdone's fellow-feeling, in *Measure for Measure*, about the fate of prostitutes in other brothels competing with hers (Singh 1994: 44).

In his plays maids, as we saw in the last chapter, may want to rise above their situation, and sometimes do; oppression in their work is not emphasized, though as in *The Comedy of Errors* ridicule may be. One sort of feminist analysis finds that Shakespeare shows many women with a sense of agency about their work as well as about their initiative in love; another sort emphasizes the way comic plots, and sometimes plotters among the other characters, such as Prospero in *The Tempest*, are, nevertheless, controlling them. One kind of feminist critic values the fact that Shakespeare made mothers important characters in many of his now lesser-known plays; others note their flaws and defeats, to which the first kind might respond that male characters have flaws and defeats as well. The fact that women worked to support Shakespeare's theatre in many different capacities, as well as contributing to the plays' success by their attendance, could suggest that many of these women found the plays' representations of women enjoyable – but on the other hand, some critics would say this shows their false consciousness or simply their need for employment.

What some have called suspicious reading may be the dominant academic practice now (Sedgwick 2003: 123–51). Theoretical analyses showing continuing patriarchal structures in the plays, for example, have sometimes been striking partly because they contrast with spectators' impressions of female characters' power. Critics' skills in finding subtexts confining women may have been heightened by reading much canonical literature in which the restrictions on female characters are in some ways more obvious than in Shakespeare. What cannot be disputed, however, is that, in spite of their early enactment by boys, Shakespeare's female characters have fascinated many audiences when played by both women and men and have inspired many writers, male and female, to rewrite or take their stories further. These rewritten characters, and Shakespeare's own versions, are still speaking to readers and spectators of later times.[19] And feminist theory can still add to these conversations.

APPENDIX

Podcast interviews with the authors of many of the titles in the *Arden Shakespeare and Theory* series are available. Details of both published and forthcoming titles are listed below.

Shakespeare and Cultural Materialist Theory, Christopher Marlow
http://blogs.surrey.ac.uk/shakespeare/2016/11/04/shakespeareand-contemporary-theory-31-shakespeare-and-cultural-materialist-theory-with-christopher-marlow/

Shakespeare and Ecocritical Theory, Gabriel Egan
http://blogs.surrey.ac.uk/shakespeare/2016/05/20/shakespeareand-contemporary-theory-24-shakespeare-and-ecocritical-theory-with-gabriel-egan/

Shakespeare and Ecofeminist Theory, Rebecca Laroche and Jennifer Munroe
http://blogs.surrey.ac.uk/shakespeare/2016/06/07/shakespeareand-contemporary-theory-25-shakespeare-and-ecofeminist-theory-with-rebecca-laroche-and-jennifer-munroe/

Shakespeare and Economic Theory, David Hawkes
http://blogs.surrey.ac.uk/shakespeare/2016/05/05/shakespeareand-contemporary-theory-22-shakespeare-and-economic-theory-with-david-hawkes/

Shakespeare and Feminist Theory, Marianne Novy
http://blogs.surrey.ac.uk/shakespeare/2016/05/13/shakespeareand-contemporary-theory-23-shakespeare-and-feminist-theory-with-marianne-novy/

Shakespeare and New Historicist Theory, Neema Parvini
http://blogs.surrey.ac.uk/shakespeare/2016/08/29/shakespeareand-contemporary-theory-27-shakespeare-and-newhistoricist-theory-with-evelyn-gajowski-and-neema-parvini/

Shakespeare and Postcolonial Theory, Jyotsna Singh
http://blogs.surrey.ac.uk/shakespeare/2016/07/19/shakespeareand-contemporary-theory-26-shakespeare-andpostcolonial-theory-with-jyotsna-singh

Shakespeare and Posthumanist Theory, Karen Raber
http://blogs.surrey.ac.uk/shakespeare/2016/09/30/shakespeareand-contemporary-theory-28-shakespeare-andposthumanist-theory-with-karen-raber/

Shakespeare and Presentist Theory, Evelyn Gajowski
http://blogs.surrey.ac.uk/shakespeare/2016/04/29/shakespeareand-contemporary-theory-21-the-arden-shakespeareand-theory-series-with-evelyn-gajowski/

Shakespeare and Queer Theory, Melissa E. Sanchez
http://blogs.surrey.ac.uk/shakespeare/2016/10/18/shakespeareand-contemporary-theory-29-shakespeare-andqueer-theory-with-melissa-e-sanchez/

NOTES

Introduction

1. Closest in time to Shakespeare among the English authors Kelly discusses are Rachel Speght and Ester Sowernam, who both responded to Joseph Swetnam's diatribe against women in 1617. Linda Woodbridge (1984) discusses their writing – and much other – relating to the controversy about women in England, including drama and poetry. Constance Jordan (1990) considers feminist writing in French, Italian and Latin, as well.

2. It would be harder to find feminism in the plays using bell hooks' definition – 'a movement to end sexism, sexist exploitation, and oppression' (2000: viii) – but easier using Chimamanda Ngozi Adichie's: 'a feminist is a man or woman who says, "Yes, there's a problem with gender as it is today and we must fix it, we must do better"' (2015: 48).

3. Alice Echols (1989) explains how and why the celebration of female difference came to be more prevalent in feminist language than the critique of gender.

4. See Wendy K. Kolmar and Frances Bartkowski (2010: 40–1). Iris Young argues for a combination of equality and difference approaches, which she calls humanist and gynocentric (2006); Ruth Hubbard and others agree about combining approaches (Kolmar and Bartkowski 2010: 41). In my chapter 'Likeness and Difference' I explain Young's use of 'humanist' in this context, a use I will also follow. Anne Fausto-Sterling takes account of transexual and intersex experience as well (2000).

5. See Ann Rosalind Jones (1985). For critiques of both masculinity and femininity, see Catharine Stimpson (1974: 237–8) and many of the early radical feminists discussed by Echols (1989), as well as hooks (2000) and Adichie (2015).

6 Sheryl Sandberg (2013) emphasizes individual effort. Some feminists would place the habit of seeing women as sexual objects as the origin of most problems.
7 *The Woman's Part: Feminist Criticism of Shakespeare* (1980), the collection in which Park's essay appears, exemplifies how important collaborative work has been in feminist criticism overall.
8 Her apparently paradoxical argument follows the deconstructive methodology of Jacques Derrida, who will be discussed shortly.
9 This paragraph draws on Ann Rosalind Jones (1985: 81–3).
10 For example, the British Donmar Warehouse production, which came to St Ann's Warehouse in Brooklyn in 2015.
11 For criticism of inattention to gender, see Lynda Boose (1987) and Carol Thomas Neely (1988).
12 Presentist criticism is explicit about its relevance to the contemporary world, though this need not preclude historical awareness. See Evelyn Gajowski (2009).
13 Some less academic feminist critics see difference feminism in Shakespeare: Marilyn French (1981) and Tina Packer (2015).

1. Likeness and difference

1 See also Joan W. Scott (1988: 44).
2 Greenblatt (1988) draws on ideas developed further in Thomas Laqueur (1990).
3 Katherine may be making the argument for pragmatic reasons: see Novy (1984: 58–60).
4 The belief that male supremacy was under threat often motivated attempts to control women. See Orgel (1997: 25, 138).
5 Shapiro (1994: 129–30) points out this faint is not in the source, Lodge's prose romance *Rosalynde*.
6 See for example Henry Smith: 'If thou be learned, choose one that loveth knowledge; if thou be Martiall, choose one that

loveth prowess; if thou must live by thy labour, choose one that loveth husbandry' (1591: 25).

7   See Chapter 2, 'Desire'.
8   Everett (1970 [1961]: 281–89) links both Beatrice and Benedick with the fool.
9   Woodbridge (1984) discusses Castiglione (52–8), Agrippa (1984: 38–45; I modernize her quotation on 39) and many other defenders and attackers of women.
10 At one point in his *Treatise of the Nobilitie and Excellencye of woman kynde,* Agrippa argues that women are superior because Adam was made out of earth; see Kathleen Crowther (2010: 107). Beatrice wishes that men were made 'of some other metal than earth. Would it not grieve a woman to be overmastered with a piece of valiant dust?' (2.1.54–6).
11 Shakespeare died in 1616. The 1997 Arden 3 editor, E. A. J. Honigmann, believes that the discrepancy between the texts on this speech is more likely to involve 'a cut in Q than an afterthought in F'; see 294n.
12 See also Jordan (1990).
13 The feminist debate between essentialism and constructivism – both sides observing differences between women and men but the latter arguing that most of them are historically and socially conditioned – is not argued in those terms in Shakespeare. However, in 1620 the speaker in the anonymous tract *Haec Vir* declares women 'as free-borne as men', and critiques customs of difference. Woodbridge (1984: 146–9) discusses this.

2. Desire

1   Cora Kaplan (1985) shows similarly that materialist feminist critic Judith Lowder Newton (1981) critiques the focus on courtship in Victorian women's fiction, while psychoanalytic feminist critic Mary Jacobus (1979) emphasizes the possible revolutionary element in women's romantic desires.
2   Erickson (1985) exemplifies the first; Traub (1992) and Belsey (1985b), the second.

3   Chapter 5, 'Language', discusses Shakespeare's men's use of Petrarchan language.
4   Belsey (2014: 79–81) discusses Brooke's preface and its complication of views vs greater cultural sympathy for love in the 1590s, when *Romeo and Juliet* was written.
5   Cooper notes, however, that Lewis neglects the importance of love leading to marriage in many medieval romances (2004: 308).
6   Quotations in this paragraph are from this source, or from Shakespeare quoted within it.
7   The *Complete Arden* reads 'when I shall die' in 3.2.21, instead of 'when he shall die'.
8   Cf. Gajowski (1992: 16).
9   Rosalie Colie refers to 'unmetaphoring' in *Romeo and Juliet* (1974: 11).
10 For more on the Ovidian and the Petrarchan discursive traditions, see Gajowski (1992: 51–85, 26–50).
11 Juliet Dusinberre relates this as well to the boy actor's presumably larger hands (2006a: 34). References to her 'blackness' might have also suggested the then unglamorous suntan that poorer people of the time received from working outside. See Chapter 6, 'Between Women'.
12 However, Celia's mockery of Orlando can be read in this way.
13 See Crawford on how the final marriage reinforces Rosalind's relationship with Celia, as well as analyses of similar structures in *The Merry Wives of Windsor* and *All's Well that Ends Well* (2003: 151–3).

3. Marriage

1   Requiring the consent of the couple, at least privately, goes back to the medieval Catholic Fourth Lateran Council, 1215. See E. J. Graff (1999: 196). However, even if companionship was valued in marriage, in Catholic tradition marriage was still second to virginity.

2. On estrangements among couples in the aristocracy, see Lawrence Stone (1967: 297).

3. David Underdown sees increased conflicts in marriage in all classes at this time (1985). On the perhaps related fascination with fears and narratives of wives plotting their husbands' deaths, see Belsey (1985a: 129–37).

4. I thank Julie Crawford for this reference.

5. In the Quarto, Folio and Arden 3 *Much Ado about Nothing*, edited by Claire McEachern, these words are Leonato's, and McEachern argues that this suggests a more egalitarian marriage (2006b: 316 n.97). Most editors give them to Benedick and often add that Benedick kisses her.

6. Detmer relates *The Taming of the Shrew* to humanists' arguments against physical violence (1997).

7. In her 'Introduction', Barbara Hodgdon (2010) discusses these and many other productions. See also Martha Andresen-Thom (1982); Graham Holderness (1989); and Marianne Novy (1993: 7–9, 13–14).

8. Holderness argues that many in the original audience would have noticed this critically because of more recent emphasis on companionship in marriage (1991: 82).

9. These similarities and more are noted by Laurie Maguire (1992).

10. See the discussion of *Macbeth* in Chapter 1, 'Likeness and Difference'.

11. The word was already sometimes being used to mean 'frivolous or disreputable woman' as well as 'woman in charge of a house'. See Iago's ambiguous insult to women, 'housewives in … / Your beds!' (2.1.112–13).

12. On Othello, Iago and Desdemona as all outsiders, see Novy (2013).

13. See the discussion in Chapter 4, 'Motherhood', of his fantasies of Lady Macbeth as a mother.

14. Gajowski emphasizes the inadequacy of Antony's commitment early in the play and finds him growing into maturity later on (1992: 89).

15 Neely points out that earlier versions of the story sympathetic to the lovers by Chancer, Boccaccio, Cinthio, Garnier and Daniel explicitly present them as married (1985: 243). Gajowski emphasizes the 'marital terms' they use about their relationship near their deaths (1992: 110).

16 See Evelyn Gajowski and Phyllis Rackin (2015). I would like to acknowledge the influence of the 2012 Shakespeare Association seminar that these scholars led on my understanding of this play.

17 Psychological force, however, was recommended to husbands. See Dolan (2008: 45).

18 Research from 2014 shows that even mothers who work full-time will still put in one-and-a-half weeks' worth more time on household tasks than their male partners each year.

19 Loomba puts *Othello* in the context of dowry murders, wife-battering and other examples of violence against women in India in the modern world (1989).

20 Belief that it is inevitably oppressive, even if it is open to same-sex couples, is associated with queer theory, though not exclusively. Nor is evaluation of marriages in Shakespeare linked to a division between equality and difference feminist theory. With regard to theories of marriage, it is hard to find a feminist who does not value equality.

21 Compare Belsey's Lacanian analysis of *Romeo and Juliet* quoted in Chapter 2, 'Desire'.

22 See especially the essays by Elizabeth F. Emens, Drucilla Cornell, Wendy Brown and Brenda Cossman in Shanley (2004).

4. Motherhood

1 See the discussion in the 'Introduction' of the need to combine the difference and equality approaches.

2 Neely comments on these statistics and also on the large number of surviving older women in Shakespeare's family and environment (1990).

3 Hero's mother, Innogen, is present according to the stage

directions of the Quarto edition of *Much Ado about Nothing*, but she says nothing.

4   Katherine, Bianca, Lucentio, Hermia, Jessica, Hero (except in the Quarto), Rosalind, Celia, Silvia and Proteus (the last two from *The Two Gentlemen of Verona*) all have fathers in the play but no mothers. Outside comedy, the same is true of Cassandra, Cressida, Desdemona, Ophelia, Lavinia, Lear's daughters, the Jailer's Daughter, Antiochus' Daughter, Thaisa and Miranda.

5   In *All's Well that Ends Well*, a sixth woman, Violenta, is named in the *dramatis personae*. She appears in one scene but has no lines. The fifth, Mariana, appears only in that scene. Early modern plays with more parts for women, Middleton's *A Chaste Maid in Cheapside* (seven) and Lyly's *Galathea* (ten), were written for children's companies, which would have had more actors who could play female roles. More recently, according to the Annenberg School for Communications, out of 4,475 characters in films on screen in the US, in 2012, still only 28.4 per cent were female. The ratio in *As You Like It* is about 25 per cent.

6   'Humanist' here refers to a scholar in ancient Greek or Latin, studies which were revived as part of new learning in the Renaissance. Vives wrote this book in Latin. He may have briefly been the tutor of Princess Mary (the future Mary I), but left England during Henry VIII's move away from Roman Catholicism.

7   Note references to Beatrice's, Jessica's, Lancelot's and Sebastian's mothers in *Much Ado about Nothing*, *The Merchant of Venice* and *Twelfth Night*.

8   However, some feminist critics observe that wanting to be considered honest (sexually faithful) still keeps her within a framework of patriarchal values, in a society where sexual fidelity was often not considered important for men. See, for example, Neely (1985: 7).

9   In the 'Introduction' to their edition of *3 Henry VI*, John D. Cox and Eric Rasmussen note this, as well as the similarity of Margaret's language to a medieval poem about Mary's grief (2001: 46).

10 Her acknowledgement of adultery is discussed in Chapter 2, 'Desire'.

11 Note for example Sara Ruddick's full title, *Maternal Thinking: The Politics of Peace*.

12 Adelman says, 'That this image has no place in the plot, where the Macbeths are strikingly childless, gives some indication of the inner necessity through which it appears' (1992: 138). But women who have lost a child may feel not so much childless as between identities.

13 About a quarter of all children died before they were ten, with heaviest mortality in the first year of life (Schofield and Wrigley 1979: 61, 65; cited by Wrightson 1982: 105).

14 Deborah Willis notes the contrast with the lower-class associations of the weird sisters, like those historically accused of witchcraft at the time, and the 'lower-class wet nurse' (1995: 217). Her analysis links *Macbeth*'s witches with the fantasies about mothers that she has found in early modern texts about witches throughout her book.

15 In early modern England, mothers were frequently criticized in advice books and sermons for not nursing their children. Aristocratic mothers were least likely to.

16 Plutarch, much read in Elizabethan England where Latin books were grade school texts, elsewhere emphasized Roman mothers' roles in educating their sons as warriors. Volumnia is even more like the Spartan mothers described in Plutarch's 'Sayings of Spartan Women'. See Kahn (1981: 145–9).

17 However, Theodora Jankowski considers her successful as a mother because she has raised her son to succeed in Roman terms (1992: 107).

18 For a critic who analyses Volumnia's role without context, see D. W. Harding (1969).

19 See also Gajowski on the scene's suggestion of 'maternal bliss' and 'a prepatriarchal goddess' (1992: 118).

20 Adrian Kiernander, 10 April 1997, SHAKSPER.net (accessed 1 March 2017). I saw the Stratford production. The Propeller Company's staging is described in detail in Mario DiGangi (2008, quotation from 425).

21 Cf. Rackin's comparison of the attention to *The Taming of the Shrew* and the neglect of *The Merry Wives of Windsor* (2005).

5. Language

1 Jerome and Augustine preferred a hierarchical model placing both virgins and widows above wives, on the basis of lack of sexual activity, but a less hierarchical life stage model had wider social dominance in the Middle Ages, according to Cordelia Beattie (2007: 15–16).
2 On this and other examples, see Muriel Schulz (1975: 64–75).
3 See Alan Stewart on the multitude of letters written or read in the plays (2008).
4 Latin was so much a part of boys' schools and so absent as a subject from girls' schools that learning Latin has been referred to as a 'Renaissance male puberty rite' by Walter J. Ong (1971). Tutors might teach it to girls in unusual situations.
5 Neely discusses this transformation as a movement to 'mad prophet', through which Ophelia finally influences other characters (1985: 103).
6 Wofford engages with the theory of words as performative developed in J. L. Austin's *How to Do Things with Words*.
7 Rosalind's behaviour here is one of Shakespeare's changes from his source, where she asks her father's permission: see Thomas Lodge (1997 [1590]: 222).
8 Madonne M. Miner emphasizes this alliance (1980: 45–8).
9 Siemon also notes that the words 'mother' and 'children' (and cognates) are 'more numerous than in any other Shakespearean play' (2009: 18).
10 See also Irene Dash on the cutting of Margaret (1981: 197–8).
11 See Chapter 4, 'Motherhood', for more on these characters as well as Margaret.
12 Bloom argues that Constance's breath 'lingers on as an agent of critique' in her absence (2007: 95).

13 The classic treatment of the 'male gaze' is Laura Mulvey (1975), but she later qualifies her argument (1979).

14 Clifford is praised as an orator in that same scene after a speech of thirty-four lines.

15 Laurie Maguire discusses this issue and finds the argument for 'his' convincing (2000: 61–3). She also discusses other aspects of feminist editing, e.g. identifying misogynist phrases as such when explaining them in glosses and counteracting biases in the listing and identification of characters.

16 Boose (1991) notes the relevance of the woman's kneeling in the Sarum rite of marriage, still a living memory in Shakespeare's time. Chapter 3, 'Marriage', contrasts productions with some of these alternatives.

17 Edward Pechter points out that Desdemona is not silent in the murder scene, though some critics claim she is. He emphasizes the sarcastic anger in her one soliloquy, which begins, ''Tis meet I should be used so, very meet' (4.2.109) (2004: 378–9).

18 References in this paragraph are to McGuire's (1985) book.

6. Between women

1 Chodorow denies that this capacity is inevitably linked with femaleness but argues that it arises from the social history of assigning childrearing to women, and that sharing this role with fathers would be not only more equitable for mothers but also lead to a more balanced psychology in children who are raised partly by men (1978: 188).

2 However, Pollitt has reconsidered her views (Reed and Pollitt 2015). See also Valerie Miner and Helen E. Longino (1987).

3 Cicero's view of women as unsuitable for friendship was still a commonplace. See Laurie Shannon (2002: 54–5).

4 This work and the character are usually referred to as Rosalynde, but this edition modernizes spelling.

5 See Chapter 2, 'Desire'.

6 See Chapter 2, 'Desire', for more on this relationship.

7   Shirley Nelson Garner sees continued brokenness, for example between Hermia and Helena (1981).
8   See Diane Purkiss for a discussion of radical feminist uses and mythologization of witchcraft history (1996: 1–29).
9   Eagleton cites Kristeva (1981, 1984).
10 Both Adelman (1992) and Willis (1995) are discussed in Chapter 4, 'Motherhood'.
11 Laurie Maguire discusses the relation of the contrasting women to traditions of Ephesus and the way Shakespeare complicates that contrast (2007: 162–82).
12 Ann Rosalind Jones writes, 'ladies in waiting are gentlewomen, close in rank to the queens or aristocrats they serve' (1999: 21). Entering into service was often a life cycle stage for people of all classes. However, historically most maidservants at the time were further down the social ladder.
13 See Chapter 2, 'Desire'. For Rosalind's scorn, see Carolyn Sale (2011). I use 'class' as does Susan Amussen to mean 'the socio-economic hierarchy and the social relations imposed by it' (1988: 4). A maid is below her mistress in class in this sense.
14 Carol Rutter shows Imogen Stubbs and Zoe Wanamaker suggesting this in Trevor Nunn's 1989 production (2001: 142–77).
15 This speech is discussed in Chapters 1, 'Likeness and Difference'; 2, 'Desire'; and 3, 'Marriage'.
16 See Peter Erickson on Othello's use of 'fair' (2014: 161).
17 However, Iago twice calls Bianca 'pale' (5.1.104–5), when blaming her for Cassio's injury.
18 The Julie Taymor production performed by Brooklyn's Theater for a New Audience and circulated on film in 2015 deconstructs the assumptions in these lines further by casting a black woman as Helena and a white blonde as Hermia.
19 Laurie Maguire emphasizes how much Helen of Troy was an icon of beauty in Shakespeare's time (2007: 76).
20 'Complexion' could mean appearance at this time; Portia is repelled by Morocco's 'complexion' when all that she knows is that he is from Morocco.

21 M. Lindsay Kaplan discusses Lorenzo's frequent references to her as fair and the tradition of seeing Jewish women as easier to incorporate into Christianity (2007).

22 Mary Janell Metzger shows that Jessica's positioning is contradictory (1998).

23 The first is in the Trevor Nunn film of 2004, the second in the Michael Radford film the same year and the third in the 2010 New York production with Al Pacino as Shylock, directed by Daniel Sullivan.

24 In 152, the speaker acknowledges some guilt in his relation to the woman, but that finally seems to consist in having sworn that she is fair.

25 In *Cymbeline*, Posthumus forgives Imogen for the adultery he thinks she has committed but she has actually been faithful to him.

26 This at the time could have been seen as an allusion to both suntan and dark skin associated with Egyptian ancestry, since exposure to the sun was sometimes considered a cause of Egyptians' (and other Africans') blackness. See Hall (1995: 94–7).

27 Most of Plutarch's few mentions can be found in David Quint's edition of *Antony and Cleopatra* (2008: 184, 185, 189).

28 Elizabeth A. Brown points out that Cleopatra follows the advice of her women more often after the defeat at Actium (1999: 137).

29 For the view that the deaths of Charmian and Iras distance the audience from Cleopatra, see Jyotsna G. Singh (2003: 426–7).

30 On literal and figurative brothers in Shakespeare, see Joel Fineman (1980) and Louis Montrose (1981).

31 Dolan discusses violence against servants (by both sexes) in *The Taming of the Shrew* (2008: 122–7). David Evett contrasts the treatments of Shakespeare's master-servant and mistress-servant relationships, especially in *Antony and Cleopatra* (2005: 159–81).

7. Work

1. For further discussion, including references to recent scholarship showing how the separation of spheres was constructed in specific cultures and historical periods, see Susan M. Reverby and Dorothy O. Helly (1987: 1–26).
2. For more critique of Clark and discussion of more recent research, see Laura Gowing (2012: 41–6).
3. See also Korda (2011: Ch. 1).
4. On feminist views, see Maggie O'Neill (2001: 15–41).
5. Helena's role has a context in the historical women healers discussed in M. A. Katritzky (2007) and Bella Mirabella (2005).
6. Many widows and never married women were heads of household in London at the time; see Froide (2005).
7. On service as a stage of life, see Schalkwyk (2008: 22–3).
8. These pages are the source of all the quotations in this paragraph.
9. On other kinds of work that women might do, such as teaching letters or knitting to pauper children, see Diane Willen (1992).
10. The surgeon John Hall, who would later become Shakespeare's son-in-law, noted in 1565 that mummy was being used by London apothecaries (Sugg 2011: 22).
11. Shaping marzipan desserts into letters, as Imogen does with roots, was a skill known to many women beyond the court, as Wendy Wall shows (2016: 146), citing Hugh Plat's popular 1602 cookbook, *Delights for Ladies*.
12. Schalkwyk draws on Peter Laslett and Richard Wall (1972: 57).
13. In addition to Helena's power as a healer, the Countess has power as an educator, see Dowd (2009: 161–71).
14. Howard emphasizes the importance of women's presence in the theatre as paying spectators (1994: 76–9, 90–2).
15. See statistics at VIDA, http://www.vidaweb.org/about-vida/ (accessed 1 March 2017).

16 The Catholic countries of Italy, France and Spain allowed women to act in their public theatres. Germany, like England split with Protestant dominance, did not, until later than England (Katritzky 2007: 262). Protestants sometimes attacked Catholicism as being too theatrical. However, Orgel argues that the English 'took boys for women' on the stage because heterosexuality was considered more dangerous than homoeroticism (1997).

17 However, other polemicists disagreed.

18 The *commedia* performers often improvised as well as following scripts.

19 See for example the Hogarth Shakespeare project, launched 2015, including Anne Tyler's *Vinegar Girl* (2016), and Novy (1999).

REFERENCES

Adamson, S., L. Hunter, L. Magnusson, A. Thompson and K. Wales (eds) (2001), *Reading Shakespeare's Dramatic Language: A Guide*. Arden Shakespeare, London: Bloomsbury.

Adelman, J. (1992), *Suffocating Mothers: Fantasies of Maternal Origin in Shakespeare's Plays, Hamlet to The Tempest*. New York: Routledge.

Adelman, J. (1999), 'Making Defect Perfection: Shakespeare and the One-Sex Model', in V. Comensoli and A. Russell (eds), *Enacting Gender on the Renaissance Stage*, 23–52. Urbana: University of Illinois Press.

Adelman, J. (2003), 'Her Father's Blood: Race, Conversion and Nation in *The Merchant of Venice*', *Representations* 81: 4–30.

Adichie, C. N. (2015), *We Should All Be Feminists*. New York: Anchor.

Amussen, S. (1988), *An Ordered Society: Gender and Class in Early Modern England*. Oxford: Blackwell.

Andresen-Thom, M. (1982), 'Shrew-Taming and Other Rituals of Aggression: Baiting and Bonding on the Stage and in the Wild', *Women's Studies* 9 (2): 121–42.

Bamber, L. (1983), *Comic Women, Tragic Men*. Stanford: Stanford University Press.

Bate, J. (2002 [1995]), 'Introduction', W. Shakespeare, *Titus Andronicus*, J. Bate (ed.). Arden 3, London: Bloomsbury.

Beattie, C. (2007), *Medieval Single Women: The Politics of Social Classification in Late Medieval England*. Oxford: Oxford University Press.

Beauvoir, S. de (1974 [1952]), *The Second Sex*, trans. H. M. Parshley. New York: Vintage.

Belsey, C. (1985a), *The Subject of Tragedy: Identity and Difference in Renaissance Drama*. London: Methuen.

Belsey, C. (1985b), 'Disrupting Sexual Difference: Meaning and Gender in the Comedies', in J. Drakakis (ed.), *Alternative Shakespeares*, 166–90. London: Methuen.

Belsey, C. (1999), *Shakespeare and the Loss of Eden: The Construction of Family Values in Early Modern Culture*. New Brunswick: Rutgers University Press.

Belsey, C. (2014), *Romeo and Juliet: Language and Writing*. Arden Shakespeare, London: Bloomsbury.

Berry, P. (1999), *Shakespeare's Feminine Endings: Disfiguring Death in the Tragedies*. New York: Routledge.

Bliss, L. (2010), 'Introduction', W. Shakespeare, *Coriolanus*, L. Bliss (ed.), updated edn. Cambridge: Cambridge University Press.

Bloom, G. (2007), *Voice in Motion: Staging Gender, Shaping Sound in Early Modern England*. Philadelphia: University of Pennsylvania Press.

Boose, L. (1991), 'Scolding Brides and Bridling Scolds: Taming the Woman's Unruly Member', *Shakespeare Quarterly* 42 (2): 179–213.

Boose, L. (2004), '"Let it be Hid": The Pornographic Aesthetic of Shakespeare's *Othello*', in L. C. Orlin (ed.), *Othello: New Casebooks*, 22–48. New York: Palgrave Macmillan.

Bradley, A. C. (1985 [1904]), *Shakespearean Tragedy*. London: St Martin's.

Bray, A. (1994), 'Homosexuality and the Signs of Male Friendship in Elizabethan England', in J. Goldberg (ed.), *Queering the Renaissance*, 40–62. Durham: Duke University Press.

Brissenden, A. (ed.) (1993), W. Shakespeare, *As You Like It*. Oxford: Clarendon Press.

Brown, E. A. (1999), '"Companion Me with My Mistress": Cleopatra, Elizabeth I, and Their Waiting Women', in S. Frye and K. Robertson (eds), *Maids and Mistresses, Cousins and Queens: Women's Alliances in Early Modern England*, 131–45. Oxford: Oxford University Press.

Brown, P. A. (2003), *Better a Shrew than a Sheep: Women, Drama, and the Culture of Jest in Early Modern England*. Ithaca: Cornell University Press.

Brown, P. A. (2012), '"Cattle of this Color": Boying the Diva in *As You Like It*', *Early Theater* 15 (1): 145–66.

Brown, P. A. and P. Parolin (eds) (2005), *Women Players in England, 1500–1660: Beyond the All-male Stage*. Aldershot: Ashgate.

Butler, J. (1990), *Gender Trouble: Feminism and the Subversion of Identity*. New York: Routledge.

Callaghan, D. (2000a), *Shakespeare without Women: Representing Gender and Race on the Renaissance Stage*. London: Routledge.

Callaghan, D. (ed.) (2000b), *A Feminist Companion to Shakespeare*. Oxford: Blackwell.

Callaghan, D. (2001), 'Looking Well to Linens: Women and Cultural Production in *Othello* and Shakespeare's England', in J. E. Howard and S. C. Shershow (eds), *Marxist Shakespeares*, 53–81. London: Routledge.

Callaghan, D., L. Helms and J. Singh (1994), *The Weyward Sisters: Shakespeare and Feminist Politics*. Oxford: Blackwell.

Cameron, D. (1992), *Feminism and Linguistic Theory*, 2nd edn. New York, Macmillan.

Cameron, D. (2014), 'Language', in C. R. Stimpson and G. Herdt (eds), *Critical Terms for the Study of Gender*, 231–49. Chicago: University of Chicago Press.

Capp, B. (2004), *When Gossips Meet: Women, Family, and Neighborhood in Early Modern England*. Oxford: Oxford University Press.

Carroll, W. C. (2001), 'Description', in S. Adamson, L. Hunter, L. Magnusson, A. Thompson and K. Wales (eds), *Reading Shakespeare's Dramatic Language: A Guide*, 89–101. Arden Shakespeare, London: Bloomsbury.

Chodorow, N. (1978), *The Reproduction of Mothering: Psychoanalysis and the Sociology of Gender*. Berkeley: University of California Press.

Christensen, A. C. (2014), 'Words about Women's Work: The Case of Housewifery in Early Modern England', *Early Modern Studies Journal* 6. Available online: http://www.earlymodernstudiesjournal.org/wp-content/uploads/2014/10/1.-Christensen1.pdf (accessed 8 January 2017).

Cixous, H. (1980 [1976]), 'The Laugh of the Medusa', in E. Marks and I. de Courtivron (eds), *New French Feminisms*, 245–64. Amherst: University of Massachusetts Press.

Cixous, H. (1986), 'Sorties: Out and Out: Attacks/Ways Out/Forays', in H. Cixous and C. Clément, *The Newly Born Woman*, trans. B. Wing, 63–134. Minneapolis: University of Minnesota Press.

Colie, R. (1974), *Shakespeare's Living Art*. Princeton: Princeton University Press.

Cook, C. (1995 [1986]), '"The Sign and Semblance of her Honor": Reading Gender Difference in *Much Ado about Nothing*', in

D. Barker and I. Kamps (eds), *Shakespeare and Gender: A History*, 75–103. London: Verso.

Cooper, H. (2004), *The English Romance in Time: Transforming Motifs from Geoffrey of Monmouth to the Death of Shakespeare*. Oxford: Oxford University Press.

Cott, N. (1986), 'Feminist Theory and Feminist Movements: The Past Before Us', in J. Mitchell and A. Oakley (eds), *What Is Feminism? A Re-examination*, 29–62. New York: Pantheon.

Cox, J. D. and E. Rasmussen (2001), 'Introduction', W. Shakespeare, *3 Henry VI*, J. D. Cox and E. Rasmussen (eds). Arden 3, London: Thompson Learning.

Crawford, J. (2003), 'The Homoerotics of Shakespeare's Elizabethan Comedies', in R. Dutton and J. E. Howard (eds), *A Companion to Shakespeare's Works, Vol. III: The Comedies*, 137–58. Oxford: Blackwell.

Crenshaw, K. (1991), 'Mapping the Margins: Intersectionality, Identity Politics, and Violence against Women of Color', *Stanford Law Review* 43 (6): 1241–99.

Crowther, K. (2010), *Adam and Eve in the Protestant Reformation*. Cambridge: Cambridge University Press.

Dash, I. (1981), *Wooing, Wedding and Power: Women in Shakespeare's Plays*. New York: Columbia University Press.

Detmer, E. (1997), 'Civilizing Subordination: Domestic Violence and *The Taming of the Shrew*', *Shakespeare Quarterly* 48: 273–83.

DiGangi, M. (1997), *The Homoerotics of Early Modern Drama*. Cambridge: Cambridge University Press.

DiGangi, M. (2008), 'An Account of Edward Hall's Watermill Theatre Production by Propeller', in W. Shakespeare, *The Winter's Tale: Texts and Contexts*, M. DiGangi (ed.), 424–7. Boston and New York: Bedford/St. Martin's.

Dolan, F. E. (2008), *Marriage and Violence: The Early Modern Legacy*. Philadelphia: University of Pennsylvania Press.

Dowd, M. M. (2009), *Woman's Work in Early Modern English Literature and Culture*. New York: Palgrave.

Dusinberre, J. (1989), '*King John* and Embarrassing Women', *Shakespeare Survey* 42: 37–52.

Dusinberre, J. (2003 [1975]), *Shakespeare and the Nature of Women*, 3rd edn. New York: Palgrave Macmillan.

Dusinberre, J. (2011), 'Squeaking Cleopatras: Gender and Performance in *Antony and Cleopatra*', in W. Shakespeare, *Antony and Cleopatra*, A. Loomba (ed.), 227–47. Norton Critical Editions, New York: Norton.

Eagleton, T. (1986), *William Shakespeare*. Oxford: Blackwell.

Echols, A. (1989), *Daring to Be Bad: Radical Feminism in American 1967–1975*. Minneapolis: University of Minnesota Press.

Eliot, G. (1981 [1855]), 'Saint-Marc Girardin's *Love in the Drama*', in *A Writer's Notebook, 1854–1879, and Uncollected Writings*, J. Wiesenfarth (ed.). Charlottesville: University Press of Virginia.

Engle, L. (1993), *Shakespearean Pragmatism: Market of his Time*. Chicago: University of Chicago Press.

Erickson, P. (1985), *Patriarchal Structures in Shakespeare's Drama*. Berkeley: University of California Press.

Erickson, P. (2014), 'Race Words in *Othello*', in R. Espinosa and D. Ruiter (eds), *Shakespeare and Immigration*, 159–76. Farnham: Ashgate.

Everett, B. (1970 [1961]), '*Much Ado about Nothing*', in J. L. Calderwood and H. Toliver (eds), *Essays in Shakespearean Criticism*, 273–90. Englewood Cliffs, NJ: Prentice-Hall.

Evett, D. (2005), *Discourses of Service in Shakespeare's England*. New York: Palgrave.

Ewbank, I.-S. (1978), 'Shakespeare's Portrayal of Women: A 1970s View', in D. Bevington and J. L. Halio (eds), *Shakespeare: Pattern of Excelling Nature*, 222–9. Newark: University of Delaware Press.

Fausto-Sterling, A. (2000), *Sexing the Body: Gender Politics and the Construction of Sexuality*. New York: Basic Books.

Ferguson, M., M. Quilligan and N. J. Vickers (eds) (1986), *Rewriting the Renaissance: The Discourses of Sexual Difference in Early Modern Europe*. Chicago: University of Chicago Press.

Fineman, J. (1980), 'Fratricide and Cuckoldry: Shakespeare's Doubles', in M. Schwartz and C. Kahn (eds), *Representing Shakespeare: New Psychoanalytic Essays*, 70–109. Baltimore: Johns Hopkins University Press.

Fletcher, A. (1999), *Gender, Sex, and Subordination in England, 1500–1800*. New Haven: Yale University Press.

French, M. (1981), *Shakespeare's Division of Experience*. New York: Summit.

Friedan, B. (1963), *The Feminine Mystique*. New York: Dell.
Froide, A. M. (2005), *Never Married: Singlewomen in Early Modern England*. Oxford: Oxford University Press.
Gajowski, E. (1992), *The Art of Loving: Female Subjectivity and Male Discursive Traditions in Shakespeare's Tragedies*. Newark: University of Delaware Press; London and Toronto: Associated University Presses.
Gajowski, E. (ed.) (2009), *Presentism, Gender, and Sexuality in Shakespeare*. Houndmills: Palgrave Macmillan.
Gajowski, E. and P. Rackin (eds) (2015), *The Merry Wives of Windsor: New Critical Essays*. London: Routledge.
Garner, S. N. (1981), '*A Midsummer Night's Dream*: "Jack Shall Have Jill; / Nought Shall Go Ill"', *Women's Studies: An Interdisciplinary Journal* 9: 47–63.
Gilligan, C. (1982), *In a Different Voice: Psychological Theory and Women's Development*. Cambridge, MA: Harvard University Press.
Gohlke, M. [Sprengnether] (1980), '"I Wooed Thee with my Sword": Shakespeare's Tragic Paradigms', in C. R. S. Lenz, G. Greene and C. T. Neely (eds), *The Woman's Part: Feminist Criticism of Shakespeare*, 50–70. Urbana: University of Illinois Press.
Gowing, L. (1996), *Domestic Dangers: Women, Words, and Sex in Early Modern London*. Oxford: Oxford University Press.
Gowing, L. (2012), *Gender Relations in Early Modern England*. New York: Pearson.
Graff, E. J. (1999), *What is Marriage For?* Boston: Beacon.
Greenblatt, S. (1988), *Shakespearean Negotiations: The Circulation of Social Energy in Renaissance England*, 66–93. Berkeley: University of California Press.
Greene, G. and C. Kahn (eds) (1985), *Making a Difference: Feminist Literary Criticism*. New York: Methuen.
Greer, G. (1971 [1970]), *The Female Eunuch*. New York: Bantam.
Griffin, S. (1978), *Woman and Nature: The Roaring Inside Her*. New York: Harper and Row.
Hackel, H. B. (2005), *Reading Material in Early Modern England: Print, Gender, and Literacy*. Cambridge: Cambridge University Press.
Hackett, E. and S. Haslanger (eds) (2006), *Theorizing Feminisms: A Reader*. Oxford: Oxford University Press.

Hall, K. F. (1995), *Things of Darkness: Economies of Race and Gender in Early Modern England*. Ithaca: Cornell University Press.

Haller, W. and M. Haller (1942), 'The Puritan Art of Love', *Huntington Library Quarterly* 5: 235–72.

Hankey, J. (ed.) (2005), Othello: *Shakespeare in Production*, 2nd edn. Cambridge: Cambridge University Press.

Harding, D. W. (1969), 'Women's Fantasy of Manhood', *Shakespeare Quarterly* 20: 245–53.

Hartman, M. S. (2004), *The Household and the Making of History: A Subversive View of the Western Past*. Cambridge: Cambridge University Press.

Hendricks, M. and P. Parker (eds) (1994), *Women, 'Race', and Writing in the Early Modern Period*. New York: Routledge.

Herman, V. (1995), *Dramatic Discourse: Dialogue as Interaction in Plays*. New York: Routledge.

Hochschild, A. and A. Machung (1989), *The Second Shift*. New York: Avon.

Hodgdon, B. (1998), *The Shakespeare Trade: Performances and Appropriations*. Philadelphia: University of Pennsylvania Press.

Hodgdon, B. (2010), 'Introduction', W. Shakespeare, *The Taming of the Shrew*, B. Hodgdon (ed.). Arden 3, London: Methuen.

Holderness, G. (1989), *The Taming of the Shrew: Shakespeare in Performance*. New York: Manchester University Press.

Holderness, G. (1991), '"A Woman's War": A Feminist Reading of *Richard II*', in I. Kamps (ed.), *Shakespeare Left and Right*, 167–83. New York: Routledge.

Holinshed, R. (1999 [1587]), 'From *The Chronicles of England, Scotland, and Ireland*', in W. Shakespeare, *Macbeth*, W. C. Carroll (ed.), 135–50. Texts and Contexts, Boston and New York: Bedford/St. Martin's.

Holstun, J. (1988), '"Will You Rend Our Ancient Love Asunder?" Lesbian Elegy in Donne, Marvell, Milton', *English Literary Renaissance* 54 (4): 835–67.

hooks, b. (2000), *Feminism Is for Everybody*. Cambridge, MA: South End Press.

Hopkins, L. (1998), *The Shakespearean Marriage: Merry Wives and Heavy Husbands*. London: Macmillan.

Howard, J. E. (1986), 'The New Historicism in Renaissance Studies', *English Literary Renaissance* 16: 13–43.

Howard, J. E. (1994), *The Stage and Social Struggle in Early Modern England*. New York: Routledge.

Howard, J. E. and P. Rackin (1997), *Engendering a Nation: A Feminist Account of Shakespeare's English Histories*. New York: Routledge.

Huston, J. D. (1981), *Shakespeare's Comedies of Play*. New York: Columbia University Press.

Jacobus, M. (1979), 'The Buried Letter: Feminism and Romanticism in *Villette*', in M. Jacobus (ed.), *Women Writing and Writing about Women*, 42–60. London: Croom Helm.

Jankowski, T. (1992), *Women in Power in the Early Modern Drama*. Urbana: University of Illinois Press.

Jankowski, T. (2000), *Pure Resistance: Queer Virginity in Early Modern English Drama*. Philadelphia: University of Pennsylvania Press.

Jardine, L. (1989 [1983]), *Still Harping on Daughters: Women and Drama in the Age of Shakespeare*, 2nd edn. New York: Columbia University Press.

Jensen, E. (1975), 'The Boy Actors: Plays and Playing', *Research Opportunities in Renaissance Drama* 18: 5–11.

Jones, A. R. (1985), 'Inscribing Femininity: French Theories of the Feminine', in G. Greene and C. Kahn (eds), *Making a Difference: Feminist Literary Criticism*, 80–112. New York: Methuen.

Jones, A. R. (1999). 'Maidservants of London: Sisterhoods of Kinship and Labor', in S. Frye and K. Robertson (eds), *Maids and Mistresses, Cousins and Queens: Women's Alliances in Early Modern England*, 21–32. Oxford: Oxford University Press.

Jordan, C. (1990), *Renaissance Feminism: Literary Texts and Political Models*. Ithaca: Cornell University Press.

Kahn, C. (1981), *Man's Estate: Masculine Identity in Shakespeare*. Berkeley: University of California Press.

Kahn, C. (1986), 'The Absent Mother in *King Lear*', in M. W. Ferguson, M. Quilligan and N. J. Vickers (eds), *Rewriting the Renaissance: The Discourses of Sexual Difference in Early Modern Europe*, 33–49. Chicago: University of Chicago Press.

Kahn, C. (1997), *Roman Shakespeare: Warriors, Wounds, and Women*. New York: Routledge.

Kaplan, C. (1985), 'Pandora's Box: Subjectivity, Class, and Sexuality in Socialist Feminist Criticism', in G. Greene and

C. Kahn (eds), *Making a Difference: Feminist Literary Criticism*, 146–76. New York: Methuen.

Kaplan, M. L. (2007), 'Jessica's Mother: Medieval Constructions of Jewish Race and Gender in *The Merchant of Venice*', *Shakespeare Quarterly* 58: 1–30.

Katritzky, M. A. (2007), *Women, Medicine and Theater 1500–1750*, 135–50. Aldershot: Ashgate.

Kelly, J. (1987), 'Early Feminist Theory and the *Querelle des Femmes* 1400–1789', *Signs* 8 (11): 16–28.

Kiernander, A. (1997), online comment, SHAKSPER: The Global Shakespeare Discussion List, 10 April, Available online: http://shaksper.net (accessed 1 March 2017).

King, Y. (1983). Talk at Columbia University Seminar on Women and Society.

Knights, L. C. (1946), 'How Many Children Had Lady Macbeth?', in L. C. Knights, *Explorations*, 1–39. London: Chatto.

Kolmar, W. K. and F. Bartkowski (eds) (2010), *Feminist Theory: A Reader*, 3rd edn. New York: McGraw-Hill.

Korda, N. (2002), *Shakespeare's Domestic Economies: Gender and Property in Early Modern England*. Philadelphia: University of Pennsylvania Press.

Korda, N. (2011), *Labors Lost: Women's Work and the Early Modern Stage*. Philadelphia: University of Pennsylvania Press.

Kristeva, J. (1981): 'Women's Time', *Signs* 7 (1): 13–35.

Kristeva, J. (1984), *Revolution in Poetic Language*. New York: Columbia University Press.

Kristeva, J. (1987), *Tales of Love*, trans. L. S. Roudiez. New York: Columbia University Press.

Kuhn, M. S. (1977), 'Much Virtue in *If*', *Shakespeare Quarterly* 28: 40–50.

Lakoff, R. (1975), *Language and Woman's Place*. New York: Harper and Row.

Lanyer, A. (1993 [1611]), *Salve Deus Rex Judaeorum*, S. Woods (ed.). New York: Oxford University Press.

Laqueur, T. (1990), *Making Sex: Body and Gender from the Greeks to Freud*. Cambridge, MA: Harvard University Press.

Laroche, R. and J. Munroe (2017), *Shakespeare and Ecofeminist Theory*. Arden Shakespeare and Theory Series, London: Bloomsbury.

Laslett, P. and R. Wall (eds) (1972), *Household and Family in Past Time*. Cambridge: Cambridge University Press.

Lenz, C. R. S., G. Greene and C. T. Neely (eds) (1980), *The Woman's Part: Feminist Criticism of Shakespeare*. Urbana: University of Illinois Press.

Lewis, C. (1997), *Particular Saints*. Newark: University of Delaware Press.

Lewis, C. S. (1958 [1936]), *The Allegory of Love*. Oxford: Oxford University Press.

Lodge, T. (1997 [1590]), *Rosalind*, D. Beecher (ed.). Ottawa: Dovehouse Editions.

Loomba, A. (1989), *Gender, Race, Renaissance Drama*. Manchester: Manchester University Press.

Loomba, A. (2002), *Shakespeare, Race, and Colonialism*. Oxford: Oxford University Press.

Lorde, A. (1984), 'Age, Race, Class and Sex: Women Redefining Difference', in *Sister Outsider: Essays and Speeches*, 114–23. Freedom, CA: Crossing.

Luckyj, C. (2002), *A Moving Rhetoricke: Gender and Silence in Early Modern England*. Manchester: Manchester University Press.

Lull, J. (1999), 'Introduction', W. Shakespeare, *King Richard III*, J. Lull (ed.). Cambridge: Cambridge University Press.

Macfarlane, A. (1986), *Marriage and Love in England: Modes of Reproduction: 1300–1840*. Oxford: Blackwell.

MacKinnon, C. (2006), 'Difference and Dominance: On Sex Discrimination', in E. Hackett and S. Haslanger (eds), *Theorizing Feminisms*, 244–55. Oxford: Oxford University Press.

Magnusson, L. (1999), *Shakespeare and Social Dialogue: Dramatic Language and Elizabethan Letters*. Cambridge: Cambridge University Press.

Magnusson, L. (2001), 'Style, Rhetoric, and Decorum', in S. Adamson, L. Hunter, L. Magnusson, A. Thompson and K. Wales (eds), *Reading Shakespeare's Dramatic Language: A Guide*, 1–30. Arden Shakespeare, London: Bloomsbury.

Maguire, L. (1992), '"Household Kates": Chez Petruchio, Percy, and Plantagenet', in S. P. Cerasano and M. Wynne-Davies (eds), *Gloriana's Face: Women, Public and Private, in the English Renaissance*, 129–65. Detroit: Wayne State University Press.

Maguire, L. (2000), 'Feminist Editing and the Body of the Text', in D. Callaghan (ed.), *A Feminist Companion to Shakespeare*, 59–79. Oxford: Blackwell.

Maguire, L. (2007), *Shakespeare's Names*. Oxford: Oxford University Press.

Marowitz, C. (1978), *The Marowitz Shakespeare*. London: Marion Boyars.

Martin, R. (2001), 'Introduction', W. Shakespeare, *3 Henry VI*, R. Martin (ed.), 83–8. Oxford: Oxford University Press.

Masten, J. (1997), 'Textual Deviance: Ganymede's Hand in *As You Like It*', in M. Garber, P. B. Franklin and R. L. Walkowitz (eds), *Field Work: Sites in Literary and Cultural Studies*. CultureWork, 153–63, New York: Routledge.

McCandless, D. (1990–1) '"Verily Bearing Blood": Pornography, Sexual Love, and the Reclaimed Feminine in *The Winter's Tale*', *Essays in Theatre/Etudes theatrales* 9: 61–81.

McConnell-Ginet, S. (2011), *Gender, Sexuality and Meaning: Linguistic Practice and Politics*. Oxford: Oxford University Press.

McGuire, P. (1985), *Speechless Dialect: Shakespeare's Open Silences*. Berkeley: University of California Press.

McKewin, C. (1980), 'Counsels of Gall and Grace: Intimate Conversations between Women in Shakespeare's Plays', in C. R. S. Lenz, G. Greene and C. T. Neely (eds), *The Woman's Part: Feminist Criticism of Shakespeare*, 117–32. Urbana: University of Illinois Press.

McLuskie, K. (1985), 'The Patriarchal Bard: Feminist Criticism and Shakespeare: *King Lear* and *Measure for Measure*', in J. Dollimore and A. Sinfield (eds), *Political Shakespeare: New Essays in Cultural Materialism*, 88–108. Ithaca: Cornell University Press.

McLuskie, K. (1989), *Renaissance Dramatists*. Hemel Hempstead: Harvester Wheatsheaf.

McNeill, F. (2007), *Poor Women in Shakespeare*. Cambridge: Cambridge University Press.

Metzger, M. J. (1998), '"Now by My Hood, a Gentle and No Jew": Jessica, *The Merchant of Venice*, and the Discourse of Early Modern English Identity', *PMLA* 113: 52–63.

Millett, K. (1970), *Sexual Politics*. New York: Doubleday.

Miner, M. M. (1980), '"Neither Mother, Wife, Nor England's Queen": The Roles of Women in *Richard III*', in C. R. S. Lenz,

G. Greene and C. T. Neely (eds), *The Woman's Part: Feminist Criticism of Shakespeare*, 35–55. Urbana: University of Illinois.

Miner, V. and H. E. Longino (eds) (1987), *Competition: A Feminist Taboo?* New York: Feminist Press of City University of New York.

Mirabella, B. (2005), '"Quacking Delilahs": Female Mountebanks in Early Modern England and Italy', in P. A. Brown and P. Parolin (eds), *Women Players in England, 1500–1660: Beyond the All-male Stage*, 89–105. Aldershot: Ashgate.

Mitchell, J. (1974), *Psychoanalysis and Feminism: Freud, Reich, Laing, and Women*. New York: Pantheon.

Montrose, L. (1981), '"The Place of a Brother" in *As You Like It*: Social Process and Comic Form', *Shakespeare Quarterly* 32: 28–54.

Morrison, T. and R. Traore (2012), *Desdemona*. London: Oberon.

Mulvey, L. (1975), 'Visual Pleasure and Narrative Cinema', *Screen* 16: 6–18.

Mulvey, L. (1979), 'Afterthoughts on "Visual Pleasure and Narrative Cinema" Inspired by *Duel in the Sun*', *Framework* 10: 3–10.

Neely, C. T. (1985), *Broken Nuptials in Shakespeare's Plays*. New Haven: Yale University Press.

Neely, C. T. (1988), 'Constructing the Subject: Feminist Practices and the New Renaissance Discourses', *English Literary Renaissance* 18: 5–18.

Neely, C. T. (1990), 'Shakespeare's Women: Historical Facts and Dramatic Representation', in N. Holland, S. Homan and B. Paris (eds), *Shakespeare's Personality*, 116–34. Berkeley: University of California Press.

Neill, M. (2004), 'Unproper Beds: Race, Adultery, and the Hideous in *Othello*', in W. Shakespeare, *Othello*, E. Pechter (ed.), 306–28. Norton Critical Editions, New York: Norton.

Neill, M. (2006), 'Introduction', W. Shakespeare, *Othello*, M. Neill (ed.). Oxford: Oxford University Press.

Newton, J. L. (1981), *Women, Power and Subversion: Social Strategies in British Fiction 1778–1860*. Athens, GA: University of Georgia Press.

Novy, M. (1984), *Love's Argument: Gender Relations in Shakespeare*. Chapel Hill: University of North Carolina Press.

Novy, M. (ed.) (1993), *Cross-Cultural Performances: Differences in Women's Re-Visions of Shakespeare*. Urbana: University of Illinois Press.

Novy, M. (ed.) (1999), *Transforming Shakespeare: Contemporary Women's Re-Visions in Literature and Performance*. New York: St. Martin's Press.

Novy, M. (2013), *Shakespeare and Outsiders*. Oxford: Oxford University Press.

Okin, S. M. (1989), *Justice, Gender and the Family*. New York: Basic Books.

Oliver, H. J. (1984), 'Introduction', W. Shakespeare, *The Taming of the Shrew*, H. J. Oliver (ed.). New York: Oxford University Press, 1984.

O'Neill, M. (2001), *Prostitution and Feminism: Towards a Politics of Feeling*. Oxford: Blackwell/Polity.

Ong, W. J. (1971), *Rhetoric, Romance and Technology: Studies in the Interaction of Expression and Culture*. Ithaca: Cornell University Press.

Orgel, S. (1997), *Impersonations: The Performance of Gender in Shakespeare's England*. Cambridge: Cambridge University Press.

Orlin, L. C. (1999), 'Three Ways to be Invisible in the Renaissance: Sex, Reputation, and Stitchery', in P. Fumerton and S. Hunt (eds), *Renaissance Culture and the Everyday*, 192–203. Philadelphia: University of Pennsylvania Press.

Oxford English Dictionary (1987), R. W. Burchfield (ed.), compact edn, vol. 3. Supplement, Oxford: Oxford University Press.

Packer, T. (2015), *Women of Will: Following the Feminine in Shakespeare's Plays*. New York: Knopf.

Park, C. C. (1980), 'As We Like It: How a Girl Can Be Smart and Still Popular', in C. R. S. Lenz, G. Greene and C. T. Neely (eds), *The Woman's Part: Feminist Criticism of Shakespeare*, 100–16. Urbana: University of Illinois Press.

Parker, P. (2004), '*Othello* and *Hamlet*: Dilation, Spying and the "Secret Place" of Woman', in W. Shakespeare, *Othello*, E. Pechter (ed.), 329–49. Norton Critical Editions, New York: Norton.

Paster, G. K. (1993), *The Body Embarrassed: Drama and the Disciplines of Shame in Early Modern England*. Ithaca: Cornell University Press.

Pateman, C. (1988), *The Sexual Contract*. Stanford: Stanford University Press.

Pechter, E. (2004), '"Too Much Violence": Murdering Wives in *Othello*', in W. Shakespeare, *Othello*, E. Pechter (ed.), 366–87. Norton Critical Editions, New York: Norton.

Plutarch (1976), 'The Life of Caius Martius Coriolanus', in W. Shakespeare, *Coriolanus*, P. Brockbank (ed.). Arden 2, London: Methuen.

Pollitt, K. (2015 [1992]), 'Are Women Morally Superior to Men?', *Nation*, 23 March. Available online: https://www.thenation.com/article/are-women-morally-superior-men/ (accessed 8 January 2017).

Purkiss, D. (1996), *The Witch in History: Early Modern and Twentieth-Century Representations*. New York: Routledge.

Rabkin, N. (1967), *Shakespeare and the Common Understanding*. New York: Free Press.

Rackin, P. (2005), *Shakespeare and Women*. Oxford: Oxford University Press.

Reed, B. and K. Pollitt (2015), 'Spreading Feminism Far and Wide', *Nation* 300 (14): 56–60.

Reverby, S. M. and D. O. Helly (1987), 'Introduction: Converging on History', in *Gendered Domains: Rethinking Public and Private in Women's History*, 1–26. Ithaca: Cornell University Press.

Rich, A. (1986 [1980]), 'Compulsory Heterosexuality and Lesbian Existence', in *Blood, Bread, and Poetry: Selected Prose 1979–1986*, 23–75. New York: Norton.

Roberts, J. A. (2002), 'Sex and the Female Tragic Hero', in N. C. Liebler (ed.), *The Female Tragic Hero in English Renaissance Drama*, 199–215. New York: Palgrave.

Rose, M. B. (1988), *The Expense of Spirit: Love and Sexuality in English Renaissance Drama*. Ithaca: Cornell University Press.

Rose, M. B. (1991), 'Where are the Mothers in Shakespeare? Options for Gender Representation in the English Renaissance', *Shakespeare Quarterly* 42: 291–314.

Rougemont, D. de (1956 [1940]), *Love in the Western World*. New York: Fawcett.

Rowbotham, S. (1973), *Women's Consciousness, Man's World*. New York: Pelican.

Ruddick, S. (1989), *Maternal Thinking: Toward a Politics of Peace*. New York: Ballantine.

Rutter, C. (1988), *Clamorous Voices: Shakespeare's Women Today*. London: Women's Press.

Rutter, C. (2001), *Enter the Body: Women and Representation on Shakespeare's Stage*. London: Routledge.

Sale, C. (2011), 'The Problem with Rosalind, or, Phebe's Leathern Hand', seminar paper, Shakespeare and the New Feminisms, Shakespeare Association of America, 11 April.

Sandberg, S. (2013), *Lean In: Women, Work, and the Will to Lead*. New York: Knopf.

Schalkwyk, D. (2008), *Shakespeare, Love and Service*. Cambridge: Cambridge University Press.

Schofield, R. and E. A. Wrigley (1979), 'Infant and Child Mortality in England in the Late Tudor and Early Stuart Period', in C. Webster (ed.), *Health, Medicine and Mortality in the Sixteenth Century*. Cambridge: Cambridge University Press.

Schulz, M. (1975), 'The Semantic Derogation of Woman', in B. Thorne and N. Henley (eds), *Language and Sex: Difference and Dominance*, 64–75. Rowley, MA: Newbury House Publishers.

Scott, J. W. (1988), 'Deconstructing Equality-Versus-Difference: Or, the Uses of Post-Structuralist Theory for Feminism', *Feminist Studies* 14 (1): 32–50.

Sedgwick, E. K. (2003), *Touching Feeling: Affect, Performativity, Pedagogy*, Durham: Duke University Press.

Shakespeare, W. (1980), *Romeo and Juliet*, B. Gibbons (ed.). Arden 2, London: Methuen.

Shakespeare, W. (1993), *All's Well that Ends Well*, S. Snyder (ed.). Oxford: Clarendon.

Shakespeare, W. (1997), *Othello*, E. A. J. Honigmann (ed.). Arden 3, London: Thomson Learning.

Shakespeare, W. (2011 [1998]), *Arden Shakespeare Complete Works*, R. Proudfoot, A. Thompson and D. S. Kastan (eds), rev. edn. London: Arden Shakespeare.

Shakespeare, W. (2001), *3 Henry VI*, J. D. Cox and E. Rasmussen (eds). Arden 3, London: Thomson Learning.

Shakespeare, W. (2004), *Othello*, E. Pechter (ed.). Norton Critical Editions, New York: Norton.

Shakespeare, W. (2006a), *As You Like It,* J. Dusinberre (ed.). Arden 3, London: Thomson Learning.

Shakespeare, W. (2006b), *Much Ado about Nothing*, C. McEachern (ed.). Arden 3, London: Thomson Learning.

Shakespeare, W. (2008), *Antony and Cleopatra*, D. Quint (ed.). New York: Longman.

Shakespeare, W. (2010), *The Taming of the Shrew*, B. Hodgdon (ed.). Arden 3, London: Methuen.

Shanley, M. L. (ed.) (2004), *Just Marriage*. Oxford: Oxford University Press.

Shannon, L. (2002), *Sovereign Amity: Figures of Friendship in Shakespearean Contexts*. Chicago: University of Chicago Press.

Shapiro, M. (1994), *Gender in Play on the Shakespearean Stage: Boy Heroines and Female Pages*. Ann Arbor: University of Michigan Press.

Siemon, J. R. (2004), '"Nay, That's Not Next": *Othello* [5.2] in Performance, 1760–1900', in W. Shakespeare, *Othello*, E. Pechter (ed.), 289–305. Norton Critical Editions, New York: Norton.

Siemon, J. R. (2009), 'Introduction', W. Shakespeare, *Richard III*, J. R. Siemon (ed.). Arden 3, London: Bloomsbury.

Singh, J. (1994), 'The Interventions of History: Narratives of Sexuality', in D. Callaghan, L. Helms and J. Singh, *The Weyward Sisters: Shakespeare and Feminist Politics*, 7–58. Oxford: Blackwell.

Singh, J. G. (2003), 'The Politics of Empathy in *Antony and Cleopatra*: A View from Below', in R. Dutton and J. E. Howard (eds), *A Companion to Shakespeare's Works: Vol. I: The Tragedies*, 411–29. Oxford: Blackwell.

Slights, C. W. (1993), *Shakespeare's Comic Commonwealths*. Toronto: University of Toronto Press.

Slights, J. (2001), 'Rape and the Romanticization of Shakespeare's Miranda', *Studies in English Literature* 41 (2): 357–79.

Smith, B. (1995), *Homosexual Desire in Shakespeare's England*. Chicago: University of Chicago Press.

Smith, H. (1591), *A Preparative to Marriage*. London: n.p.

Stallybrass, P. (1986), 'Patriarchal Territories: The Body Enclosed', in M. W. Ferguson, M. Quilligan and N. J. Vickers (eds), *Rewriting the Renaissance: The Discourses of Sexual Difference in Early Modern Europe*, 123–42. Chicago: University of Chicago Press.

Stanton, K. (2000), '"Made to write 'whore' upon?": Male and Female Use of the Word "Whore" in Shakespeare's Canon', in D. Callaghan (ed.), *A Feminist Companion to Shakespeare*, 80–102. Oxford: Blackwell.

Stewart, A. (2008), *Shakespeare's Letters*. Oxford: Oxford University Press.

Stimpson, C. R. (1974), 'The Androgyne and the Homosexual', *Women's Studies: An Interdisciplinary Journal* 2: 237–47.

Stimpson, C. R. and G. Herdt (eds) (2014), *Critical Terms for the Study of Gender*. Chicago: University of Chicago Press.

Stone, L. (1967), *The Crisis of the Aristocracy 1558–1641*, abridged edn. Oxford: Oxford University Press.

Sugg, R. (2011), *Mummies, Cannibals and Vampires: The History of Corpse Medicine from the Renaissance to the Victorians*. London: Routledge.

Suzuki, M. (2000), 'Gender, Class, and the Ideology of Comic Form: *Much Ado about Nothing* and *Twelfth Night*', in D. Callaghan (ed.), *A Feminist Companion to Shakespeare*, 121–43. Oxford: Blackwell.

Thomas, K. (1959), 'The Double Standard', *Journal of the History of Ideas* 20: 195–216.

Thompson, A. (1984), 'Introduction to *The Taming of the Shrew*', W. Shakespeare, *The Taming of the Shrew*, A. Thompson (ed.). Cambridge: Cambridge University Press.

Thompson, A. (ed.) (2006), *Colorblind Shakespeare: New Perspectives on the Power of Performance*. New York: Routledge

Thompson, A. and S. Roberts (eds) (1997), *Women Reading Shakespeare 1660–1900*. New York: Manchester University Press.

Tilney, E. (1992 [1568]), *The Flower of Friendship*, V. Wayne (ed.). Ithaca: Cornell University Press.

Traub, V. (1992), *Desire and Anxiety: Circulations of Sexuality in Shakespearean Drama*. London: Routledge.

Traub, V. (2002), *The Renaissance of Lesbianism in Seventeenth-Century England*. Cambridge: Cambridge University Press.

Underdown, D. (1985), 'The Taming of the Scold: The Enforcement of Patriarchal Authority in Early Modern England', in A. Fletcher and J. Stevenson (eds), *Order and Disorder in Early Modern England*, 116–36. Cambridge: Cambridge University Press.

Vickers, N. (1981), 'Diana Described: Scattered Women and Scattered Rhyme', *Critical Inquiry* 8: 265–79.

Wales, K. (2001), 'Varieties and Variations', in S. Adamson, L. Hunter, L. Magnusson, A. Thompson and K. Wales (eds), *Reading Shakespeare's Dramatic Language: A Guide*, 192–209. Arden Shakespeare: London: Bloomsbury.

Wall, W. (2002), *Staging Domesticity: Household Work and English Identity in Early Modern Drama*. Cambridge: Cambridge University Press.

Wall, W. (2016), *Recipes for Thought: Knowledge and Taste in the Early Modern Kitchen*. Philadelphia: University of Pennsylvania Press.

Watson, B. B. (1975 [1927]), 'On Power and the Literary Text', *Signs* 1 (1): 111–18.

Wayne, V. (1991), 'Historical Differences: Misogyny and *Othello*', in V. Wayne (ed.), *The Matter of Difference: Materialist Feminist Criticism of Shakespeare*, 153–80. Ithaca: Cornell University Press.

Wayne, V. (1998), 'The Sexual Politics of Textual Transmission', in L. E. Maguire and T. L. Berger (eds), *Textual Formations and Reformations*, 179–210. Newark: University of Delaware Press.

Willen, D. (1992), 'Women in the Public Sphere in Early Modern England: The Case of the Working Poor', in D. O. Helly and S. M. Reverby (eds), *Gendered Domains: Rethinking Public and Private in Women's History*, 183–98. Ithaca: Cornell University Press.

Williams, R. (1977), *Marxism and Literature*. Oxford: Oxford University Press.

Willis, D. (1995), *Malevolent Nurture: Witch-Hunting and Maternal Power in Early Modern England*. Ithaca: Cornell University Press.

Wimsatt, W. K. (1963), 'The Morality of *Antony and Cleopatra*', in L. Lerner (ed.), *Shakespeare's Tragedies*. Harmondsworth: Penguin.

Wofford, S. (1994), '"To You I Give Myself, for I Am Yours": Erotic Performance and Theatrical Performatives', in R. McDonald (ed.), *Shakespeare Reread: The Texts in New Contexts*, 147–75. Ithaca: Cornell University Press.

Wollstonecraft, M. (1995 [1792]), *A Vindication of the Rights of Woman*, A. Tauchert (ed.). London: J. W. Dent.

Woodbridge, L. (1984), *Women and the English Renaissance: Literature and the Nature of Womankind 1540–1620*. Urbana: University of Illinois Press.

Woodford, D. (2007), 'Nursing and Influence in *Pandosto* and *The Winter's Tale*', in K. R. McPherson and K. M. Moncrief (eds), *Performing Maternity in Early Modern England*. Studies in Performance and Early Modern Drama, New York: Routledge.

Woolf, V. (1989 [1929]), *A Room of One's Own*. New York: Harcourt.

Wrightson, K. (1982), *English Society 1580–1680*. London: Hutchinson.

Yachnin, P. (2001), 'Magical Properties', in A. B. Dawson and P. Yachnin, *The Culture of Playgoing in Shakespeare's England: A Collaborative Debate*, 111–30. Cambridge: Cambridge University Press.

Young, I. (2006), 'Humanism, Gynocentrism, and Feminist Politics', in E. Hackett and S. Haslanger (eds), *Theorizing Feminisms: A Reader*, 174–86. Oxford: Oxford University Press.

INDEX

Adelman, Janet 16, 81, 83, 88, 89–90, 92–5, 127, 169 n.11
Adichie, Chimamanda Agozi 162 nn.2, 5
adoption 76, 82, 83
adultery 35, 36, 37, 70–1, 72
  and acceptable desire 47–50
  in *Cym* 96–7
  infrequent in Shakespeare 47
  jokes in drama 69
  in *KJ* 86, 169 n.10
Agrippa, H. C. 24–5, 164 n.9
Alexander, Bill (director) 110–11
All's Well That Ends Well 5
  Countess 76
  as educator 174 n.13
  Helen as healer 104, 147, 174 n.5
  mothers and fantasies of mothers in 82–3
  source 82
  women's power in 104, 155
Amazon 45, 85
Amussen, Susan 172 n.13
Antony and Cleopatra 23
  Antony 95, 166 n.14
  breaks down dichotomy between good and bad women 68
  Cleopatra 18, 33, 34, 104, 112
  gender fluidity in 8
  Iras and Charmian 142–3, 173 nn.27–9, 31
  maternal sexuality 95
  opposition between Cleopatra and Octavia 122–3, 142
  partnership and definition of marriage 67–8, 95
  political and theatrical power 147
  revises associations of dark skin 141, 173 n.26
  Rome vs. Egypt 141–2
  sources of 68, 142, 147, 173 n.27
As You Like It 32
  agency in marriage 54, 170 n.7
  Audrey 29
  boy actor in epilogue 54
  Celia–Rosalind relationship 46, 74, 123–4
  and *commedia dell'arte* 157
  gender ambiguity in text 115–16
  language censored 114–15
  patriarchal structures 54
  Phebe 41–5, 46

Rosalind/Ganymede 18–19, 28, 32, 38, 44, 50, 56–7
Ashcroft, Peggy (performer) 85
audience response 159
    to boy actors 41, 44
    to Desdemona 112, 117
    to disguise 39–40
    divided 113
    to eloquence 105
    to end of *AC* 95
    to end of *TS* 57–9
    to mothers in Shakespeare 100
    to power of female characters 159
    by women in audience 174 n.14
Augustine 103, 170 n.1

Bamber, Linda: *Comic Women, Tragic Men* 6–7
Barton, John (RSC director) 6
Bate, Jonathan 113
Beauvoir, Simone de: *The Second Sex* 2
Belsey, Catherine 7, 9, 10, 37, 40, 54, 165 n.4, 166 n.3 167 n.21
Berger, Harry 40
Berry, Philippa 129–30
bias against women 1, 11, 66, 69, 107
    in language 65
    protested against 35
Bible 17, 25, 29, 52, 164 n.10
biology
    and mother's authority 84–5
    one-sex model 15–16
    and women's subordination 17

blackness, darkness in women 10, 137–40
    and casting 140, 141, 172 n.18
    Cleopatra on 141
    related to suntan and class 134, 139, 140, 173 n.26
    and ugliness 139
blazon 43, 104
Bloom, Gina 105, 110, 111, 170 n.12
body, women associated with 34, 71, 76, 77
Bogdanov, Michael (director) 59
Boose, Lynda 58, 112, 163 n.11, 171 n.16
boy actors of women 6, 11, 15–17, 25, 42, 44, 54, 78, 116, 155, 157, 159, 165 n.11, 175 n.16
    limited number in company 79
Bradley, A. C. 88
Branagh, Kenneth (actor/director) 132
Brissenden, Alan 115
Brooke, Nicholas 35, 165 n.4
brothers 173 n.30 *see also* friendship between men
Brown, Elizabeth 173 n.28
Brown, Pamela A. 103, 157
    and Peter Parolin 155
Bunker, Archie (TV character) 35
Butler, Judith 18

Callaghan, Dympna 15, 104, 153
Cameron, Deborah 103

capitalism 145
Capp, Bernard 53
Carroll, William 113
Castiglione 24, 164 n.9
Catholic tradition 34, 36, 105, 165 n.1, 168 n.6, 175 n.16 *see also* Christian tradition
Ceres (mythological figure) 94
Chodorow, Nancy 75, 121, 171 n.1
Christensen, Ann 146
Christian tradition 52, 156, 173 n.21 *see also* Augustine
Cixous, Hélène 8, 9, 23, 77
Clark, Alice 145, 174 n.2
class 9, 29, 42, 88, 121–3, 155, 157–8
  between women of different households 133–7
  maidservant–mistress relations 130–3, 135–6, 142–3, 149–55, 172 n.13, 173 n.31
  and sexual morality 134–7, 146–8
  and speech 106–7
Colie, Rosalie 165 n.9
colour, women of 141, 142
  casting 10, 172 n.18
  see also fairness, darkness
Comedy of Errors, The
  Courtesan 148
  division of spheres 149
  on double standard 71
  kitchen-maid 154, 158
  on male privilege 29
  maternal power of Abbess 81
  mother added to source 80–1
  relationship between sisters 128
commedia dell'arte 155, 175 n.18
  actresses as model for Shakespeare's women 157
companionship, partnership
  in marriage 17, 21, 52, 53–4, 61, 63, 64, 133
  in marriage sermons 19, 34, 61, 166 n.8
competition and women 109, 121–3, 128, 129, 130, 134, 141–2
constructivism 3, 39
Cook, Carol 8, 20
cooking 154–5
Cooper, Helen 33, 165 n.5
co-operation by women 110, 121–2, 124–7
Coriolanus 90–3, 123, 130
  celebrity 155
  Virgilia 91–2
  Volumnia 91–3, 169 nn.16–18
  Young Marcus, 92
Cott, Nancy 13
courtesan 136, 148
Cox, John D. and Eric Rasmussen 168 n.9
Crawford, Julie 46, 124, 165 n.13
Crenshaw, Kimberlé 121–2
cultural materialism 9 *see also* materialist feminism
cursing, women's 22, 85, 110, 111 *see also* prophets, women as

custom 1, 62, 164 n.13 *see also* constructivism
Cymbeline 23, 69
  disguise 96, 154
  Imogen's cooking skills 154
  Posthumus 70, 96, 173 n.25
  wicked stepmother 97

Dash, Irene 146, 170 n.10
daughters
  and fathers 27, 53–4, 65, 78, 93–4, 97, 113, 168 n.4
  and mothers 37, 76–8, 82, 83–4, 94, 97–8, 99–100, 168 n.7
deception
  associated with women 28
  believed by men 28, 96
  practiced by Maria in *TN* 133
  practiced by men 28, 96
  practiced by Paulina in *WT* 97
  practiced by women competing 128–9
  self-deception 35
  see also disguise
Dench, Judi (performer) 92
Derrida, Jacques 7, 163 n.8
desire
  adulterous 32, 47–9
  and disguise 38–40
  giving women power 36
  same-sex 11, 41
  sport or sincere passion 49–50
Detmer, Emily 58, 166 n.6
difference feminism, cultural feminism 3–4, 14, 20, 28, 76–7, 158, 162 nn.3, 4, 167 n.20 *see also* essentialism
DiGangi, Mario 15
Dionisotti, Paola (performer) 59
disguise
  of desire 39–40, 42–3
  masculine 11, 14, 18–19, 26–7, 28, 38, 96, 131, 132, 154, 158
  promoting education and companionship 39
Dolan, Frances 51, 52, 166 n.17, 173 n.31
domestic *see* household, public vs. private
Donmar Warehouse 163 n.9
double standard 69–70
  causes of 71
  critiqued 70–1, 72, 136, 168 n.8
Dowd, Michelle 150
Dryden, John 115, 141
Dusinberre, Juliet 5, 39, 51, 52, 85, 111, 141, 165 n.11

Echols, Alice 162 n.3
editing Shakespeare
  feminist editing 11, 171 n.15
  removing 'improper' lines from women 25–6, 105–6, 114–15
  removing possible gender ambiguity 115–18
educators, women as 39, 174 nn.9, 13
Egypt, Egyptian ancestry and colour, values 141–3, 173 n.26
Eliot, George (novelist) 31

Elizabeth I 34, 147
empathy, associated with women 121, 143 *see also* sympathy
Engle, Lars 108
Ephesus 172 n.11
equality feminism 1, 11, 14, 16, 17, 25, 39
  combining with difference feminism 5, 167 n.1
  liberal vs. materialist 4
  see also humanism
Erickson, Peter 7, 23, 51, 54, 58, 95, 154, 172 n.16
essentialism 4, 164 n.13
Everett, Barbara 19–20, 164 n.8
Evett, David 173 n.31
Ewbank, Inga-Stina 104

fairness, whiteness 10, 20, 64, 134, 137–40, 173 nn.21, 24
fairy-tale-like wicked women
  Bawd in *Per* 135
  Queen in *Cym* 97
fantasy
  evil mother 96–7, 169 n.14
  female power after marriage 5
  forgiveness 99
  image of Hermione 97
  male nurture 9
  male parthenogenesis 96
  maternal care 93–4, 101
  TS ending presented as 59
  of women 6, 9
fathers *see* daughters, and fathers
Fausto-Sterling, Anne 162 n.4

feminism, definitions of 1, 162 n.2
  diversity of 157–8
  liberal 2–4
  materialist 3–5
  psychoanalytic 3–4
  see also difference feminism; equality feminism; feminist theory
feminist activism, history of 2–3
  current issues 4
  work 145
  see also under films; housework; intersectionality; language; marriage; pornography; prostitution
feminist Shakespeare criticism, varieties of 5–12, 105, 157–9
feminist theory, development of and contrasts within 1–5, 7–9, 10–12, 157–8, 159 *see also* difference feminism; equality feminism; humanism; essentialism; gynocentric feminism; materialist feminism; psychoanalytic feminism
films 132, 171 n.13, 172 nn.8, 14, 18, 173 n.3
  male gaze 112, 171 n.13
fool 20, 164 n.8
Fletcher, Anthony 53
Fletcher, John: *Woman's Prize or The Tamer Tamed, The* 57–8

freedom for women 19, 24, 29, 35, 36, 38–9, 40, 50, 54, 98
Freud, Sigmund 3, 8, 36
Friedan, Betty: *Feminine Mystique, The* 2
friendship between men 39, 99, 144, 171 n.3
   competing with marriage 65–6, 73–4, 123
friendship between women 40–1, 97–8, 123–7, 142–3
   competing with love for men 45, 73, 123–4
   set in past or surviving marriage 46, 124
Froide, Ann M. 74, 174 n.6

Gajowski, Evelyn 163 n.12, 165 n.10, 166 n.14, 167 n.15, 169 n.19
Galen *see* Laqueur
Ganymede (mythological) 43
Garner, Shirley N. 172 n.7
Garrick, David 115
gender
   critiques of 162 nn.2–5
   deconstruction of 18, 23–30, 116
   generalizations about 14–15
   metaphors of 13, 14, 21
   as performance 18
   see also polarization
gestures
   end of MM productions 117
   end of *TS* productions 116
   in *Oth* 117
   in *WT* text and production 99

Gilligan, Carol: *In a Different Voice* 14, 121
Globe Theatre 147, 155
Gohlke [Sprengnether], Madelon 6, 75
Gower, John: *Apollonius of Tyre* 81
Gowing, Laura 86, 174 n.2
Greenblatt, Stephen 9, 15, 40
Greene, Robert: *Pandosto, or the Triumph of Time* 97–8
Greer, Germaine: *Female Eunuch, The* 3, 39
Griffin, Susan: *Women and Nature* 3, 14
gynocentric feminism 86, 110, 162 n.4 *see also* difference feminism

Hack, Keith (director) 117
Hackel, Heidi 106
Haec Vir 164 n.13
Hall, Edward (director) 99
Hall, John (surgeon) 174 n.10
Hall, Kim 10, 137, 139, 173 n.26
Haller, William and Malleville 52
Hamlet 26
   Gertrude 26, 27
   language 107, 170 n.5
   Ophelia 27
   relation between Gertrude and Ophelia 126
Harding, D. W. 169 n.18
Hartman, Mary 52–3
healers, women 104–5, 147, 174 n.5
Helen of Troy 172 n.11

Hendricks, Margot 10
Henry IV, Part 1
　all-female production 8
　contrast of marriages in 61
Henry IV, Part 2
　class 133
　Doll Tearsheet 148
　Lady Percy 61
Henry V
　Isabel 62–3
　Katherine and Alice 130
　marriage negotiations 61–3
　TS comparisons 61–2
Henry VI, Parts 1, 2 and 3 171 n.14
　Joan of Arc 147
　Margaret 48–9, 84–5, 114, 134, 147, 168 n.9
Henry VIII
　Bullen, Anne 49
　Katherine 99–100, 109, 152
　prophecy about Elizabeth 147
　sewing 152
Herzog, Don 53
heterosexuality
　assumption of 44
　compulsory 8, 31, 41
Hodgdon, Barbara 11, 166 n.7
Hogarth Shakespeare Project 175 n.19
Holderness, Graham 59–60, 165 n.8
Holinshed: *Chronicles* 88, 127
Holstun, James 46
homoerotic desire 11, 15, 31, 32, 41–7, 175 n.16
　circulating among characters 45, 124
　merging with heterosexual desire 47
hooks, bell 162 nn.2, 5
Hopkins, Lisa 51, 61
household, housework 145–6, 149–55
　justice in 72, 167 n.18
Howard, Jean 9, 16, 17, 39, 174 n.14
　and Phyllis Rackin 48, 60, 110, 147
humanism
　and classical knowledge 166 n.6
　and equality feminism 14, 110, 162 n.4
Huston, Dennis 132

imitation
　maidservants, of mistresses 131–3, 142–3
　women's, of masculine aggression 20–2
India 11, 167 n.19
infant mortality 88, 169 n.13
intersectionality 10, 121–3, 131–2, 134, 136–7, 144
Irigaray, Luce 8, 14
Italy 35, 155, 175 n.16

Jacobus, Mary 164 n.1
Jameson, Anna 91
Jankowski, Theodora 146, 147, 169 n.17
Jardine, Lisa 6, 15, 17, 44, 51
jealousy, unwarranted 65, 67, 68–71, 95, 96–8, 131–2, 135–6
Jensen, Ejner 15

Jews, gender and assimilation 139–40, 144, 173 n.22
Jones, Ann Rosalind 7–8, 172 n.12
Jordan, Constance 162 n.1
Julius Caesar, marital companionship vs. male-dominated society 22–3, 63–4

Kahn, Coppélia 6, 9, 37, 92, 93
Kaplan, Cora 164 n.1
Kaplan, M. Lindsay 173 n.21
Katritzky, M. A. 174 n.5, 175 n.16
Kelly, Joan 1
Kiernander, Adrian 99
King John
  Constance and Eleanor 85–7, 111, 170 n.12
  Lady Faulconbridge 49, 86
King Lear 9
  adultery 47, 48–9
  competition between Goneril and Regan 128
  fantasies of good and bad maternal care 93–4
King Leir (source) 93
kitchen-maids 154–5
Klein, Melanie 36
Knights, L. C. 88
Korda, Natasha 11, 58, 145–6, 152, 155–7, 174 n.3
Kristeva, Julia 8, 9, 36–7, 48, 127
Kuhn, Moira 116
Kyle, Barry (director) 111, 117

Lacan, Jacques 7–8, 36, 37, 167 n.21
Lakoff, Robin 108
language
  ambiguous relation to women's power 108–11
  restricting women's behavior 104
  restricting women's language 103, 114, 118
  women's about men they love 34
  women's, about sex, cut by directors and editors 26, 33, 114–15
  'women's language' strategic in relation to social context 108–9
  women's resisting objectification 112–13
Lanyer, Aemilia 1, 29
Laqueur, Thomas 15–16
Laroche, Rebecca and Jennifer Munroe 11
Latin 106, 168 n.6, 170 n.4
laundry 153–4, 156, 157
Lenz, Carolyn Ruth Swift Lenz, Gayle Greene and Carol Thomas Neely 163 n.7
Lewis, C. S. 35
Lewis, Cynthia 95, 135
life cycle, categories of women, 103, 151, 170 n.1
  service as stage of cyle, 149–50, 172 n.12, 174 n.7
likeness vs. differences of women and men, 3
  of Shakespeare's women to men 13–17, 18–30

limitations on women 13,
    protest against 14, 22,
    112
  see also double standard
literacy and gender 106, 133,
    150, 170 nn.3, 4
Lodge, T.: *Rosalynde* 80, 116,
    123, 163 n.5, 170 n.7
Loomba, Ania 10, 141, 167
    n.19
Lorde, Audre 121
Love's Labour's Lost 155
    Berowne's ambivalence
    about female blackness
    138
Luckyj, Christina 117
Lull, Janis 111

Macbeth 66
  association of women and
    evil debated 89–90
  child's death imagined 87–8,
    169 n.12
  Lady Macbeth 17–18, 21,
    66, 76
  popular culture 90
  relationship to Lady
    Macduff 89
  Witches, deconstructive,
    psychoanalytic and class
    approaches 126–7
Macfarlane, Alan 52
McConnell-Ginet, Sally 108
McEachern, Claire 21, 166
    n.5
McGuire, Philip 117
McKewin, Carole 122
McLuskie, Kathleen 6, 10, 16
McNeill, Fiona 151–2
madness 27

and Ophelia's speech style
    107, 170 n.5
Magnusson, Lynne 106, 107,
    109
Maguire, Laurie 11, 171 n.15,
    172 nn.11, 19
maidservants, companions
    130–3, 135–6, 142–3,
    149–51, 172 n.12
male domination 3, 6, 14, 17,
    29, 58, 63, 65, 90, 163
    n.4
Marlowe, Christopher 41
Marowitz, Charles (director) 59
Martin, Randall 85
Mary, mother of Jesus 34, 85,
    94, 168 n.9
Mary I, Queen of England 100,
    168 n.6
marriage
  and bonds between men
    52, 54
  and bonds between women
    124
  dynastic in history plays 60
  economics of 34, 52, 152
  historically closer to equal
    in England 52–3
  husband's power over wife's
    emotions 52
  idealization of 73, 79
  inequities in 72
  inherent inequality 52, 72,
    167 n.20
  opposed to passion 36, 73
  and parental authority 35,
    52, 53
  permanence and
    exclusiveness critiqued
    73

prizes for men 32–3
as punishment 56
same-sex 73–4
scarcity and violence 52, 78
several kinds contrasted 53
social glue 51, 56
social pressure for 19, 31, 40, 57
tensions dramatized 53, 73
unhappy 166 nn.5–6
women's choice in 5
see also compulsory heterosexuality
Marx, Karl 3
Masten, Jeff 116
materialist feminism 2–3, 4, 5, 110, 126–7, 145, 158, 164 n.1
McConnell-Ginet, Sally 108
McEachern, Claire 21, 166 n.5
McGuire, Philip 117
McLuskie, Kathleen 6, 10, 16
McNeill, Fiona 151–2
Measure for Measure
double standard 71
Isabella's eloquence 105
late twentieth-century stagings of end 117
marriages 55–6
Mistress Overdone 133, 148, 158
Medea 100
men as maternal 76, 86, 95, 97
and maternal language 100
Mendes, Sam (director) 111
Merchant of Venice, The 32
Jessica 38, 140, 173 n.23
Portia 18, 32, 54, 71, 104, 108, 144, 146–7

mercy, as feminine 21–2 *see also* empathy; sympathy
Merry Wives of Windsor, The 69–70
class lines somewhat porous 134–5
friendship defeats jealousy 124
household management 145–6, 152–3
imperfect motherhood 81
laundry and men's shame 153–4
Quickly's work 150–1
women's financial power 70
women's language outside aristocracy 106–7
Metzger, Mary Janelle 173 n.22
Middleton, Thomas
Chaste Maid in Cheapside, A 168 n.5
Witch of Edmonton, The 127
Midsummer Night's Dream, A 5
adulterous desire 47
desire and agency 36
women's colour in 138, 172 n.18
women's friendships and conflicts 46, 126, 172 n.7
militarism 22, 63, 91–2
Millett, Kate: *Sexual Politics* 3
Mirabella, Bella 174 n.7
misogyny 35, 171 n.15 *see also* bias against women
Mitchell, Juliet: *Psychoanalysis and Feminism* 3
Montrose, Louis 2, 54, 173 n.30

Morrison, Toni: *Desdemona* 119
mothers 158
   absent vs. present 80, 93–4, 98, 100
   added to sources 80, 81, 82
   adoptive vs. biological 76
   agency 98
   biology and authority 92
   blamed 96, 127
   bliss 37, 169 n.19
   dangerous 100, 101
   difference vs. equality feminism on 76–7
   have lives outside motherhood 100
   in literary tradition 101
   men fleeing mother's influence 83–4, 92–3, 96
   power 81, 102
   pregnant 97
   Roman and Spartan 167 n.16
   self-sacrifice 77, 79, 94
   sentimental image 101
   and sons 100
   unease about maternal sexuality 81, 96, 99
   vindicated 96
   violent 85–6, 88–9, 90–1
   witty 97
mother, the (name given to hysteria-like disease in early modern England) 93
mourning, women's power in 61, 84–5, 109–10
Much Ado About Nothing 57, 68–9, 166 n.5
   Beatrice and Benedick 19–21, 39–40
   Claudio and Hero 20–1
   critique of male dominance 29
   Don Pedro 40
   Friar 29
   Innogen 167–7 n.3
   Margaret's imitation of Hero and Beatrice 131–2
Mulvey, Laura 171 n.13
mummy (medicinal liquid) 153, 174 n.10

Neely, Carol Thomas 7, 68, 83, 95, 97, 98, 125, 126, 167 nn.2, 15, 168 n.8, 170 n.5
Neill, Michael 112, 136
new historicism 9–10
Newman, Karen 10
Newton, Judith Lowder 164 n.1
Novy, Marianne 163 n.3, 166 n.12
Nunn, Trevor (director) 172 n.14, 173 n.23
nursing (of children) 87–8, 91, 95, 169 n.15

Ong, Walter J. 170 n.4
Orgel, Stephen 44, 163 n.4, 175 n.16
Orlin, Lena Cowen 152
Othello 49–50, 77, 117, 118, 137, 166 nn.11, 12
   Bianca critiques scorn of her morality 136
   Desdemona's speeches 35, 106, 112, 113, 171 n.17

destruction of partnership in marriage 64
handkerchief 152–3
household management 145–6
Iago 35
idealized love part of polarized attitude to women 65
'Let husbands know' speech 24–6, 49–50, 70–1
re-imagined by Toni Morrison 119
relationship between Desdemona and Emilia 107, 135–6, 172 n.14
sources of 35
outsider, othering 38, 65, 139, 140, 166 n.12
Ovid: *Metamorphoses* 37, 38, 100, 165 n.10
Oxford English Dictionary 1

Park, Clara Claiborne 6
Parker, Patricia 10, 112
Paster, Gail Kern 81, 98
patriarchy *see* male domination
patrilineality 90
Pechter, Edward 135, 171 n.17
Pericles 77–8
  Bawd 135, 147–8
  Marina's friendship with Philoten 46
  Thaisa 100
Petrarchan language 32, 104, 137, 165 n.10
  contrasts with 33, 34, 36, 38, 43, 113
  by Henry V 61

  mocked by female characters 112
  shows male characters' immaturity 35
  used by Phebe and Silvius 41–3
Phillips, Robin (director) 117
Pickford, Mary (performer) 59
Plat, Hugh 174 n.11
Plautus 80
plots as confining women 158
  love-death in tragedies 36
  marriage in comedies 41
  in *TNK* 46
Plutarch 91, 142, 169 n.16, 173 n.27
polarization
  deconstruction of gender opposition 4–5, 7, 8, 23
  gender associations in Western culture 4
  good vs. bad mothers 77, 87, 95–6
  good vs. bad women 65
Pollitt, Katha 4, 116, 121, 171 n.2
pornography 112
postcolonial criticism 11
post-structuralism vs. structuralism, unified meaning 32, 40, 41, 164 n.2
poverty 150–2
power and women's language use
  ability vs. dominance 105
  marital self-commitment 108
  mourning and cursing 109–11

resisting and mocking 112
self-deprecation 108–9
pregnancy 97
presentism 163 n.20
projection, by men onto women 5, 27–8, 65, 71, 98
Propeller Company 99, 169 n.20
prophets, women as 110, 152–3, 170 n.5
prostitution 44, 135, 147–8, 152, 158
  ambiguity about 134, 136
  'whore' as stigma 104
Protestant Reformation 168 n.6
  and marriage 5, 6, 34, 35, 52, 72
  and theatre 5, 6, 34, 35, 52, 72
  and women 5, 6
psychoanalysis 6
psychoanalytic feminist criticism
  on *AC* 95
  on *AW* 83
  on *Cor* 92–3
  on *KL* 93–4
  on *Mac* 88–90, 93
  on *Oth* 94
  on *RJ* 36–7
  on women's fiction 164 n.1
  on *WT* 98–9
public vs. private/domestic spheres 145–9, 152, 154, 174 n.1
  and motherhood 101
Purkiss, Diane, 172 n.8

queer theory 167 n.20
  see also homoerotic desire; sexuality as early modern identity category debated; Traub, Valerie

race, racism 65, 121, 137, 139–40, 144
Rackin, Phyllis 170 n.21 *see also* Howard, Jean
Radford, Michael (director) 173 n.23
radical feminism 33, 172 n.8
  see Echols, Alice; male domination; Wittig, Monique
rape 61, 113, 129–30
Reverby, Susan M. and Dorothy O. Helly 174 n.1
Rich, Adrienne 31, 41
Richard II 166 n.8
Richard III
  frequency of words 'mother' and 'children' 170 n.9
  Margaret 22, 60, 110, 111
  women often cut in productions 110, 170 n.10
Roberts, Jeanne 92
Roman comedies 32–3 *see also* Plautus
romance (pre-Shakespearean narrative) 33, 35, 165 n.5
romance (Shakespearean dramatic genre) *see under* Shakespeare, William, genres

Rome, Roman values 22–33, 90–2, 129–30, 140–1, 169 nn.16, 17
Romeo and Juliet 32, 48, 154
  feminist psychoanalytic readings 36–7
  Friar Lawrence 36
  Juliet 23, 26–8, 32, 33, 112
  Lady Capulet 37
  Nurse 37
  sources 35, 165 n.4
Rose, Mary Beth 34, 75, 79, 81, 97, 101, 104
Rougemont, Denis de 35, 36
Rowbotham, Sheila: *Women's Consciousness, Man's World* 3
Rowe, Nicholas (editor) 114, 116
Ruddick, Sara 76, 169 n.10
Rutter, Carole 59, 141, 142, 172 n.14

Sale, Carolyn 42, 172 n.13
Sandberg, Sheryl 163 n.6
Schalkwyk, David 174 nn.7, 12
scolds, punishment of 58
Scott, Walter (novelist) 139
sexuality as early modern identity category debated 15, 45
Shakespeare, William, genres 7, 17, 22
  comedies 53–60, 78, 79–84, 111
  histories 60–3, 79, 84–7, 109–11
  romances 75, 95–100
  tragedies 37–8, 63–8, 79, 87–95
  see also sonnets; *Venus and Adonis*
Shakespeare, William, representations of women
  agency 5, 31, 32, 36, 54, 60, 98, 104, 107, 158
  alliances or rapprochement 89, 92, 96, 173
  direct and/or sexual language 33
  eloquence 43, 103–5, 111
  idealization 47, 98–9
  intelligence 28
  literacy 106
  mobility outside home 149
  quieter, as background 107
  subordination 6, 7, 17, 58, 101, 135
  teachers 105
  wit 112
  see also friendship between women; mothers
Shanley, Mary Lyndon 167 n.22
Shannon, Laurie 171 n.3
Shapiro, Michael 163 n.5
Shaw, George Bernard 13, 55
Siemon, James 110, 117, 170 n.9
silence 54–6, 62, 107
  different meanings 117–18
  Innogen 167–7 n.3
  meanings in different stagings of end of *MM* 117
  urged on women 103
  Virgilia 91, 98
  Volumnia 92
Singh, Jyotsna 158, 173 n.29
single women 74, 151

sisters 126–8
  among feminists, metaphorical for allies 121
slavery 140
Slights, Camille 29
Slights, Jessica 115
Smith, Henry 64, 163–3 n.6
sonnets, Shakespeare's 42
  'dark lady' language 137, 140, 173 n.24
Sowernam, Ester 162 n.1
Speght, Rachel 162 n.1
Stallybrass, Peter 54, 103
Stanton, Kay 148
Stewart, Alan 170 n.3
stereotypes of women 66
  applied to men 25–8
  changeable 5, 23, 25, 26, 29, 129
  deceptive 22
  irrational 17, 23
  loquacious 103, 106–7, 114
  lustful 23, 34–5, 65, 69, 71, 77, 103–4
  lustful if black 138, 140, 141
  male fear of becoming like 18
  nurturing 4
  passionless 34
  Petrarchan 104
  self-sacrificing 77, 153
  weak 17, 18–9, 26–7, 63, 66
  see also body, women associated with; polarization
Stimpson, Catharine 162 n.5
Stone, Lawrence 166 n.2
Stubbs, Imogen 172 n.14

subordination of women 6, 7, 58, 101
Sugg, Richard 174 n.10
Sullivan, Dan (director) 173 n.33
Suzuki, Mihoko 39, 132
Swetnam, Joseph: *Arraignment of Women, The* 35, 162 n.1
sympathy
  associated with women 19, 143
  between women 49, 125, 158
  expected of mothers 76
  lacking in mothers 86–7
  see also under Shakespeare, William, representations of women

Taming of the Shrew, The 57–60, 155, 166 n.6
  competition between Katherine and Bianca 128
  Garrick adaptation 115
  gestures at end 116, 171 n.16
  Katherine's long speech 62, 108
  male supremacy 17
  productions aiming to shock or relieve audience 59–60
  violence against servants 173 n.31
  Woman's Prize or Tamer Tamed 57–8
Taymor, Julie (director) 100, 172 n.18
Tempest, The 54
  Miranda's speech removed by editors 115

Prospero's appropriation of maternal language and Taymor's revision into Prospera 100
textile work, gendered female 151–4
Theater for a New Audience 172 n.18
theatres
  helped by women workers 156–8
  masculinity as legitimation in England 156
  women spectators 174 n.14
Thomas, Keith 71
Thompson, Ann and Sasha Roberts 31
Thompson, Ayanna 10
Tilney, Edmund 25
Timon of Athens, prostitutes 148
Titus Andronicus
  Marcus on Lavinia 113
  opposition between Tamora and Lavinia 129–30
  Tamora 47, 48–9
transgender, intersex 162 n.4
Traub, Valerie 11, 20, 31–2, 41, 42, 44–5
Trevis, Di (director) 59
Tristan and Isolde 36
Troilus and Cressida
  Cressida called changeable 129
  women's colour 138, 139
Tudor ideology 110
Twelfth Night 55, 112
  Maria as Olivia's servant 132–3, 150
  Olivia's household management 149
  Olivia's relation with Viola/Cesario 43–5
  service romanticized 149–51
  Viola's disguise 38–9
Two Gentlemen of Verona
  disguise 38
  Julia on tanned skin as black 139
Two Noble Kinsmen, Emilia and Flavina 45, 126
Tyler, Anne: *Vinegar Girl* 175 n.19

Underdown, David 166 n.3

Venice 136, 148
Venus and Adonis 32
Vickers, Nancy 104
Victorian period 31, 34, 111, 164 n.1
violence
  and adulterous women 48, 92
  against servants 58, 173 n.13
  instigated by mothers 84–5, 87–90, 129–30
  language inadequate 113
  linked with masculinity 20, 22, 37–8, 61–2, 72–3
  punishing scolds 58
  source of value 66
  unconscious 36
  see also militarism
virgins, virginity 34, 81, 94, 153, 165 n.1
Vives, Juan Luis 80, 105, 167 n.6

Wales, Katie 106
Wall, Wendy 11, 145, 173 n.11
Wanamaker, Zoe (performer) 172 n.14
Watson, Barbara Bellow 105
Wayne, Valerie 34, 148
whiteness 64
  fairness 137–40
widows 82, 174 n.6
Willen, Diane 174 n.9
Williams, Raymond 17
Willis, Deborah 88, 90, 92, 110, 169 n.14
Wimsatt, William 67
Winter's Tale, The 69
  ending and revisions in productions 98–9
  female friendship 125
  Hermione 77–8, 97–9
  Paulina 98, 114
witches 22, 89, 90, 100, 110, 126–7, 144, 169 n.14
Wittig, Monique 8
Wofford, Susanne 108, 170 n.6
Wollstonecraft, Mary:
  Vindication of the Rights of Women (1792) 2

women, early modern activism 1, 53, 110 *see also* feminist activism
women, exclusion from
  banquet scenes 154–5
  political scenes 22, 60
  stage 15, 146, 156
  survivors in *Mac* 89–90
women performers
  in *commedia dell'arte* 157
  in English pageants, courts, households 155
Woodbridge, Linda 35, 103, 162 n.1, 164 nn.9, 13
Woolf, Virginia 2, 13
work, women's 4, 8, 145–58
  law, medicine, governing, warfare 146–7
  household 149–55
  see also educators; prostitution; theatres, helped by women workers; women performers
Worth, Irene (performer) 92

Yachnin, Paul 117
Young, Iris 14, 162 n.4